D1605823

C

228106

$19.95

DATE		
12-08		

Die

BAKER & TAYLOR

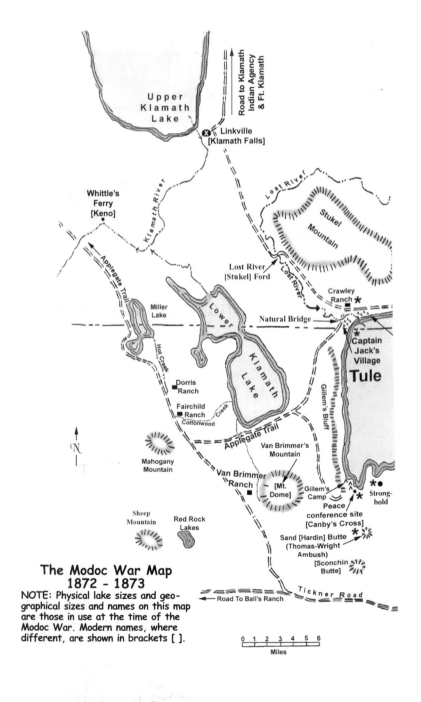

Upper
Klamath
Lake

Road to Klamath
Indian Agency
& Ft. Klamath

⊗ Linkville
[Klamath Falls]

Klamath River

Lost River

Stukel
Mountain

Whittle's
Ferry
[Keno]

Applegate Trail

Lost River
[Stukel] Ford

Lost River

Crawley
Ranch ✱

Miller
Lake

Hot Creek

Lower

Klamath
Lake

Natural Bridge →

✱
Captain
Jack's
Village

Tule

Dorris
Ranch

Fairchild
Ranch
Cottonwood

Cottonwood Creek

Gillem's Bluff

Applegate Trail

Van Brimmer's
Mountain

Mahogany
Mountain

Van Brimmer
Ranch

[Mt.
Dome]

Gillem's
Camp

✱ •
Strong-
hold

Peace
conference site
[Canby's Cross]

✱ ✺

Sheep
Mountain

Red Rock
Lakes

Sand [Hardin] Butte
(Thomas-Wright
Ambush)

[Sconchin ✺
Butte]

N

The Modoc War Map
1872 - 1873
NOTE: Physical lake sizes and geo-
graphical sizes and names on this map
are those in use at the time of the
Modoc War. Modern names, where
different, are shown in brackets [ ].

Tickner Road

← Road To Ball's Ranch

0 1 2 3 4 5 6
Miles

MODOC

The Tribe That Wouldn't Die
by Cheewa James

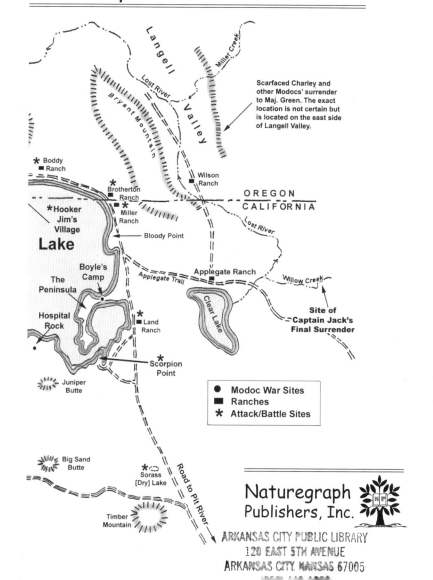

Scarfaced Charley and other Modocs' surrender to Maj. Green. The exact location is not certain but is located on the east side of Langell Valley.

Langell Valley

Lost River

Miller Creek

Bryant Mountain

Boddy Ranch

Brotherton Ranch

Miller Ranch

Wilson Ranch

OREGON
CALIFORNIA

Lost River

Hooker Jim's Village

Lake

Bloody Point

Boyle's Camp

Applegate Trail

Applegate Ranch

Willow Creek

The Peninsula

Clear Lake

Hospital Rock

Land Ranch

Site of Captain Jack's Final Surrender

Scorpion Point

Juniper Butte

● Modoc War Sites
■ Ranches
* Attack/Battle Sites

Big Sand Butte

Sorass [Dry] Lake

Road to Pit River

Timber Mountain

Naturegraph
Publishers, Inc.

Library of Congress Cataloging-in-Publication-Data

James, Cheewa.

Modoc : the tribe that wouldn't die / by Cheewa James.

p. cm.

Includes bibliographical references and index.

ISBN-13: 978-0-87961-275-7

ISBN-10: 0-87961-275-4

1. Modoc Indians--Wars, 1873. 2. Modoc Indians--History. 3. Modoc Indians--Relocation--Oklahoma. 4. California--History. 5. Oregon--History. 6. Oklahoma--History. I. Title.

E83.87.J35 2008

979.4004'974122--dc22

2008012723

Copyright © 2008 by Cheewa James

Cover photo: Clyde L. "Chief" James, author's father

Cover photo by: Peter Haley

Back cover photo by: Doug Austin

Cover design by: Allen Snyder and Cheewa James

Modoc War map by: Bill Johnson, Karen Tofell Weatherby, and Cheewa James

Naturegraph Publishers has been publishing books on natural history, Native Americans, and outdoor subjects since 1946. Free catalog available

Books for a better world

Naturegraph Publishers, Inc.
PO Box 1047 • 3543 Indian Creek Rd.
Happy Camp, CA 96039
(530) 493-5353
www.naturegraph.com

This book is dedicated in love and respect to my father, Clyde LeClair James (1900 - 1982), who gave me my prized Modoc blood

—and to my mother, Luella Katherine Mueller James (1904 - 1962), for her great efforts in preserving Modoc history, culture, and art.

Clyde L. James—1900 · 1982
Author's father
with Modoc gambling mats and bones.

Table of Contents

Table of Illustrations

Foreword

Writing this book has been the emotional journey of my life—unlike any other path I have ever followed. I have Modoc blood and know that with the war, disease, and death that dogged the footsteps of Modocs, it is a miracle that I even exist. I am Modoc, of the tribe that wouldn't die.

My name, Chee-wa-wee, was given to me by Jennie Clinton, the last survivor of the 1873 Modoc War. The name means "beginning of a basket." The Modocs were great basket makers, and the start of the basket was the most important—if the beginning was symmetrical and tightly woven, the sides would grow as they should. The symbolism of this to a human life has always sparked my imagination.

A tiny wisp of life flickered into existence during the Modoc War of 1873 in a cave located in what today is the Lava Beds National Monument, California. Born to the Modoc warrior Shkeitko, known as Shacknasty Jim, and his wife Anna, this infant, my grandfather, struggled to survive that snowy, bloody winter of the war. Even after being hauled over miles of treacherous terrain under unbelievable battle circumstances, that delicate thread of life dug in and held on. He then faced the arduous exile to Oklahoma Indian Territory, the fate of the Modocs who remained at war's end.

In three short generations, my Modoc blood from Jim and Anna has mingled with blood rooted in Germany and Ireland. I served in the Lava Beds National Monument in 1989 and 1990 as a seasonal ranger-interpreter for the U. S. National Park Service. My job was to find meaning in the silent, sagebrush-dotted land and to interpret the history of the phenomenal Modoc War, opening people's minds—and hopefully their hearts—to the vast panorama of human social evolution.

The rigorous life of the early Modocs was by no means a way of life to me, only a history. But it was a history with so many mysteries and half-hidden truths that it begged me for clarification and understanding. Often at dusk as I sat in front of my cabin in the Lava Beds, I would conjure up images in the fading light of the shadowy, ancient Indians who lived in the lake lands adjoining the Lava Beds. Sometimes, in the dimming light, I thought I could see distant silhouettes of Modocs and U. S. soldiers as they locked in brutal battle. During the time I lived in the Lava Beds, even in the silence of that land, I never felt I was alone.

It is important to me that readers know the total story of the Modoc people from ancestral times to the present. As I wrote, I marveled at the intricacy and antiquity of the early Modoc culture. Writing in the dead of night, I shed tears thinking of the fear my great-grandfather must have felt as he fought a battle that he couldn't win, all the while trying to care for his family, who were with him through the entire war. I was overcome with immense distress as I imagined the long, miserable train trip for my Modoc forebears to Oklahoma Indian Territory.

But I also was deeply touched and saddened by the tragedy of settlers Louisa Boddy and Sarah Brotherton as their husbands and sons were shot dead by Modocs in a settler attack. They were brave and ingenious women. As I read the long lost letters of Second Lt. Harry De Witt Moore, written over 130 years ago in the bleakness of the lava fields, I wished I could have been there to comfort him.

I wrote this book through months and years of extensive research. But some of it came through the hand of fate reaching out and placing incredible material in my hands—sometimes through chance meetings, some through the miracle of unsolicited e-mails through my web site (www.cheewa.com). I am a professional keynote speaker, and as you will see as you read this book, the early Modocs honored oratory skills. They would have loved the fact that I have a way with words. This book has been written in hotels and planes all over the United States and Canada. My apologies to the passengers in the front half of the late-flight plane that I woke up when I found the buried story of my great-grandmother fighting troops herself.

This book was written on the fading fringes of time. Since finishing the writing of this book, Helen Crume Smith of the Klamath Tribes has passed on. Likewise Arnold Richardson, 102 years old and honorary member of the Modoc Tribe of Oklahoma, has passed on. These two people, who never met, shared great memories and stories, a wonderful wit, and a love for the Modocs. I will miss them both.

My biggest message for those who choose to journey with me on this book odyssey is that we need to understand and honor people as the human beings they are, regardless of race, gender, religion, and all the other walls and barriers of diversity that can be concocted.

Acknowledgments

This is a book that exists because so many people cared and contributed. I am eternally grateful—but future generations will be even more indebted to these people, although none of us will be around to know. Such is the march of time.

Daniel Woodhead, thank you for your kind and giving spirit in letting me use the thorough newspaper and photograph files you have painstakingly collected. Karen Tofell Weatherby, you stepped in at a critical time and rescued me. I appreciate the time you spent on photographs. Thanks to Laddie Tofell for his help. Lon Cantor, what an act of friendship to edit the first writing of the Modoc War. Jim Hackbarth, thanks for the great photographs you gave your time and talent to obtain. To my friend, Peter Haley, now of the *Tacoma News Herald*, thank you for the wonderful cover photo of my father, Clyde. Jimmy Sexton, thanks for the Oklahoma photos. Pat Seawell, your quick eyes and willing spirit in indexing made you a real team member.

To Allen Snyder, thank you, thank you. I will always appreciate your help on research trips and the immense work with photographs that you did. Thanks for being there with the right word when I needed one, reading, proofing, and re-proofing sections of the book.

I cannot imagine where I would be without my sons and their children. Thanks to my sons David and Todd and to Todd's children, my grandchildren, Tanner and Tayla, for their care and love. I love you, too.

I thank my sister Doris Hartshorn, who shared a mother with me, for her caring and support in writing this book. Thanks to my sister, Viola Colombe, for tracking down the photograph of our grandfather, Clark James. To my brother Sonny Jim-James, I acknowledge his interest in the Modoc.

Austin Meekins and Nina McMillan: you should know what a contribution to history you made by allowing me to use the powerful and moving letters of your ancestors Charles Pentz and Harry De Witt Moore. These two men, long deceased, have become dear friends to me.

The Klamath Tribes was always there to help—special thanks to Taylor David and Gerald Skelton. Tribal members Bert Lawvor and Alvin Lawver went out of their way time and again to help. Thanks also to tribal members Helen Crume Smith, Coke Crume, Allen Foreman, Joe Kirk, Marvin Garcia, Debra Herrera, Harold Wright, Bill Duffy, and Buttons Bodner for the help they gave me. To Yvonne Lawver Kays, a very special thanks for giving me information and insight that was invaluable.

Patty Trolinger, former historian for the Modoc Tribe of Oklahoma, who has always been my right hand in working with Oklahoma Modoc history, my gratitude to you. Thanks to Jack Shadwick, who put in so much time, and Bill Follis. Also, thanks to honorary tribesman, centenarian Arnold Richardson, for his wonderful stories on early Oklahoma Modocs.

How blessed I am to have a publisher who understands the tremendous import of the information on the Modocs in this book—but also takes such good care of me as a writer and friend. Thank you, Barbara Brown. To her son, Keven, a note of gratitude for the careful editing and positive reinforcement. Sonny Vanderhoof, thanks for your good help in getting the book ready to print.

To my wonderful new friend from Spain, Jose Manuel de Prada, thank you for sharing your careful research on Jeremiah Curtin and Martha Lawver. Thanks to Gerry Milhorn and Bruce Cox, now deceased, experts on Modoc genealogy, and to Bill Quinn, Bill Johnson, and Richard Silva, who know so much about Modoc War history and land. Their help was invaluable.

Thanks to students in the literary editing and publishing certificate program at California State University, Chico, for copyediting an early version of the manuscript. Students were under the capable guidance of Casey Huff, the coordinator of that program.

Although now gone, I remember Francis "Van" Landrum, Gary Hathaway, and Carrol Howe—valued friends and historians, who always kept me in the loop of Modoc knowledge they uncovered. I also am grateful to the many historians who have written books and built a foundation before me. The goal in writing history is to add new building blocks to the groundwork already there.

Harold Porterfield, thanks for the wonderful four-wheel drive through Modoc lands, especially to the site of my own roots, the Hot Creek village.

I appreciate information on the Quakers from Jo Anne Tuning Magee, Floyd Watson, and Lyle Wheeler. Ann Miles and Herb Adams filled me in on the Portland, Maine, connection to the Modocs. Thanks to Klamath County Museum's Todd Kepple, Lynn Jeche, Kevin Fields, and Susan Rambo; Terry Harris and Kale Bowling, Lava Beds National Monument; Anne Hiller-Clark, Shaw Historical Society; the Oklahoma Historical Society staff; Lee Juillerat, *Klamath Falls Herald and News*; Sam Howard, Dr. Albert Hurtado, Dr. Lisa Jorgensen, Margaret McAuliffe, Bob Ernst, Bernita Tichner, Tina Lawver, Val Trudeau, Lynn Schonchin, Ricky Phillips, Don Moore, Sunshine Jim-Martin, Gail Ottoman, Tamara Mitchel, and Helenrose Nickols.

Chronology of Modoc War

November, 1852	Ben Wright Massacre
February, 1864	Valentine's Day Treaty
October, 1864	Treaty of 1864
November 29, 1872	Lost River Battle
January 17, 1873	First Battle for the Stronghold
January 29, 1873	Peace Commission Established
April 11, 1873	Peace Commissioners and Lt. Sherwood Killings
April 14 - 17, 1873	Second Battle for the Stronghold
April 26, 1873	Thomas-Wright Battle
May 10, 1873	Sorass [Dry] Lake Battle
May 22, 1873	Hot Creek Modocs Surrender
June 1, 1873	Captain Jack Surrenders
July 1 - 9, 1873	Trial of Modoc Leaders
October 3, 1873	Hanging of Modoc Leaders

Chronology of Post-war Events

October 10, 1873	Exiled Modocs Leave Ft. Klamath, Oregon
October 23, 1873	Board Train in Redding, California
November 16, 1873	Arrive in Baxter Springs, Kansas
Late November, 1873	Moved to Quapaw Agency, Oklahoma Indian Territory
1874	Redpath Lecture Tour Begins
1877	Jesse Carr's "China Wall" Building Begins
April, 1879	Agent Hiram Jones Removed
1880	Modoc Tribal Government Abolished
1884	Linguist Jeremiah Curtin Interviews Modocs
February 25, 1885	Carr's "China Wall" Ordered Torn Down
March 3, 1909	Oklahoma Modocs Allowed to Return to Klamath Reservation
12 pm Aug.13, 1954	Federal Supervision Over Modocs Ends
May 25, 1978	Oklahoma Modocs Restored to Federal Recognition
August 27, 1986	Klamath Tribe Restored to Federal Recognition

Luella Mueller James—1904-1962
Author's mother
in Navajo dress at Bandelier National Monument, New Mexico.

Modoc
The Tribe That Wouldn't Die

Part One
The Modoc War

Trench in Captain Jack's Stronghold
*Lava Beds National Monument, California - This natural lava fortress was
where the Modocs took their stand against enemy troops. Trenches
running through the uneven and rugged lava allowed Modocs to
move back and forth.*
(Photo courtesy of Lava Beds National Monument)

Prelude

In war it is tempting, but simplistic, to label the warring factions as "right" or "wrong," "good" or "bad." War spawns cruel acts but also brings humane actions on both sides. The complexity of any war asks that naïve, one-dimensional conclusions not be drawn. War itself is the true evil.

The Modoc War of 1873 stands as an amazing conflict in United States history.

- **It was the most costly Indian war in United States military history, in terms of both lives and money, considering the small number of Indians who battled.**

- **By the end of the six-month war, over 1,000 United State military troops were engaged in bringing 50 - 60 Modoc men, who had their families with them throughout the entire war, under control. Army troops outnumbered Modoc fighting men about 20 to 1.**

- **The Modoc War is the only Indian war in American history in which a full-ranking general, General E. R. S. Canby, was killed.**

Were it not for the George Armstrong Custer fight at the Little Bighorn against the Lakota and Cheyenne only three years after the Modoc War, the Modoc conflict would probably be remembered as the most significant Indian confrontation in America's western history. The Modoc War involved only one relatively small group of American Indian people. However, it is a riveting example of what happened across the United States as non-Indian settlers, landowners, and military persevered in efforts to continue western expansion.

The Modoc saga is one that belongs equally to California and Oregon. But by the end of the war, Oklahoma became a part of this poignant story.

Archaeological research has documented that for many millenniums the Modocs had inhabited an area in northern California and southern Oregon. They were spread over about 5,000 square miles of territory. The Modocs' summer hunting ranged from Mount Shasta eastward and north to Goose Lake. Their permanent villages were in Lost River country, including Tule Lake, on what is today the central Oregon-California border. The Modocs were water people, much of their livelihood and culture stemming from their waterways.

19

Examining the findings from Night Fire Island, a recent archeological site in ancestral Modoc land, author Carrol Howe says, "It seems doubtful that any place will be found that was continuously occupied longer than the Modoc homeland."

Their population fluctuated between 400-800 at any given time. Over those many centuries, the Modocs' culture, theology, and life had become perfectly tuned to their environment and the richness of the resources it provided them. Their nomadic patterns took them to the right places at the right times for their hunting, fishing, and food gathering activities. Then the last move of the year brought them back to the favored areas for building their winter homes and storing their winter food caches. Above all, the Modocs loved their land. It was, in every sense, their world.

The environment sometimes could be adversarial, but Modocs knew ways to cope. They understood the land. It was that knowledge that made them powerful in combat. Neighboring tribes regarded them as skilled fighters. They were masters at using the land to their advantage against the enemy. This trait was a major factor in their ability to battle the U. S. military so successfully.

Too often the Modocs have been stigmatized as warring savages, with little understanding given to other facets of their culture. Their tenacious staying power over thousands of years refutes this narrow stereotype. Investigation into the past reveals the Modocs as a solid, enduring people with a vast history. The aspects of their lives that dealt with social customs, family, theology, and art were well developed.

The Modocs were never a unified tribe but instead several autonomous bands. Each band had its own leadership and operated independently, except in war when they joined forces and selected a war chief. Modoc bands were not dictatorships. Both military and civil decisions were made by consensus of the entire group. This held true in the Modoc War, and the assembly of Modoc fighters met often to strategize.

The roots of the war began sometime in the mid-1800s. Increasing numbers of Anglo-Europeans, in their quest for new land, began to infiltrate and encroach on ancestral Modoc land. In the fall of 1847 the immigrants brought smallpox. It is unknown how many Modocs died, although there have been estimates as high as 130. Other Indian groups to the north suffered losses between 25 and 50 percent of their people. Some bands in the Columbia Valley of present day Oregon were eliminated completely. The impact of this plague on the Modoc culture can only be imagined. The very young and the elderly are especially susceptible in an outbreak of this sort. The elders had always been the leaders and were the greatest reservoirs of knowledge and tradition. With the passing of the older people, there can be no doubt that Modoc culture and leadership were adversely affected.

The bloody and tragic Modoc War could have been averted. The underlying cause of the war can be summed up in one four-letter word—land. Land to the immigrants meant ownership. To the Modocs, land could not be owned any more than could air or water or clouds. It was inconceivable to the Modocs that they could be forced to leave their home and environment and to relinquish their lifestyle. The case of the Modocs is similar to that of many other Indian tribes of mid-nineteenth century America. As more and more non-Indians poured westward, more and more land—the richer, more fertile Indian land—was being claimed by these immigrants.

The issue of how land was now to be parceled out and lived upon created great chasms between the two cultures. There was even dissention among the immigrant settlers, landowners, and government as to who should get the land and how. When Yreka, California, gold fields opened in 1850, conflicts became more frequent between Indians and non-Indians. There was violence and bloodshed as the two cultures clashed.

But other things also generated and prolonged the war. Missed opportunities existed on both sides to solve problems and live cooperatively. Racial bias and stereotyping influenced decisions. Errors in judgment and miscalculations contributed. Military and government blunders, such as launching an attack with too few men and not notifying civilians of an imminent war, were staggering.

The war resulted in great devastation, almost beyond comprehension, to the Modoc people. It placed them on the brink of cultural destruction. Even more severe were events after the war, but directly related to the war, that decimated their already small population. The death and suffering of U. S. soldiers was also great. Families of the wounded and slain dealt for years with the results of the Modoc War. Certainly among both Indian warriors and U. S. Army soldiers the feeling of "Why am I here?" was present. Settlers, caught in the middle of the battle, suffered death and destruction as well.

During the Modoc War there was dissention internally within both the Indian and military sides. On the side of the military, for example, dislike of a commanding officer by many of his own men caused disruption and even the disobeying of orders. On the other hand, internal dissention at the close of the war caused the Modocs to split back into their separate bands. Bands thought differently about how to handle surrender and defeat. There were accusations of deception between separate Modoc bands, and they turned on each other.

Through centuries of existence, the Modoc were a people without a written language. At the time of the war, many Modocs did not speak fluent English. Much of what is known is the interpretation by others of what Modocs did and said. Modocs were viewed by the U. S. government as "the other side," a foe of U. S. military troops. Much of the history of the Modoc War is written from that perspective.

The Modoc War is often viewed and discussed without a comprehensive knowledge of the Modocs. Little has been written on the Modoc culture to enlighten people on this much talked about but little known tribe. To honestly interpret the war, the impact of Modoc culture on the war must be taken into account. My hope is that this book will provide readers with a greater understanding of the Modocs. The appendix of this book has a section, "The Ancestral Modocs," which examines what we know of this ancient group of people,

Certain aspects of Modoc culture related to the war and the ultimate removal of the Modocs were reported in newspapers, military documents, and letters of that era. These aspects include the Modocs' surprise at being attacked in winter, as they traditionally did not fight in winter; the right of a Modoc to kill a shaman or healer who failed at his task; grieving mourners wailing for long lengths of time and covering their hair with tree pitch and ashes; the occasional circumstance of a man having more than one wife.

Most of what has been written on the Modoc War has not given sufficient emphasis to the fact that for the entire six months of the war, Modoc women and children lived and moved with the men of the tribe and experienced the battles. I have explored what little we know of the Modoc women and tried to give them faces and voices.

There were also settler women pulled into the war in tragic circumstances. The first names of these women are not found in the bulk of writing on the Modoc War. Mrs. Brotherton, Mrs. Boddy, and Mrs. Schira did not have first names. They do in my book. I am proud of the Modoc, settler, and military women who handled the war with strength and grace.

The Modoc War was riveting and highly emotional. The story of the Modocs as prisoners of war in Oklahoma Indian Territory is equally compelling. These events are not dry history, and I want people—especially children and young people—to feel the significance and drama. Accordingly, I have inserted fictionalized vignettes throughout the book to tell particular stories connected to the history of the Modoc people. The historical details in the fictionalized vignettes are precise. Read them and experience the excitement, bewilderment, pain, horror, pride, sorrow, or wonderment they evoke.

It is also important that an accurate record exists. This book is heavily researched and documented for those who wish to explore further. There are also new sources that offer fresh reading for Modoc history buffs.

Even though I am of Modoc descent, I have tried to show all sides of this conflict in an unbiased, well-researched way. As a result, I have a solid understanding of the background and pattern of the war, know the Modocs better as individuals, and have come to know certain settlers, soldiers, and government officials well. I feel related to them all.

What I know is that the bitterness of the past must be just that—past. The understanding and lessons derived from the war must be used to build a better, more tolerant world today and a stepping-stone to the future. We must acknowledge, in the Indian way of thinking, that all living things, including human beings, are interrelated. We are here to care for one another.

—Cheewa Patricia James, 2008

Soldiers in formation during Modoc War

Soldiers in lava rocks

Chapter 1
Roots of War

The Modoc guns are sure.
The Modoc hearts are strong.
The white men are many. They will come again.
No matter how many the Modocs kill, more will come.
We will all be killed in the end.[1]

Captain Jack, Modoc War leader, 1873

He walked with a swagger. Ben Wright was the stuff from which legends are made. Wright was a charismatic man, considered a natural leader by some, a barbarous, unthinking killer by others of his time. He was born in 1828 in Indiana. After the death of his mother when he was eighteen years old, he hopped a wagon train and headed west for the frontier. He did not like farming and turned to hunting beaver and Indians.

With the coming of the immigrants onto Modoc land, blood flowed as the two sides struggled to survive in the same area. But with no check on what really happened, myths grew, especially with respect to how many people the Modocs killed. Numbers jumped dramatically from a handful to dozens and into the hundreds. Those statistics were often used as political tools to show the vengeance of the Modocs and to encourage their ouster.[2]

Ben Wright

Wright was at home in this country. Letting his naturally curly hair grow long, Indian-style, he bragged of the noses, fingers, and scalps he had taken from fallen Indians. By the time he was twenty-three years of age, he was acknowledged as the most notorious of the Indian fighters in northern California. "Ben Wright was an

Indian killer," wrote pioneer newspaperman Samuel A. Clarke. "That was what he thought Indians were made for. He generally kept an Indian woman, too, for convenience, but he was hostile to the men whenever he had an excuse." One thing was for sure. Wright wanted to eliminate Modocs—to get them off the land, which was rapidly filling with settlers.[3]

In November 1852, Wright made his move on the Modocs. After stationing his men around a Modoc encampment, Wright rode into the camp unchallenged, a white truce flag paving the way. Once there he opened fire, and his men rode into the camp to support him. They shot Modocs in violent gunfire. Some Modocs tried to grab their bows, but most ran and were hunted down mercilessly. Some fled into the water and were shot as they came up for air. Others in the sagebrush were rounded up and destroyed as soon as they were found.

On that fateful day, one Modocs would never forget, over thirty Modoc men, women, and children were slaughtered. Considering the small total population of the Modocs, the massacre was devastating. Only a few Modocs, less than five, lived through the carnage.[4]

The meaning of a white flag was forever changed in the eyes of the Modocs. The ghost of Ben Wright would ride again years later when at the height of the Modoc War, a peace conference was called under a white flag of truce.

Wright was a hero upon his return to Yreka, California, a small mining town on the western boundary of traditional Modoc lands. In 1854, Wright was appointed Indian agent to all tribes south of Coos Bay, Oregon, an act that many Indians considered a step toward extermination. Many non-Indians saw it as a means to finally control the Indian problem.

Wright had a major flaw. He was not a temperate man in his habits and behavior, especially when it came to alcohol. For Ben Wright, drinking was a precursor to violence.

* * * * *

— An Act of Revenge —

Chetcoe Jennie had never considered herself a person of revenge. Quite to the contrary, as a government interpreter in 1855, the Indian woman worked to create bridges between people. Women didn't have many chances to do something like this, and Jennie was understandably proud. From the time she was a small child, her natural curiosity and gift for language and words had been a source of pride to her parents. She was also unusually outgoing for a girl and connected with people easily.

It had been a long, hard day for Chetcoe Jennie, with more duties than usual. Night was already falling as she started home from her interpreter job in Port Orford, Oregon. As she scurried along the wooden sidewalk, she saw a shadow a few yards in front of her. She stopped abruptly, realizing that the man moving toward her was Indian Agent Ben Wright, his long hair hanging free, frontier-style. She felt a tiny bubble of anxiety—this man had a reputation for being rough when he was drinking. In a town filled with miners, rough was a good thing for women to avoid.

Chetcoe Jennie stepped to her left to allow him to pass. Suddenly he grabbed her, forcing her against the building wall. His lips moved to her face, and she could smell the stench of whiskey. She lashed out at him with a hand and a foot. He screamed in rage and in one swift movement ripped her blouse up the front and threw her to the street. "No-good Indian. You'll pay for hitting at me."

In his drunken rage, Wright ordered her to strip off the rest of her clothing. When she did not obey, he reached over and tore her clothing from her body. The commotion attracted people from inside the building. They watched in horror, but no one made a move to interfere with the violent man. Grabbing his whip from his belt, Wright landed a vicious stroke across Chetcoe Jennie's bare legs. Blood surged to the surface. As she attempted to run from him, Wright followed her, landing blow after blow. The violence displayed that night shocked even the most toughened miners of Port Orford.

It took Chetcoe Jennie more than a month to recover from this horrific beating. As her wounds healed, her thirst for revenge festered and her fury flamed. Chetcoe Jennie changed into a person hell-bent for vengeance. She knew she alone was no match for Ben Wright. But she sought out and found another person who had reason to hate Wright. A former guide named Enos, who was working for Wright, had a similar vendetta. Enos had also received a lash from a whip when he hadn't moved fast enough to obey Wright's order.

It took little to persuade Enos to help her in the quest for retribution. Their plan was simple. On the night of February 25, 1856, Chetcoe Jennie and Enos accosted Wright on his way home from the tavern. She was armed with a knife and Enos wielded an ax. Wright drew a knife with his left hand and swung his ever-present whip in his right hand. He landed one lash on Jennie's shoulder, but the ax whirled through the air and found its mark.

Revenge takes strange turns. Chetcoe Jennie's need for revenge was not yet satisfied. She cut Ben Wright's heart from his body and ate a portion of it.

* * * * * *

Yreka, California - Mid 1800s
(Photo courtesy of Siskiyou County Museum)

The dilemma of the Modocs reached a crescendo by 1864. Lost River country was a favored destination for settlers and potential landowners pouring westward. The solution, it seemed to the non-Indians of the area and eventually to the government, was to place the Modocs on a reservation where conflict could be avoided. An official treaty—the Treaty of 1864—was accordingly drawn up, although it was not ratified until 1869. It provided that the Modocs be placed on a reservation located north of what then was Linkville, Oregon, and is today Klamath Falls. Ft. Klamath had been established as an army post just the year before the treaty was signed so that the Indians could be watched by the army.[5]

The Modocs were to share the Klamath Reservation with the Klamaths, with whom the Modocs had maintained a strained relationship, and the Yahooskin band of Snake Indians. The Treaty of 1864 was a standard treaty. It provided for the cession of all land claimed by the three tribes. In return they would reside on the Klamath Reservation and receive $8,000 worth of supplies for the first five years, $5,000 worth for the next five years, and $3,000 worth for the third five years. Presumably they would be self-supporting after fifteen years. The government promised to build shops and mills and establish schools.

The signing of the treaty took place in October of 1864 on the Klamath Reservation. Present for the signing were 339 Modocs and 771 Klamaths. Only twenty-two Snakes were there. For a short period of time, they all lived on the reservation.[6]

Captain Jack of the Sour Stomach

It was at this time that one Modoc emerged who was destined to stand out in Modoc history above all others. His name was Keintpoos, translated as "Having-the-Waterbrash" (pyrosis or heartburn), probably referring to his stomach problems. But his Indian name was not the one people would remember. Keintpoos became known as Captain Jack. Stories differ as to where he got his name. The most commonly accepted version involves Yreka lawyer Elijah Steele, a good friend of the Modocs. He named Captain Jack after a miner to whom he bore a resemblance.[7]

Jack was stocky in build, somewhere around 5'8". He was described as "a man of square mold." He was rather small, weighing around 145 lbs., with small hands and feet and thin arms. He had a large head, a round, square-jawed face with prominent cheekbones, and a large mouth. He was in his early thirties when trouble began building between the Modocs and United States government. Unlike some Modocs of that time, he did not speak English. Steele, in a letter to his brother, said, "Captain Jack talks no English, except the names of a few articles in trade, and no jargon, and as far as my knowledge of him is concerned, he always brought to the conference an interpreter."[8]

Captain Jack—Keintpoos
Photo was taken prior to the Modoc War,
probably by Yreka photographer Louis Heller in his studio.
The clothing is not traditional Modoc.

This means that the words of Captain Jack that are read today are through the ears and words of others. Interpreters were used extensively throughout the Modoc War. A lot of faith would have to be placed with interpreters. They could change intent and meaning in translations to suit their own purposes. Whether by error or by design, words may have been changed, omitted, or added. How this might have affected events in Modoc history, especially during the Modoc War, will never be known.

There was a disagreement among the Modocs on the reservation over leadership. The primary discord was between Captain Jack and Old Schonchin, a leader who favored staying on the reservation. Finally, in 1865 Captain Jack and a small group of Modocs left the reservation and went back to Lost River country. There Captain Jack found settlers had already moved onto traditional Modoc land even though the official Treaty of 1864 had not been ratified. The bulk of the Modoc population, under the leadership of Old Schonchin, remained on the reservation.

For four years the Modocs who had left the reservation continued to live in the ancestral lands. But in late December 1869, Captain Jack and the Modocs living in Lost River country were coerced by the government back onto the reservation. They were assured that the Treaty of 1864, which granted Modocs basic care from the government, would be honored. It took eight large government wagons with mule teams to haul the Modocs with all their belongings to the reservation. They were placed at the northern end of Klamath Lake, about eight miles south of Klamath Agency, which had been established near Ft. Klamath as administration headquarters for overseeing the reservation Indians. The spot is today known as Modoc Point, named for the Modocs settling there.

Modocs as Lumberjacks

Within a few days of returning to the reservation, Captain Jack requested chopping axes, cross-cut saws, wedges, and maul rings to put his men to work making rails. The Modocs were off and running with their new industry.

But trouble was ahead. The Modocs were greatly outnumbered by the Klamath Indians on the reservation. The Klamaths demanded that the Modocs turn over a certain portion of their cut timber as rent for living on their part of the reservation. The Klamaths began to harass and dominate the Modocs. They hampered the Modocs at fishing and struck the Modoc women who gathered seeds at the lake. Moreover, mysterious fires ignited, destroying Modoc property. This was much more than the Modocs could endure. They were a proud people with a heritage of strong leadership and family values and, when necessary, they were superior warriors. Within the narrow confines of the reservation, the two tribes were at odds.[9]

Captain Jack, to his credit, made an effort to keep the peace. He went to the Klamath Agency to talk with Indian Agent Capt. O. C. Knapp, who had been appointed reservation sub-agent shortly before Captain Jack and his Modocs had returned. He had replaced Lindsay Applegate, who had served since 1865. Applegate was an explorer who, with brothers Jesse and Charles, had helped establish the Applegate Trail, which, coupled with existing trails, produced a shorter, easier southern route from Ft. Hall, Idaho, to Oregon. He was the choice of the Klamath Reservation Indians for an agent. After thirty years on the frontier, he thoroughly understood the habits and customs of his charges, and he liked the Indians in his care. Under his leadership the Indians made rapid advances. A federal political change in policy moving control of Indian agencies back to the military ousted Applegate.[10]

Knapp, in contrast, had no heart for the job and largely went through the motions of administering the agency. He knew nothing of Indian character and felt the contempt for the Indian so nearly universal among officers of the U. S. Army.[11]

The visit to Knapp by Captain Jack took place on the front porch of the agency. Jack was not invited into Knapp's office, and the meeting resulted in a brusque promise that the agency would "make it all right."[12]

Captain Jack and his Modocs continued to make rails. One snowy day, five or six Klamaths drove up with their wagons and began to load rails. Captain Jack urged his men to ignore them and keep working, which they did. He told the Modocs that the Klamaths were just picking a fuss and that if it happened again, he would go to the agent. The Klamaths filled their wagons and left but returned shortly to refill the wagons. This time Jack walked over to one old Klamath man and asked him who had told them they could take away the rails. He replied, "I did. This is my land. You have got no business to cut my trees down. This is not your country or land. Tule Lake is your home. Go there and live." Land occupation had now become an issue with Indians, too.[13]

Once again Captain Jack with Bogus Charley as interpreter arrived at the agency to talk with Knapp. A crowd of Klamaths confronted them, jeering the Modocs as cowards. Jack asked that the agent do something about the unacceptable conditions under which Modocs were living. Knapp suggested that Captain Jack let the rails go to the Klamaths and move up the Williamson River a few miles. He assured Captain Jack that, "I will attend to the fellows [Klamaths], but by all means, Jack, don't fight any of them."[14]

Captain Jack and the Modocs agreed and moved, settling about five miles farther up on the river. The winter passed, and in the spring the resettled Modocs again began making rails. Just as before, the Klamaths appeared and took the rails. Captain Jack appeared in late April before Knapp with an accounting of the growing problem.

* * * * * *

— "I Am Not A Dog" —

The Modocs were a difficult people, no doubt about it, Capt. Knapp concluded with a disparaging shake of his head. Sitting in his office with the sun pouring through the window, the Union Army veteran moved his hand from his neck to his shoulder, pushing hard on the knotted muscles, as he once again reflected on the unhappy state of life that had cast him into the role of agent for the Klamath Reservation.

He knew he'd been a fine soldier during his stint in the Civil War. A small smile of pride graced his face briefly as he remembered his two promotions, a direct result of what they'd called his gallantry and meritorious service in action. The smile quickly faded as he thought of his present situation. He was now somewhere between a baby-sitter and a chaperone for a bunch of illiterates who....His thoughts broke off with a sigh. If someone were to say he was indifferent to the Indians that he was overseeing on the Klamath Reservation, he would have to acknowledge, in all honesty, that they were right. His assignment was an unwelcome chore.

When he had first come into contact with the Modocs, he had tried to reform this ragged, heathen group of Indians. They had a reputation for being fighters, and he planned to break that spirit immediately. He also did not agree with the government's lenient way of subsidizing these people. Until the work ethic was solidly instilled in the Modocs, he saw no way they could become reasonable citizens of the reservation. But to date, Knapp and the Modocs had locked horns.

It wasn't just the Modocs causing him problems. It was the government as well. They were idiots back there in Washington, D. C. They knew nothing about the situation on the reservation, took forever to get anything done, and gave him no relief or tools to deal with the situation.

The latest problem was the government's inability,

or more likely their incompetence, to provide rations, food, and supplies to Knapp for the Indians. It was this last example of lack of support that prompted him to ask to be relieved of his duties on the Klamath Indian Reservation.

His thoughts swung to the Modoc leader, Captain Jack. Knapp had never imagined that all his training and experience would someday bring him to dealing with a man with whom he could hardly communicate. It wasn't what Knapp felt he was cut out to do. It wasn't what he was prepared to do or wanted to do. Quite honestly, it wasn't what he deserved.

The situation with Captain Jack was becoming severe. It was beginning to attract attention from Knapp's superiors. Jack had proven to be a determined and willful man. Knapp's initial meetings with him had seemed promising in terms of reaching a working agreement in the way the Modocs were to be governed. But there was nowhere left to go in their negotiations. The same dead ends kept popping up.

The first time Jack came to him about the problems with the Klamaths, Knapp promised that the agency would take care of the problem. Knapp had really hoped it would work out that way.

Now Jack was back again. Knapp was a soldier and a good one. But he'd never planned to be a mediator. He felt he was an equitable man. But more was expected of him than he should have to produce.

The meeting with Jack was not a pleasant one. Knapp was just plain tired of herding a bunch of complaining Indians through life. He was impatient. He accused Jack of being a chronic complainer. In the heat of the quarrel, Knapp swore at Jack, curse words punctuating his sentences.

"If you come and bother me any more with your complaints, I will put you where no one will ever bother you again. Now get out of here."

Jack in his anger had cried out that he was not a dog, that he was a man. Gutsy words, Knapp reflected, for an Indian. "I and my people shall not be slaves for a race of people that is not any better than we are. If the agent does not protect my people, we shall not live here. If the government refuses to protect my people, who shall I look to for protection?" he had asked.

* * * * * *

Jack's parting words highlight one of the major causes of the Modoc War and the principles for which the Modocs were willing to fight.

Following his meeting with Knapp, Captain Jack called a meeting of all Modoc bands. He proposed that because they were not welcome in Klamath territory and Knapp did not want to interfere, the logical thing to do was return to Lost River country. Once there, he maintained, they would demand a separate reservation near Tule Lake. Old Schonchin was not present, and the meeting went Jack's way.

The third week in April, Knapp cut off rations to the Modocs on the grounds that they could now support themselves by their usual methods of food gathering. The Modocs quietly made plans to leave.

On April 25 or 26, 1870, more than 300 Modocs left the Klamath Reservation to return to their homeland on the Lost River. Only forty-three had originally arrived on the reservation with Jack. Even Old Schonchin joined the exodus.

The U. S. government was more than a little upset by the Modocs returning to Lost River country. Sub-agent Knapp and Ft. Klamath Commander H. S. Goodale blamed each other, Knapp saying Goodale had been inefficient in permitting the Modocs to get away and Goodale accusing the agent of stupidity in antagonizing Jack. As might be expected, the settlers in the Tule Lake basin were filled with concern when Captain Jack and the Modocs returned.

Old Schonchin lived only a few weeks under Jack's control and then voluntarily returned to the Klamath Reservation. Eventually, some 130 Modocs drifted back to the reservation. The Modocs returning to the reservation were separated from the Klamaths and placed at Yainax, about thirty-five miles east of Klamath Agency. Modocs moved easily back and forth between Lost River country and Yainax. Jack did visit Yainax from time to time but flatly refused to live there. [15]

Knapp's ineptness and reputation for drunkenness brought about his dismissal from Klamath Agency in October, 1870.[16]

*Modoc woman grinding seeds from the wocus plant on Tule Lake,
located in the ancestral home of the Modocs. Lost River flows into Tule
Lake. Wocus was a major food staple of the early Modocs.*

Chapter 2
Back Home in Lost River Country

"I do not want to live upon the reservation,
for the Indians there are poorly clothed, suffer from hunger, and
even have to leave the reservation sometimes to make a living."[17]

Captain Jack, May 14, 1872

In the following three years, Captain Jack and the Modocs continued to roam free. Jack watched the proceedings on the Klamath Reservation closely, and the more he saw of life there, the more convinced he became that the Modocs should try to live as their ancestors had.

Some of the Modocs spoke English, although the tribe as a whole still used the native tongue. They adopted clothing similar to the settlers around them. Dungarees, shirts, and work shoes had long replaced the skins and tule sandals of their ancestors. Most had their hair cropped short and had muzzle-loading rifles with powder horns. Only the very old Modocs carried bows and arrows.

The Modoc men worked for neighboring stockmen or farmers. Charles Putnam, Jesse Applegate's grandson, was especially fond of Boston Charley, who worked on his grandfather's ranch near Clear Lake, on the eastern side of traditional Modoc land:

> He was the best-natured indian [sic] I ever knew in my life. He had a keen wit and a deep sense of humor and a happy disposition. Sometimes he would get so tickled at our jokes that he would lie down on the ground and roll with laughter.

The first time Putnam ever saw Captain Jack was when Jack and twenty of his men rode full gallop

Boston Charley

37

into Putnam's camp near Clear Lake. Putnam and his men fed them all. Jack told them that this was his country, but that they could live there if they would be good. He also stipulated that they must "give him eat" at any time he came, but that they need not feed the others. Jack said his Modocs were the same as coyotes, meaning that if you fed them, they would constantly come back. Humor and good will were obviously a part of Jack's relationship with Putnam. After that initial meeting, Jack would arrive at Putnam's camp, come in to eat by himself, and leave the other Modocs to camp at a distance.[18]

Yreka had flamed to life at the western boundary of the traditional Modoc lands when gold was discovered in the vicinity in 1851. To the Modocs, it was a lively and vibrant place. Modoc boys could look for employment there, often as house servants. More and more, these young men came to be accepted as customers for goods and drinks.[19]

Judge Elijah Steele   *Judge A. M. Rosborough*

Before their move to the Klamath Reservation, the Modocs had found friends in Judge Elijah Steele, a Yreka lawyer, who had come to the gold fields from New York in 1850, and Steele's partner, Judge A. M. Rosborough. Both men were sympathetic to the plight of the Modocs. It was common for them to give Modocs a "pass" certifying their identity and character as they sought work. The "pass" would read something like this:

April 6, 1868

Charlie, the Indian to whom I give this paper, makes a living for himself and his family by farming, driving teams, etc., and wants me to give him this paper certifying to the fact that he is a civilian Indian and not a wild Indian—that he is an independent freeman entitled to the protection of life, liberty, and pursuit of happiness by the laws of civilization.

A.M. ROSBOROUGH,

County Judge of the County of Siskiyou and the State of California.[20]

Both Steele and Rosborough continued their friendship with the Modocs upon the Modocs' return in 1870 to Lost River country.

Who Will Tell Indians What to Do?

The challenges of running Indian affairs and administering to Indians on reservations continued to be a thorny issue in areas throughout the United States. Ulysses S. Grant was inaugurated president of the United States on March 4, 1869. It fell to him to sort out the Indian administration issue and find a way to deal with the original inhabitants of U. S. lands.

One of Grant's solutions was a unique plan widely known as the "Quaker Policy." Grant had been approached with the idea of turning the administration of Indians over to church people of various religious denominations. Who better to govern Indians than men of God? The thinking went that if Indians adopted Christianity, they would change their habits, their folkways, and their economic system. They would then become peaceable and self-reliant within the economic system of the United States.

One major flaw in this policy was that some of the men put into authority at this time knew practically nothing about Indians and their lifestyles. They were more concerned with religious issues than education, welfare, economics, and other real life issues.[21]

Alfred B. Meacham

As a result of the "Quaker Policy," a prime player in the drama of the Modoc War came into play. Alfred B. Meacham was appointed Oregon superintendent of Indian Affairs on May 1, 1869, although some individual Oregon Indian agencies, such as the Klamath, came under direct supervision of others.

Alfred Meacham was definitely qualified for his position under Grant's new policy philosophy. He was a Methodist and a God-fearing man. He was tall, portly, balding, and had a full dark beard. He looked older than a man in his forties. He was almost always meticulously dressed in a suit and tie, a definite contrast to the dress of the Westerners around him. He was a strict temperance man, who did not look kindly on alcohol.[22] A native of Iowa, he had engaged in several profitable ventures in eastern Oregon, including an inn, a toll road, and ranching. His vigorous mind made up for his lack of formal education. Snagging his appointment from President Grant as Oregon superintendent of Indian Affairs had been one of the biggest coups of Alfred Meacham's life.

Ft. Klamath, Oregon
Established in 1863 to provide military protection, the fort was abandoned on August 10, 1889, having been declared "useless for military purposes" by U. S. President Grover Cleveland. (Photo: Klamath County Museum)

Meacham hoped that "a better understanding between white and red men may be had and that justice to both may be promoted." He could speak easily and confidently, if at times flowery and verbosely. Newspaper correspondents commented that Meacham "could talk the legs off a cast-iron pot in just ten minutes," and "words roll from his silvery tongue like green peas from a hot platter."[23]

One of Meacham's official visits in his new position was to Ft. Klamath. Located on the northeastern side of Klamath Lake, Ft. Klamath had groves of ponderosa pines and tamarack that stood like sentinels behind the neat and orderly buildings of the fort. A stream of cold, crystal clear water flowed between it and the mountain. A smooth, level prairie, serene and lovely, extended far to the west.[24]

But Meacham realized that despite the outward appearance of tranquility, peace would not be his at Fort Klamath. He had not anticipated the total moral degeneration he found at Ft. Klamath—

human nature revealed at its worst. Meacham's religious hackles were raised.

Soon after assuming his position and while touring other agencies in Oregon, Meacham was stunned to have one of his agents comment that he felt the solution to the Indian problem was to "wash the color out," implying that interbreeding between whites and Indians was the solution to the Indian issue. Meacham had very dryly commented that some of his own agents "had accomplished what they were able to in that line."

Now, here at Ft. Klamath, he found the same lack of morals with "children of all shades" running about. The soldiers at Ft. Klamath took Indian women quite openly, even from their husbands. Meacham was further disturbed to find that many of those husbands then refused to take their wives back. He found many soldiers to be inept. They were dishonest and immoral in their dealings with the reservation Indians. One officer gambled with the Indians and had won thirty-seven horses.[25]

The lapse in morals caused Meacham to issue regulations across Oregon forbidding plural marriage or gambling by any Indian in Oregon. Further, any white man living on a reservation with an Indian woman had two choices: marry her or give her up. Little did Meacham know as he toured the Indian agencies of Oregon in 1869 that his fate at many junctures in the future would be indelibly and powerfully cast with one group of Indians— the Modocs.

A Six-Mile Square Proposal

The situation with the "free" Modocs led by Captain Jack was deteriorating by 1869. Settlers did not like the Modocs in their vicinity. They complained that the Modocs took hay from the settlers' fields, walked uninvited into kitchens demanding food, snatched things from cupboards, lounged on beds, threw water around in kitchens, and otherwise annoyed their settler neighbors. No one was harmed and only certain individuals did this, but the Modocs as a whole were branded. The situation was volatile.[26]

Captain Jack made his first formal request for a tract of land in 1870. It was six-miles square, lying on both sides of the Oregon and California line. This was according to the general terms of an agreement, known as the Valentine's Day Treaty of 1864, which he had worked out informally with Elijah Steele.[27]

This treaty was totally different than the Treaty of 1864, officially drawn up by the U. S. government and placing the Modocs on the Klamath Reservation. Steele, who had at one time been Indian agent for the tribes in the Yreka area, put together the Valentine's Day Treaty, although he knew his jurisdiction no longer extended to the Modocs. He felt at the time he wrote it, before the Treaty of 1864 came into existence, that an informal treaty was better than nothing. Most importantly, it would state very clearly the Modocs' desires.

The Valentine's Day Treaty stated that the Modocs agreed to stop stealing stock, cease quarreling among themselves, and concede the right of soldiers to punish them if they broke the agreement. They also had to get permission from the soldiers at Ft. Klamath if they wanted to leave the reservation. In return they could act as guides, trade, and operate ferries for a fee.[28]

The official Treaty of 1864 was adopted, and nothing had ever happened with the Valentine's Day Treaty. But it was this six-year-old agreement upon which Jack based the terms for his formal request to the government. Not sure how to get the Modocs back onto the Klamath Reservation, Meacham recommended that Jack's request for the six-mile tract of land be granted. However, the feasibility of the plan was compromised by the fact that much of the land was now occupied.

There was immediate conflict with the settlers in possession of land within these boundaries. Neighboring farmers opposed the plan. It was unthinkable having the Modocs, a degraded band to their thinking, in their vicinity. Settlers heard of Meacham's recommendation and became alarmed that their uneasy association with the Modocs might become permanent. The Modocs' presence, they felt, would drastically alter their lives, even endanger their lives. Who was to say, they wanted to know, that the Modocs would become good neighbors?[29]

The most extraordinary thing about the six-mile square proposal was that the question of establishing a reservation was ever considered in the first place. Legislation passed on March 3, 1871, by Congress put into law Sec. 2079 and Sec. 2116. This legislation prohibited the United States from recognizing or drawing up a land treaty with an Indian nation or tribe. Only land legislation enacted before that time would be recognized.[30]

Even at the highest levels, forming a new reservation was discussed. A March 24, 1873, letter from Secretary of the Interior Columbus Delano to Secretary of War W. W. Belknap says, in regard to relocating the Modocs:

> It was intended that their [the Modocs] wishes should in some respects be consulted and adopted... Lost River was suggested as a place for their location, provided they declined the Coast reservation.[31]

Killing of a Shaman

In January of 1871 a warrant was issued for the arrest of Captain Jack in the murder of a Klamath shaman, or medicine man. Jack's niece had become ill. Curley Headed Doctor, the medicine man Jack called on when a medical problem arose, was gone. Jack turned to the nearest available healer, a shaman from Klamath. The Klamath medicine man was so convinced that he could cure the girl, he accepted a fee in advance, guaranteeing a cure. The girl died, and in accordance with Modoc and Klamath custom, Jack killed the shaman for incompetence.[32]

The killing of a shaman who did not perform was not uncommon. It was a known hazard of the job among Indians considering the profession. Friends of the unsuccessful shaman reported the death to Ivan Applegate, nephew of the prosperous rancher Jesse Applegate, who in turn asked the Siskiyou County sheriff to arrest Captain Jack.

This was a vivid illustration of the clash of two cultures whose value systems collided. Defining murder was tricky. It was hard to interpret an action without understanding the thinking of a different society. Jack made a trip to Yreka and asked Elijah Steele for advice. Steele wrote a note dated January 28, 1871, advising against anyone's attempting to arrest Jack.

> The white people should not meddle with them [the Modocs] in their laws among themselves further than to try to persuade them out of such foolish notions...let them settle all these matters among themselves... [33]

But the damage was done, and even Captain Jack probably

realized his course of action was not the best. Local settlers used the killing to discredit Jack as an "indicted murderer." As for Jack, he would never forget the name Applegate.

Early Photograph of Fissure in Lava
*Volcanic activity some half million years before, had
laid down a rugged terrain to the south of Tule Lake.
Huge cracks and fissures ran throughout.
This area today is known as the Lava Beds National Monument.*

Chapter 3
The Two Jesses

*In only twenty-seven short years, a Modoc society,
primitive as it was, was chopped to bits
and scattered to the four winds.*[34]

Francis "Van" Landrum, historian, 1988

The Modoc people stood poised in 1871 on the brink of a war from which they would not recover. In order to fully understand the start and cause of the Modoc War, it is necessary to move back in time.

When historian Francis Landrum talked about the collapse of the Modoc society, he saw the start of that demise in 1847 when brothers Jesse, Lindsay, and Charles Applegate, with a party of other Oregonians, blazed the Applegate Trail through traditional Modoc Lost River country. This land was a natural range for beef cattle. That did not go unnoticed by the pioneer exploration party, especially Jesse Applegate who was a land surveyor.[35]

In the early part of the summer of 1871, Jesse Applegate had settled at Clear Lake, to the east of Tule Lake, on a tract of land owned by Jesse Carr, a wealthy California legislator and land developer. Even though the land belonged to Carr, it was known as the Jesse Applegate Ranch.

Jesse Carr, a diminutive man with a speech impediment that kept him from public speaking, was a major participant in San Francisco real estate speculation and investment. In addition to substantial land holdings, he possessed large herds of cattle and horses and in 1862 reported 2500 Spanish ewes at his ranch in Monterey County, California. He was one of the largest U. S. mail delivery contractors on the Pacific coast from 1866 to 1870, a lucrative position. He was a power in the state, frequently mentioned as a candidate for senate or governor.[36]

Just how the two Jesses met is not totally clear. It was probably through their common interests of politics, livestock, and land development. The two men, both in their mid-fifties, concocted a

Jesse Applegate

*A drawing of this prominent
figure in Modoc War events.
Reluctant to be photographed—
no known photograph is known.*

Jesse Carr

*California politician
and land baron.
(courtesy of Shaw Library,
Klamath Falls, Oregon)*

massive land development scheme that started in the years just prior to the Modoc War.

Combining their skills, energies, and ambitions, this colossal undertaking, which they referred to as their "stock rancho," took years to reach its culmination, even beyond Applegate's death in 1888. The rancho acquisition plan included vast portions of ancestral Modoc land. A key facet in the "stock rancho" plan was to get the Modocs permanently off the land.

Historian Robert Johnston, who spent many years studying the Applegate-Carr connection, concluded in a 1991 study that "... looking at the record...it can be shown that the two Jesses—one an Oregonian, the other a Californian—probably did more than all other settlers, civilian governmental officials, or the military, to cause that tragic conflict [the Modoc War]."[37]

The Strategy Behind the "Stock Ranchero"

Their plan was to move forward on two fronts: first of all, the removal of the Modocs and, secondly, the acquisition of land from the appropriate governmental agencies. Applegate was the "front man." Carr's name was rarely mentioned in relationship to the Modocs.

Alfred Meacham had joined Elijah Steele in support for a Lost River reservation, as outlined in Steele's Valentine Day Treaty. Applegate set out to squash that thinking as quickly as possible. He made his feelings about a Modoc reservation in the Lost River country very clear in a July 27, 1871, letter to Meacham.

Applegate argued that such an arrangement would not satisfy the settlers in the area. Marauding by the Modocs would increase, and the Modoc Lost River reservation would become the refuge of "every vicious and vagabond Indian in the country." On a practical level, administration of a reservation this small would be financially unfeasible. A new reservation in Lost River country would also impact the Klamath Reservation, "filling the Modocs there with discontent."[38]

Brigadier General Edward Richard Sprigg Canby was at this time in charge of the entire military Department of the Columbia, which included the Klamath-Modoc region. Appointed to his position in 1870, he was known to be empathetic to the Indian plight while concurrently performing his role in keeping the peace. Canby, who was in his mid-50s, became a central figure in the Modoc conflict.[39]

Applegate's letter was passed to Canby, who sent it on to Capt. James Jackson at Ft. Klamath. Jackson responded: "...no doubt they [Modocs] are insolent beggars but...no one has been robbed or seriously threatened."[40]

The Case for the Modocs' Removal

A hand-written, homemade looking petition to the Ft. Klamath commander against the Modocs surfaced at the start of 1872 from a Mr. True and a Mr. Burnett. The True-Burnett complaint was casual in its wording and style, obviously informally written by the two men. The petition stated that certain Modocs had come to True's home in Lost River country, where he had a land claim. They had knocked down his fence, turned their ponies into his hay, and taken some hay with them. They had also stolen household utensils. True concluded by saying that "they had threatened the lives of several white men." Mr. Burnett adds, "Any statement that Mr. True makes I will vouch for."[41]

Within a few days, an official petition, formal in all respects and much more powerful, surfaced and was sent to Meacham. Very different than the True-Burnett petition, this document bore marks of legal assistance. A serious movement was underfoot to unite settlers in a concentrated effort to get the Modocs out. More than forty "Citizens of Lost, Link, Klamath and Tule Lake country" signed it. The petition complained that the military and Indian departments had not done their job:

> ...this band of outlaws, who by your delay to enforce the treaty, have been led to despise rather than respect the authority of the Government.

> ...shall a petty Indian chief, with twenty desperados and a squalid band of three hundred miserable savages any longer set at defiance the strong arm of the Government, driving our citizens from their homes, threatening their lives, and destroying their property.[42]

The petition had a solid Applegate feel to it. Petition signers recommended Jesse Applegate's nephew Ivan, the Yainax commissary on the Klamath Reservation, as a suitable man to take charge of the Modocs' removal.[43] The True-Burnett petition and the formal settlers' petition, under a cover letter from Meacham, were forwarded to Canby. Meacham recommended to Canby that the Modocs be removed to the Yainax portion of the Klamath Reservation. Both the settlers' petition and Meacham's letter presented a prompt to Canby to act during the remaining winter because the Modocs traditionally did not fight in the wintertime.

Meacham was half-hearted about the action he had taken. In his quandry and vacillation about what to do, Meacham sought approval from Commissioner of Indian Affairs F. A. Walker in Washington, D.C. He wrote him of his request to Canby to remove the Modocs. He asked Walker to send a telegram if he did not approve of the Modoc removal. Meacham noted that the Modocs "...were ill treated by the Klamaths and the sub-agent [Capt. O. C. Knapp] failed to protect them." Meacham also reminded the commissioner, "I have suggested in my annual report an alternative [six-mile square reservation at Tule Lake], but it has not received any attention known to this office."[44]

Meacham's efforts met with silence—no response from Washington.

Canby sent a report to his superiors on Feb. 7, 1872, including copies of both petitions:

> ...no action should be taken toward a forcible removal of the Modoc Indians until the question of their permanent location is settled....I do not think that the immediate application of force as asked for [to move the Modocs back to the reservation] would be either expedient or just...

> I am not surprised at the unwillingness of the Modocs to return to any point of the reservation where they would be exposed to hostilities...(and without adequate protection) from the Klamaths.[45]

Jesse Applegate, meanwhile, in his fervent, almost poetic style of writing, took verbal aim at the Modocs. A lengthy and cynical letter written on Feb. 1, 1872, to Meacham lambasted any effort to allow the Modocs to stay in Lost River country:

> If these Indians [Modocs] were of the quiet, orderly description that the majority of Oregon Indians are, these difficulties would not exist.

> ...their [Modocs] arrogance and impudence have been greater than ever before, and the patience and forbearance of the settlers most inclined to peace is well-neigh [sic] exhausted...

> If the humanitarians who now control Indian affairs have any regard for the lives of white men, women, and children, there are reasons for the removal of these Indians to their

reservation...

Poets and moralists agree that the 'untutored savage' is also a 'wild-man,' and like other wild animals they chafe and fret under any kind of restraint...

This will cause strife between the red man and the white, and both...may come to grief in the scuffle. In tenderness, therefore, to the poor Indian, they had better be removed out of harm's way.[46]

Applegate concludes with a piece of advice to the military on strategy for the Modoc removal:

If this is not done before spring opens, it cannot be done this year. As well expect to collect the coyotes out of that region of rock, mountain, and morass, as the Indians in the summer season.[47]

The two Jesses' "stock rancho" plan was falling into place.

But not everyone was oblivious to what was going on. Both before the Modoc War and during it, certain publications and newspapermen, particularly Robert Bogart of the *San Francisco Chronicle*, hounded the Applegate family.[48] A Feb. 23, 1873, article in the *San Francisco Chronicle*, referred to "Uncle Jesse," a name often used in the paper for Jesse Applegate:

Uncle Jesse says that newspaper men are the curse of the earth... Uncle Jesse will probably be confirmed in that belief by the time the correspondents get through with their exposures of the Applegates' family management of Indian affairs.

Old Jesse hates the Indian as the devil hates holy water... This Indian business up here is a good deal like a decayed egg. Puncture the shell anywhere and you will find an Applegate flavor at the same time.

General Edward R. S. Canby *1817 - 1873*
Commander of the Department of the Columbia.
Military leader through much of the Modoc War and
generally well respected by Indian tribes.

Chapter 4
Lost River Battle

You are directed to remove the Modoc Indians to Camp Yainax on the Klamath Reservation, peaceably if you possibly can, but forcibly if you must.[49]

F. A. Walker to T. B. Odeneal, Nov. 25, 1872

Finally, in November 1872, an attempt was made to return the Modocs to the Klamath Reservation. The resulting conflict is known in history as the Lost River Battle—and the start of the Modoc War.

Meacham had been prepared to protect the Modocs and to act as a buffer against the shadow of war and land grabbing that was beginning to move menacingly across the land. He was eager to prevent war with the Modocs. Jesse Applegate and Meacham were at great odds, as Applegate vehemently opposed the Modocs staying in Lost River country. He wanted the Modocs back on the Klamath Reservation—whatever it took.

But the bulwark against war, namely Meacham, was on his way out. He was replaced in the $2500-a-year job as Oregon superintendent of Indian Affairs by Thomas B. Odeneal in the autumn of 1871. In the casual spirit of frontier politics and communication, Meacham did not know Odeneal had replaced him for five months.

So it was in this critical time of negotiations that the Interior Department sent in a man who knew practically nothing of the precarious relationship with the Modocs and had never even met Captain Jack. Odeneal displayed

Thomas B. Odeneal

little knowledge of the Modocs and even less empathy. But there he was, ready to solve pressing problems regarding the Modocs.[50]

Odeneal sent Yainax Commissary Ivan Applegate to Captain Jack's Lost River village in late November to discuss the possibility of the Modocs returning to the reservation. This seems like a strange selection on Odeneal's part because of the animosity Jack felt toward Applegate over the shaman incident. Why Odeneal did not go himself to negotiate with Captain Jack about a settlement remains a puzzle. Odeneal kept the reason for not going to himself, but his poor decision not to meet with Captain Jack left a sore and festering feeling with Modocs for a long time.[51]

The next development is what historian Herbert Bancroft has referred to as a "fatal error." The information that Applegate transferred to Odeneal as a result of his meeting with Captain Jack heavily impacted the relationship between the military and Modocs, sowing the seeds of the Modoc War.

Applegate returned with the information that the Modocs would not meet with Odeneal. He further informed Odeneal that the Modocs were talking war. It was Applegate's opinion that action should be taken immediately by the military to forcibly remove the Modocs from their Lost River villages. He also assured Odeneal that the Modoc forces were very small at this particular time and that no serious resistance would be made to the troops.[52]

A Contradiction of Orders

A major factor contributing to the start of the Modoc War involved conflicts between two branches of the U. S. government: the military and the Bureau of Indian Affairs. Although both wanted to bring the Modocs back to the Klamath Reservation, they did not work in accord.

Crucial to the action was F. A. Walker of the Bureau of Indian Affairs. It was Walker who ordered Odeneal to bring the Modocs back to the reservation. Walker's infamous words on returning the Modocs peaceably if possible, but forcibly if necessary, were destined to ring through history.

Odeneal had promised to inform Canby and Lt. Col. Frank Wheaton, who served under Canby as commander of the Klamath-Modoc region, before taking any kind of action. Instead, Odeneal gave Maj. John Green, who had taken command of Fort Klamath during the summer, the job executing Walker's order.

Green had been told earlier by Canby and Wheaton that no one was to chase after Indians until all troops were ready to act with a single purpose and in a concentrated, coordinated campaign. Canby believed that no force of less than fifty troops should attempt to take Captain Jack and his warriors. But Green had explicit orders from Odeneal. He didn't feel he needed to check with Canby.[53]

Odeneal ordered Green to move Captain Jack's Modocs back onto the Klamath Reservation immediately. He stated that he didn't expect or want war but thought a show of force would be enough to persuade the Modocs to move back to the reservation.

It is here that Ivan Applegate once again entered the Lost River fiasco, and events began to spiral inevitably toward war. Applegate relayed to Green, as he had to Odeneal, that only half the Modoc force was encamped in their winter quarters on Lost River. He did not report that the other half of the force, led by Hooker Jim, was well ensconced on the opposite bank farther down stream. This led Odeneal and Green to conclude that there were far fewer Modocs to confront. Applegate insisted that, "thirty men would be ample force, as the Modocs would not think of fighting at all."

Captain Jack's camp was located on the south side of Lost River just east of the Natural Bridge. This natural phenomenon consisted of two ridges of stone that spanned the river just beneath the water level. Used for centuries to ford the river, this was the pioneer route of the Applegate Trail blazed in 1847. Hooker Jim's camp was on the north side of the river, a little east of Jack's camp.[54]

Maj. John Green

Hooker Jim was born into the Hot Creek band of Modocs, located on the western edge of traditional Modoc land, and he was listed as a member of that band on the official POW list at the end of the war. However, he had married Curley Headed Doctor's daughter and moved into their Lost River village. Through the early part of the war, most of his interaction was with his father-in-law's band, where he became a leader.[55]

With the report from Applegate, Green saw a way to end the entire Modoc problem with little effort. The element of a surprise attack in bad winter weather must have been in his thinking.[56] He forged ahead, ordering Capt. James Jackson to lead all available men at Ft. Klamath to Captain Jack's Lost River camp. Second Lt. Frazier A. Boutelle brought the official orders to Green for his signature. Boutelle had been startled at the order to depart and reminded his superior officer that Canby had requested to be told if troops were going to be used. He was also uncomfortable with the assumption that the Modocs would not fight. He cautioned Green that he believed the Modocs would fight. Little did Boutelle know that not only would the Modocs fight, but that the name

Boutelle would be etched in history at Lost River.[57]

Green had been misled by Applegate, but surely he knew that he was ignoring the intentions of Canby, his commanding general. It is interesting to note that some time after the Lost River Battle, when the conflicting orders were discovered, there was the usual quarrel among the military and Indian departments as to how that had happened and which had been in the wrong.[58]

Jackson left Ft. Klamath with thirty-eight men, including a doctor, and four men following with the pack train. Jackson and his men found the weather had conspired to be an enemy. The sleet troops encountered on horseback turned to ice. Man and beast were coated with it. Deep and unyielding mud caused the troops to move slowly. After almost sixteen hours of steady riding, exhausted and cold to the bone, the troops arrived at daybreak at Captain Jack's camp.[59] It was November 29, 1872—a day to be remembered forever in Modoc War history.

Capt. James Jackson

Jackson found Captain Jack ensconced with about fifteen warriors and their families. Jackson was completely unaware of the nearness of the second encampment of some fourteen warriors and families across the river. In that camp were a number of the most active leaders of the Modoc force, including Hooker Jim and his father-in-law, Curley Headed Doctor.

Let the War Begin

Talk kindly but firmly...
let the Indians be the aggressors.
Fire no gun except in self-defense.[60]

Thomas B. Odeneal, 1872

It scared me when Major [sic] Jackson came...
and made me jump out of my bed without a shirt,
or anything else on.[61]

Captain Jack, commenting on Lost River Battle.

His name was Scarfaced Charley. A deep scar—the result of a childhood accident—ran down his cheek, carving through the brown skin, tanned even darker by an intense, outdoor life in the sun. It was not a name his Modoc parents had given him nor was the name one he had selected. As the first wave of fair-skinned immigrants from the east began to move into the northern California/southern Oregon area in the mid-1800s, they found the Modoc language difficult to pronounce. Although the Modocs had lived for centuries in this spot with a culture and language intact, they found themselves being renamed by the settlers.

Whether Scarfaced Charley's Modoc name was Na-lu-is, as recorded on the 1885 Modoc Census, or the more complicated Chic-chack-am Lul-al-kuel-atko (translated as "run over by a wagon and scarred"), which appeared at the end of the war on the Modoc prisoner-of-war list, the non-Modoc-speaking immigrants had no desire to tackle these names.

Shkeitko (sometimes seen as Ski-et-tete-ko), meaning "left-handed man," was given the name Shacknasty Jim. Some say it was because of his mother's untidy housekeeping, but descendants were told it was a corruption of his Modoc name. Slat-us-locks became Steamboat Frank. He was named in recognition of the deep, resounding voice of his foster mother (who later became his wife). Boston Charley was very fair, Black Jim, very dark. History has recorded the colorful names of historically well-known Modocs like Curley Headed Doctor, Bogus Charley, and Hooker Jim. But lesser known Modocs had names that make one wonder who dreamed them up: Greasy Boots, Big Duck, Old Longface, Skukum Horse, Humpy Joe, and Tee-Hee Jack.

But the man with the scarred cheek was to leave his name permanently carved on the opening days of the Modoc War.

* * * * * *

— Simultaneous Gunfire —

The bitter cold, pre-dawn hours of November 29, 1872, brought a shroud of mist to the small cluster of wickiups nestled on the banks of Lost River. Most of this band of Modoc men, women, and children still slept.

Scarfaced Charley was up early that morning, out on the river. He did not know what lay ahead of him. The frigid cold caused his body to draw inward. His breath was slung before him as he glided south across the water. He banked his canoe, picked up his rifle, and moved through the still dawn toward the sleeping village.

A movement caught his attention. His eyes, trained for most of his life to catch the subtle shifts of game, locked on the bank above him. There stood a line of obviously cold and weary soldiers wearing the blue uniform that the Modocs knew well from the short time they had been forced to live on the Klamath Reservation.

Surprised to see the soldiers, Charley felt a slight feeling of uneasiness. The three years since the Modocs had walked off the reservation had passed fairly peaceably, with many Modocs living side-by-side with settlers, even helping them farm the fields that were beginning to claim the wilderness. He could think of no reason for soldiers to be here.

As he moved up the bank, the unthinkable happened. In his concern over the appearance of the soldiers, his usual careful ways with his gun failed him. The gun discharged, the aimless bullet hitting in the ground in front of him. A pang of fear hit him. This was not a good thing to happen with a string of blue on the bank.

Boutelle did not want to be where he was on this white, frosty morning. The military troop from Ft. Klamath had ridden through fifty-six miles of penetrating sleet and ice. The numbed men even found themselves frozen to their saddles at times.

Boutelle had told the Ft. Klamath commanding officer, Maj. John Green, that the scant number of soldiers dispatched to bring the Modocs back to the reservation was "just enough to provoke a fight" but not enough to bring the Modocs into submission. Yet here he was, exhausted and drained from the cold, on guard, studying the Modoc who walked toward him. He did not know what the one shot that had rung out in the stillness meant, but Boutelle was ready for whatever happened.

Bring the Modocs in, "peaceably if you possibly can but forcibly if you must," was the command that had been handed down to the troops. It was running through Boutelle's head now. He figured he was about to find out which it would be.

The cold was bone chilling, especially since the soldiers stood coatless. The troops had halted to adjust their saddles a mile before reaching Captain Jack's village. Boutelle informed Capt. James Jackson, heading the detail of soldiers, that if he was going into a fight, "I want my deck cleared for action," and so he

*had removed his half-frozen overcoat. Most of the men
followed suit.*

*Scarfaced Charley climbed the bank and withdrew
to one end of the Modoc camp. He was talking in a very
excited manner with a number of other Modocs who had
been alerted by his accidental shot. His rifle, which he
waved defiantly, was still in his hand. Charley and
Boutelle faced each other, two men from two different
worlds, preparing to enter American history. The cold
metal of the rifle in his hand was reassuring to Charley.
He knew the time had come when he must use it.*

*In the pre-dawn hours on Lost River, the historic
moment moved into fast action. Charley tightened
his grip on his gun and raised it. Boutelle lifted his
weapon at the same time. Two shots rang out at the
same time, sounding as one.*

* * * * * *

Second Lt. Frazier Boutelle
*Thirty-three years of age at time
of Modoc War. Served in 1889 as
superintendent of
Yellowstone National Park.*

Scarfaced Charley
*Major Modoc figure in the Modoc
War. Both sides
had a high opinion of him,
and he emerged as a "hero."*

Neither man on that windy, snow-swept ridge could have
known the great significance of the first two shots of the Modoc
War, fired simultaneously in the conflict that became known as
the Lost River Battle.[62]

Boutelle gave this account after the war:

> I raised my pistol and fired at Scarfaced Charley. Great
> minds appear to have thought alike. At the same instant
> Charley raised his rifle and fired at me. We both missed, his
> shot passing through my clothing over my elbow. It cut two

holes through my blouse, one long slit in a cardigan jacket and missed my inner shirts. My pistol bullet passed through a red handkerchief Charley had tied around his head; so he afterward told me. There was some discussion after the close of the war as to who fired the first shot. I use a pistol in my left hand. The track of Scar-faced Charley's bullet showed that my arm was bent in the act of firing when he fired. We talked the matter over but neither could tell which fired first....He [Charley] told me that [the fired shot as he came up the bank] was an accidental discharge. I believed him.[63]

Those first two shots of the Modoc War did not kill a man, but they would result in huge suffering and anguish to settlers, Modocs, and the U. S. Army. The shots also signaled the beginning of a period that would profoundly and irreparably affect the destiny of the Modoc people.

Most Modocs either did not speak English or spoke it only sparingly at the time those shots pierced the silence of that frosty dawn in 1872. Three decades later, at the turn of the century in 1900, hardly a Modoc spoke the ancient Modoc language.

In the age-old Modoc culture, conflicts took place in good weather, only rarely in the winter.[64] The late November military raid caught the Modocs completely by surprise. The bedlam of the Lost River Battle—riderless horses rearing and kicking, din, and commotion—lasted only a few minutes. The Modoc village was torched. Watchman, one of Captain Jack's lieutenants, was killed. Meacham wrote that soldiers piled matting on a sick woman left behind and burned her to death. Meacham claimed he heard the story from several soldiers. Other accounts are that it was not a deliberate act.[65]

In a December 2, 1872, report to Green, Jackson outlined the Lost River encounter differently than Boutelle's account.

I directed Boutelle to...arrest the [Modoc] leaders, if possible. This order was followed by firing on the parts of the Indians, and a general engagement immediately ensued. I poured in volley after volley among their worst men, killing most of them, capturing the camp, and driving the Indians to the refuge of the brush and hills."[66]

An official report of the Lost River Battle was made by Col. Jefferson C. Davis nearly a year later, after the war had ended. The November 1, 1873, document once again used Jackson's words "opened fire upon the troops," discounting Boutelle's account of a simultaneous firing.[67]

A verbal conflict related to the shoot-out between Scarfaced Charley and Boutelle happened when Alfred Meacham sometime later wrote about the first shots fired. He maintained that, "Boutelle with blasphemous oaths and insulting epithet...enraged at the Indian [Scarfaced Charley] for presuming to 'talk back,'... said he would teach 'the d-d red skin son of a _____ a lesson.'"[68]

Jeff Riddle, who was a small boy during the Modoc War, parroted the same words, complete with the blanks for swear words, when he wrote his book in 1914.[69]

Boutelle was obviously upset with Meacham:

> You may have seen a book written by A. B. Meacham. He represented me as advancing upon Scar-faced Charley, uttering vile and insulting epithets. I did not move forward a foot...but commanded the men to fire and fired myself. I did not address a word to an Indian that morning. Meacham attempted to get an account from me and was referred to Major Jackson's official report. Hence his insults to me.[70]

Another attack at Lost River, across the river from Jackson's assault, was to seal the fate of many settlers in the area. Shortly after the exchange of the first shots, Oliver C. Applegate, a younger brother of Ivan and nephew of Jesse, and a small ragtag band of citizens attacked Hooker Jim's camp across the river. Two civilians, including Wendolin Nuss, the first permanent settler of the Klamath Basin, were killed. It is not known how many Modocs were killed, although Meacham claimed two women and a baby in its mother's arms were shot. The surprised and enraged Modocs fought back but eventually fled.[71]

The general consensus between both U. S. military and government departments was that the Lost River attack was hastily thought out and ill advised. The military put the death toll of soldiers and civilian fighters from both attacks at four losses.[72] At the highest level, a January 17, 1873, report on the Lost River episode from Canby to U. S. Secretary of War W. T. Sherman read:

> A grave mistake was no doubt committed in attempting their [the Modocs] removal before a sufficient force had been collected to secure that result beyond the probability of failure.[73]

History shrouds much of the truth of any event as time passes, people die, and interest moves elsewhere. But the words of Boutelle still stand out sharply in his analysis of the Lost River events:

> [Odeneal] sent word to Captain Jack that he was at Linkville and to meet him there. Jack not responding, he was informed that Odeneal would be at Lost River two days later to talk to him. Instead of making preparations for his suggested meeting, he [Odeneal] dispatched Mr. I. D. Applegate to Fort Klamath asking that troops be sent to move the Indians.... The greater sin lies at the door of Mr. Odeneal, who would not trust his precious skin to a council on Lost River; but preferred treacherously to send troops with guns in place of an agent of the Indian Department with an olive branch. He was sadly mistaken in believing that the Indians would not fight...

Boutelle also commented on the unexpected attack led by Oliver Applegate:

> The citizens who attacked the Indian camp on the left bank of Lost River were there without order or authority, and had

no more right for their attack than if it had been made on Broadway, New York.[74]

It is hard to assess blame for a disastrous war. But certain facts seem obvious. A major reason that the war came about was that certain individuals wished to attain Modoc land. Author Walter H. Palmberg says, "Insatiable greed for the Indian's lands was the one and only basic cause that led to the Indian's retaliation....Any cultural considerations were attending and resulting issues."[75]

There was an over-all decentralization of authority. Neither the army, the Bureau of Indian Affairs, the agents, nor the Modocs knew who was the real authority. Orders and counter-orders flew every which way.

Odeneal had promised to inform Canby and Wheaton before taking action. He did not. He made poorly thought-out provisions for alerting the settlers to the attack. Further, he took advantage of an innocent, antiquated Army regulation to override normal levels of command and gave an order to Green. Why Green took orders from a civilian rather than waiting for his commander to issue them is incomprehensible. Later Green tried to explain: "It was believed that the Modocs would submit."

The attack by Oliver Applegate and the civilians on Hooker Jim's camp, unauthorized by the military, was disastrous. It caused the senseless deaths of uninvolved settlers and set the path to war on an irreversible course.[76]

But all the events on that cold and dreary November day at Lost River did happen. Soldiers and Modocs alike scattered in every direction. The Modocs fled into the surrounding sagebrush, headed for the nearby water of Tule Lake.

* * * * * *

— A Scramble for Safety —

The fire and mayhem of the village were well behind the Modoc girl Bap-pee-Binpatokit, who would become known in later years as Jennie Clinton. Her dugout canoe, now on Tule Lake, was tossed high in the air by the stiff and vicious wind. Waves broke over the canoe, swamping its inhabitants and threatening at times to dump the fleeing Modocs into the dark, turbulent water. Jennie was in her early teens in that winter of 1872, and in addition to the crippling fear that seized her, she had never in her life been so cold. The bitter sleet had practically paralyzed her. She shook so badly, her teeth felt like they would fall out. Her body was starting to quiver uncontrollably in response to the penetrating cold.

It had fallen to Jennie, and Jennie alone, to control the canoe with her paddles, and, when she was able, to throw every piece of her slender body and arms into trying to force the vessel forward. Her fingers were frozen in numbness and pain.

The teenager felt her aunt shuddering and shivering beside her. The two of them had managed to drag a badly wounded Black Jim into the canoe as bullets landed around them. They had frantically paddled down Lost River through the day and now moved across Tule Lake. The ten-foot cedar tree canoe was not made to handle three people, even with one as small as Jennie, and the craft listed dangerously. The daylight had faded and darkness had brought an even more horrible cold.

The wind howled as if taunting the exhausted Modocs in the sorrow of their defeat. It was not so much a military defeat. In all the blood and confusion, no one seemed to know whether more soldiers or Modocs had fallen or even who had been killed or wounded. The defeat Jennie and the other Modocs felt on this awful night—with homes burned, possessions lost, family pets left behind—was the loss of security and the uncertainty of the future.

Jennie had been jarred from sleep this morning by gunfire. The wickiup in the winter camp had grown cold during the night as the fire died out, but Jennie had wrapped herself in her bearskin. When the noise had first started, Jennie had jumped to her feet only to be thrown to the floor by her mother.

"Hold the children down," her mother had screamed, and then Jennie understood. They would all be safer from bullets if they were flat on the floor. The gunfire began to die down, and Jennie believed that it would all pass. Then she smelled smoke, and the truth became apparent to her. The soldiers were burning them out.

The smoke, fire, and screams had all mingled together as Jennie ran for the river. She didn't know where her mother, father, or brother and sisters had gone. She had managed to grab Auntie, who was too frail to move by herself.

Jennie stopped rowing for just a moment to relieve her burning arms. She reached down and pulled Auntie close, pressing her cold lips to Auntie's forehead. Her aunt had always been a dear part of Jennie's existence, and now Auntie's life rested in Jennie's hands, frozen as they were. For all the panic Jennie was feeling, her aunt was far worse, emotionally and mentally ready to slip over the edge. Black Jim now moaned softly from the bottom of the canoe. He was somewhat sheltered from the wind and in his unconscious state was surely more comfortable than they, despite his wounds.

The flotilla of Modocs—Jennie could see the outline of canoes to both sides of her—were headed for the lava bed located thirteen miles across the lake. She could only wonder if her parents and siblings were somewhere in the canoes around her. Nothing could be heard above the whining of the wind. Silence and shock had settled over the Modocs

Jennie had traveled south previously to the lava bed. But that had been in another time. The lava land that had always before seemed so harsh and hostile was now a beckoning refuge. She knew its crevices and caves would offer shelter. The men had often talked of what they would do if war ever came to the Modocs. The barren wastelands across the lake would be where the Modocs would take their stand.

The land of burnt out fires, where hot volcanic lava had once flowed angrily across the landscape, now offered salvation to the Modoc people.

* * * * * *

Scarfaced Charley was one Modoc who remained behind before fleeing to the lava flow. He now rode out by himself to warn friendly settlers of their peril and to urge them to run for their lives. It is said that he even grabbed settlers' horse halters, pointing them away from danger. In particular he was concerned for the ranchers in the Hot Creek area, mainly John Fairchild and Pressley "Press" Dorris, who had long been friends of the Modocs.[77]

Some dozen other Modocs also remained behind, but with exactly the opposite motives from Scarfaced Charley. While Fairchild and Dorris began efforts to save the Hot Creek Modocs, Modocs from Hooker Jim's village that had been attacked sought vengeance against settlers.

Chapter 5
The Nightmare Escalates

*If the soldiers had come about fifty or sixty strong, with plenty of
ammunition... all this trouble
and bloodshed could have been saved.*

Louisa Boddy, Lost River settler, Jan. 8, 1873, *San Francisco Chronicle*

The result of Oliver Applegate's attack on Hooker Jim's village
left a bloody page in history. In retaliation for the Applegate
attack, enraged Modocs—smarting from the surprise attack—rode
along the north and northeast shores of Tule Lake searching for
white men to kill. Meacham claimed that among those Modocs
making the raid was the father of the baby killed in Hooker Jim's
village and relatives of the women shot and burned. This was done
without Captain Jack's knowledge or approval. The maurading
Modocs, expecting to come home in victory, instead found a very
angry Captain Jack.[78]

This group of Modocs killed fourteen settlers. Surviving settlers
later listed Modocs they had seen in the group. Three Modocs were
identified by most witnesses: Curley Headed Doctor, Hooker Jim,
and Long Jim. There was both misidentification and speculation
on whom the other Modocs were. But they were most likely minor
warriors.[79]

Henry Miller, longtime friend of the Modocs, had been out
riding the Thursday afternoon before the fateful Lost River Battle.
He had assured Modocs he encountered that he knew of no plans
for soliders to be in the area. Because of the military's neglect to
warn settlers of an impending attack, he had no idea there was
a problem. Out riding on the day of the attact, he saw a band of
Indians and raised his hand in greeting. He was shot from his
horse and went to his grave never knowing what hit him—or why.
Ironically, Miller had, the spring before, assured an army officer
that the settlers need not fear the Modocs.[80]

William Brotherton and two of his sons were shot and killed
while cutting wood. Joseph, Brotherton's fifteen year-old son, was

with neighbor John Schroeder, who tried to escape the Modocs on his horse. He did not succeed, the Modocs shooting him from his horse.

In the confusion, Joseph ran for home. Sarah Brotherton, seeing her son fleeing the Modocs, rushed to meet him with a revolver in her hand. Her younger son called to her to come back, then opened the door and followed her. Turning to the boy, she ordered him back to the house, told him to grab his father's rifle, elevate the sights to eight hundred yards, and blast away at the Modocs. This he did, with his younger sister wiping and handling the cartridges. Sarah grabbed her older son and raced back to the house. Barricading the door with freshly purchased sacks of flour, she pushed loopholes in the house walls, converting her home to a fortress. The family bombarded the Modocs with rifle fire, keeping them at bay. Finally they left, but it was not until the third day that Ivan Applegate arrived with help at the Brotherton homestead and rescued the beleaguered family.[81]

* * * * * *

— A Killing Time —

Late autumn was always Louisa Boddy's favorite time of year. It was now moving into winter, the nip in the air was sharp, and there was snow on the ground in places. The Boddy family—Louisa's husband William; son Richard Cravigan, twenty-two, and his brother Willie, eighteen; and daughter Kate and son-in-law Nicholas Schira—lived on the east side of Tule Lake, three miles from the Modoc camps on Lost River. When Louisa had first come to this hostile piece of America from Australia, where her family had lived for several generations, she hated both the life and the land. The Modocs wanted it back, and there were times she wished they had it back.

Time had mellowed her, however. The cabin that the men had built was a sturdy one. It might not be the finest house a person could have, but it had character and warmth. She had especially come to love the lake itself with its vast expanse of water. She never ceased to be awed by the waterfowl, the ducks and geese sometimes coming in such great numbers that the sky was darkened with their flight. Louisa rubbed her face with the back of her hand, leaving another smear of flour across her cheek. Friday was bread day and bread making was always good. There was a soothing nature to the constant kneading, and when she was done, she felt she'd accomplished something. She knew her husband William looked forward to bread-making day. He always stuck his head around the door, a big grin on his face, hand outstretched, begging for a piece of warm bread. It was just a few minutes before noon, and the men, who were out with the wagon gathering wood, would soon be in. Her daughter had already put lunch on the table and had gone outside to wait for her husband, Nicholas.

A shrill scream from her daughter, Kate, jerked Louisa from her thoughts. As she ran to the door, Louisa, too, saw Nicholas's team of horses running homeward. Louisa's heart gave a sick lurch as she grabbed her long skirt off the ground and ran toward her daughter and the wagon.

The wagon was covered with blood. When Kate picked up the reins, they were slippery with blood. Thinking that her husband had fallen from the wagon and been hurt, she started running up the road. Louisa paused only long enough to grab a shawl, which she wrapped around her, and a basin of water. Then she, too, ran up the road.

About a quarter of a mile from the house Nicholas was sprawled on the side of the road. Just as Louisa reached Kate, six Modocs on horseback rushed out of the brush. Louisa now felt not only fear for Nicholas, but a fear of these men, whose sudden arrival seemed out of character with the usual easy-going nature of the few Modocs that from time to time happened by the house. Why, just last Friday she'd given a piece of her fresh bread to a Modoc who had come by. His grin had been almost as big as William's.

Two of the men urged their horses forward until they loomed above her, a few feet away. One of the men leaned down, with his face only inches from hers, and asked her if there were any more men at the house. With a voice none too steady she told them that the team had run away with Nicholas's wagon. Abruptly, one of the Modocs emitted a shrill war whoop, and the two Indians whirled on their horses and joined the others. Then all six were gone as abruptly as they had come.

Sobs came from Kate. She had already discovered that her husband was dead, shot through the head.

Louisa's thoughts whirled. Why had they not killed her and Kate, too? Death had whispered in her face and passed on its way. The Indians were obviously killing only men.

Supporting each other, the two women continued down the road to where the men were supposed to be chopping wood. More horror confronted them as they found Richard killed, stripped naked, and thrown across his wagon.

The bile rose in Louisa's throat, and she wanted nothing more than to curl up in a ball, lie down, and die herself. But a sense of urgency caused her to grab her daughter and push on in a desperate search for William.

Then in the distance, Louisa saw William. But she also saw the Indians moving toward him. She knew she could do nothing now but save herself and her daughter. Feeling the greatest sorrow she had ever felt, and swallowing the greatest fear she'd ever experienced, Louisa took the last living member of her family by her hand and gently led her off the road toward the hills.

They walked until it got so dark they could not see. They sat down under a tree, their arms wrapped around each other. The bitter cold was nothing next to the pain the women felt at their unbelievable, unspeakable loss. Daylight sent them struggling through the snow again.

After traveling at times through two feet of snow, Louisa and Kate finally arrived at Lost River Bridge. There they learned there had been a fight with the Modocs the day before. The settlers had not been warned.

* * * * * *

Capt. Jackson, resting his exhausted command after the Lost River Battle, did not know until two days after the Boddy men were killed that settlers had been attacked and killed. Odeneal had sent James Brown (or "One-Armed" Brown as Louisa Boddy called him), a messenger with the Indian department, to notify settlers who were likely to be endangered. Brown afterward said he knew nothing of any settlers farther below the cabin of the settlers he warned, and that the men he notified said nothing about any more settlers.[82]

As a result of not being notified by the military that a battle with the Modocs was going to take place, many settlers in the Lost River area lost their lives. Louisa Boddy was to harbor bitterness against more than just the Modocs. In a letter written on Dec. 24, 1872, and published in the *San Francisco Chronicle* on Jan. 8, 1873, she says:

> Editor Sentinel:
>
> The Indians had told us, time and again, that if the soldiers came to take them upon the Reservation it would make them mad, and they would kill every white man; but if the soldiers did not come, they would not kill any white men, as they wanted to be good friends.
>
> We requested the Messengers never to come with soldiers without sending a runner ahead to warn the settlers. But they failed to do so... .all [my family] were murdered in cold blood within a mile and a half of the house, and all through the carelessness and negligence of the officers in command.

The reaction to the killings was one of shock and horror in the area, and it reverberated across the nation. Quite amazingly, in the midst of reaction to this atrocity, the fact that women were spared provoked commentary among both the press and the military.

The Dec. 18, 1872, *Yreka Journal* commented on the fact that the women were easy targets "but for the first time in Indian warfare in Oregon, they did not kill the women. They killed both of the husbands of the ladies and then asked for more men."

Second Lt. Harry De Witt Moore was transferred from Vancouver, Washington, to duty in the Modoc conflict. He wrote countless letters home to his aunt and uncle. Only recently have Moore's letters come to light. He wrote that the Modocs had gone "down to the valley and killed the settlers, sparing however the women and children—this is remarkable—such a course is unprecedented in the annals of Indian warfare...and they deserve a great deal of credit for it."[83]

We Want Peace

Ranchers John Fairchild and Pressley "Press" Dorris sought out the peaceable Hot Creek (sometimes referred to as the Cottonwood) band of Modocs in an attempt to get them to safety after the Lost River Battle. Under the leadership of Shacknasty Jim and including such men as Bogus Charley, Steamboat Frank, and Ellen's Man George, the Hot Creek Modocs were a separate Modoc band. The Hot Creek band was located some distance to the west of Captain Jack's and Hooker Jim's villages. They lived between the Fairchild and Dorris ranches, and many of the Hot Creeks were employed by these ranchers and others in the area. The Hot Creeks had little in common with Captain Jack's people and did not wish to now become embroiled in disorder. They could not see Captain Jack successfully holding out against the forces

Pressley Dorris

that were coming in on him.[84]

No rancher or settler in the area was more respected by the Modocs than thirty-eight-year-old John Fairchild, a local stockman, who had lived his whole life on the frontier. A man with prematurely gray hair and a squared off beard, he had come to California during the Gold Rush. But the hit-and-miss nature of mining did not appeal to him. He had undertaken ranching and successfully so.

Fairchild thought people should lead lives in their own way, and as a result, he did not like government. He did not think much of the treaty that had, with an "X" on a piece of paper, taken the ancestral Modoc lands. He respected the Modocs' claim to the land and was willing to do whatever was appropriate to show it. Fairchild had made a personal agreement with the Modocs and paid a small rent for his large ranching operation.[85]

Hot Creek Modocs showed the effects of successful integration with the non-Indian, not only in the fact that they learned and were involved in ranch work, but many of them, including women, spoke English as a result of the assimilation. They led a diplomatic existence in the Hot Creek area.

The Hot Creeks, numbering approximately fourteen men and thirty women and children, were anxious to avoid trouble. Fairchild felt that a paternalistic protection of their interests was his proper role. He contacted military officers at Ft. Klamath, asking to bring the Hot Creeks to safety and for permission to keep two of his indispensable ranch hands. Maj. John Green replied on Dec. 4, 1872:

> Your note of yesterday...in reply I would state that if you bring the forty Indians to Major Jackson's camp at the mouth of Lost River, they will be protected to the Yainax agency.
>
> The request regarding the Indians you wish to keep (Shack Nasty [sic] Jim and Frank) is acceded to so far as I am concerned.

Leadership of the Hot Creeks had passed from Old Sheepy, who was "upwards of eighty," to Shacknasty Jim. Sheepy was too old to travel with the band, so the decision was made to leave him behind with a half dozen women to care for him. Some of those women were to play a major role in the months ahead as translators and couriers. The rest of the Hot Creeks gathered their belongings and joined Fairchild.[86]

(L to R) Hot Creek Modocs Shacknasty Jim, author's great-grandfather; Hooker Jim; Steamboat Frank; and rancher John Fairchild.

Rancher Harold Porterfield, current co-owner of the Fairchild Ranch, and author Cheewa James on traditional Hot Creek land.

Fairchild, Dorris, and the other ranchers accompanying the Hot Creek Modocs were determined to keep the army, volunteer soldiers, and settlers from harming the Modocs. Unfortunately, word spread that Modocs were coming. The Modocs, as they thought about passing near Linkville, were nervous. It was immaterial that none of these Hot Creek Modocs had been involved in the Lost River Battle and that the group wanted only to avoid fighting by moving to the Klamath Reservation.[87]

The Hot Creek Modocs would never reach the Klamath Reservation. An intoxicated man by the name of Fritz Muntz, once a farmhand employed by John Fairchild, set out to avenge the death of his friend and fellow German, Wendolin Nuss, killed at Lost River in the raid on Hooker Jim's village. He single-handedly sent the Modocs on their way by the power of his words.[88]

The Dec. 6, 1872, *Yreka Union* told the story:

> [The Modocs] were met by some eight or ten men from the Linkville settlement, who were shocked at the idea of these Indians being permitted to proceed peaceably to the Reservation and declared their purpose to attack them. Fairchild and company remonstrated, stating that their word was pledged to protect the Indians, and they felt their own safety and that of their families depended upon their keeping it or dying in the attempt.

Muntz managed to talk to some of the Hot Creeks, most of whom spoke English, and his words whipped them into a frenzy. In Shacknasty Jim's words, "...we were met by a lot of drunken settlers who told us they would murder every one of us if we crossed the river."[89]

Any belief that the Modocs had that they could go to the reservation and live in peace vanished following their confrontation with the Linkville citizens. Driven by fear and anger, the Hot Creeks took the path they felt offered the least danger to them. The skittish Hot Creeks bolted from the ranchers' convoy and joined Jack in the lava bed.

What would have happened if Muntz had stayed home that night enjoying a comfortable evening in front of the fire?

These fourteen Hot Creek warriors tipped fate's scales by joining Captain Jack to fight. The Hot Creeks' coming gave him impetus toward war. Captain Jack now had a significantly larger force and a better military advantage. Shacknasty Jim and his brother Shacknasty Frank also did not stay with Fairchild as ranch hands, as he had requested. Like the rest of the Hot Creeks, they picked up weapons and became fighters.

Chapter 6
Confronting the Stronghold

I have never before encountered such an enemy,
civilized or savage, occupying a position of such great natural
strength as the Modoc Stronghold.

Nor have I ever seen troops engage
a better-armed or more skillful foe.

Lt. Col. Frank Wheaton to Gen. Canby, Feb. 7, 1873[90]

The Modocs realized that war had come. Their battlefield was in a major lava flow in northern California, today the Lava Beds National Monument. The field of harsh, jagged rock resulted from volcanic activity over the last half-million years from the Medicine Lake shield volcano to the west. The monument measures thirty-five miles, north to south, and twenty-five miles, east to west.[91]

The Modocs' natural fortress was known as Captain Jack's Stronghold. To the south of the Stronghold was no-man's land—torturous black lava as far as the eye could see. The terrain was so uneven and rough that no one ventured into it. The Stronghold was bordered on the north by Tule Lake, which provided water to those inside the lava walls of the Modoc war camp. As the weather warmed, water was a major survival issue.[92]

Captain Jack, with the older Schonchin John second in command, chose this rugged landscape because he knew that the land itself would be a wicked enemy of the army troops. The Modocs, in contrast, knew the lay of the land and how to use it. The lava flow was part of their forbears' tribal domain. They had used the ice caves for food storage and water. The warmer caves were temporary hunting lodges.[93]

The addition of the Hot Creeks brought the number of fighting men with Captain Jack to between fifty and sixty. The Modoc army was a young one. Many of the fighters could be classified as boys. A number of the better-known warriors and leaders were in their late teens and early twenties. The fighting uniform was the clothing they had adopted from the miners and ranchers in the

Schonchin John

area. Despite some of the glorified descriptions and drawings of Modoc fighters, dungarees, boots, shirts, and bandanas were worn.

One extraordinary aspect of this war is often overlooked. Modoc women and children, numbering somewhere around 100, were with their men in the lava bed throughout the entire six-month war. When battles were fought, the women and children were there. There are records of women actually being armed and fighting. The ancestral Modoc women did not go into or near battle for fear of seeing their husbands killed. The only women who went were those whose husbands wore the heavy and cumbersome elk rawhide armor, relieving their wives' fears. For the women of the Modoc War, present at almost every battle, the war must have been devastating.[94]

When the Modocs traveled from their primary camp to other parts of the lava bed, the women and children also moved. In addition to the physical and mental strain of battle that any war places on the fighter, the emotional pressure on the Modoc warriors of having their families with them was monumental. Women and children were wounded and killed in the war, but the names and numbers are unknown and not included in official war casualty records.

Captain Jack's Stronghold was two-miles long and 300-yards wide. Pit-like depressions and broken lava tubes forming caves served as dwellings for the Modoc warriors, women, and children. The Modocs had acquired a herd of 100 cattle. These animals were driven in and maintained as sustenance for the Modocs. The Stronghold had deep chasms running through the fortress allowing the Modocs to move easily from one end to the other. Jack's men dug additional trenches to strengthen their position. Where the natural terrain did not provide protection, they constructed artificial barriers of stone about four feet in height with loopholes to shoot through. Lookouts posted throughout the stronghold could easily see movement to the east and west.[95]

The Modocs knew their own battlefield intimately. In preparing for battle, they had placed piles of rocks at strategic spots. These markers had no significance for the military but had a deep importance to the Modocs as they slipped from one point of cover to another, using the rocks as guide posts. There were large mounds of rocks fortified and designed for a man or two to be stationed in each, giving the Modocs about a twenty-foot altitude advantage over the soldiers.[96]

The Stronghold was described by Lt. Thomas Wright in this way: "The match for the Modoc Stronghold has not been built and never will be....It is the most impregnable fortress in the world."[97]

The unique geology of the lava bed and the Modocs' understanding of how to survive in and use that terrain were the foremost reasons the Modocs were so successful. Bleak and forbidding, the jagged, sharp lava rocks became the allies of the Modocs, who used the land against their enemy in the truest sense of guerrilla warfare.

Curley Headed Doctor, spiritual leader and shaman to the Modocs, played a major role in the war, for it was his teachings that convinced the Modocs they were invincible. The shaman professed that no Modoc would fall in battle if they were to follow his beliefs.

Curley Headed Doctor adhered to a religious belief introduced in the 1860s by a Columbia River Indian prophet named Smohalla. The prophet's basic message was that the Indians must return to their primitive mode of life and refuse the teachings or things of the white man. He predicted the coming of massive earthquakes that would destroy all human beings. The faithful would promptly rise from the dead, and all land and belongings would revert back to the resurrected Indians.[98]

Curley Headed Doctor

* * * * * *

— Powerful Medicine —

As night fell, Curley Headed Doctor knew that the next morning would be his test. He could hear the measured chanting in the sacred circle in the Stronghold. He had very carefully selected the location for the circle. The towering Mt. Shasta, whose slopes were covered most of the year with snow, formed a backdrop for the sacred circle.

The throb of the drums matched Curley Headed Doctor's excitement as he prepared himself for the greatest day of his life.

The medicine man had moved into the shadows

of the fortress. He pulled his robe tighter about his shoulders, throwing back the long wavy hair that was so different from his kinsmen around him. He took great pride in his mane while always secretly wondering where it had come from.

He, more than any Modoc, understood the need for freedom and independence from government control. Of all Indian traditions, religion topped the list as that which the intruders found most offensive and wanted to obliterate. Reservation life and the taming of the Modocs would threaten that most precious thing in his life: the spiritual belief of the people who would on the next day be fighting for their very existence. He felt a surge of anger—not only was the forced removal from their homeland an insult to the Modoc people, it was an affront to the sacred ones inhabiting the supernatural world of the Modoc.

Curley Headed Doctor was a survivor of the Ben Wright massacre. Although the scars had smoothed over enough to allow him to deal on friendly terms with the early settlers on Modoc land, the buried emotions from the massacre flared up when the suggestion was made that the Modocs might be better off on a reservation. He was adamantly against the move. His first recorded words on the subject, spoken in 1869, were simple: "We won't go there."

In preparation for the battle, the medicine man had ordered a rope of tule fiber to be braided and painted red. Many hundred feet of fiber rope and hours of labor had gone into the braiding. That rope now surrounded the Stronghold, waiting for him to make the medicine that would give it power. In the darkness beyond him, he sensed the rope's mystical presence.

Curley Headed Doctor remembered the doubt that had first met his demand that the rope be completed. He had told his tribesmen that no soldier would cross that rope. No Indian would die. The medicine man had never wavered in his belief. The magnetism, the power of belief he created, pulled the Modocs to him.

But on this night, for all the feeling of power, Curley Headed Doctor's emotions were terribly mixed. He lifted his head and contemplated the bowl of sky above him. Thousands of stars filled the circle. From the time he was a boy and his vision quest had told him he would move in metaphysical paths, the patterns of the stars had always spoken to him of the omnipotence of a force beyond that of humans.

He shivered at his own knowledge of the other world. He felt so small and alone. His hand raised slowly into the air. He waited as he had so many times for the voice within him to speak and reassure him. For months he had been promising the Modocs that if they believed his teachings, no harm would come to them. He also knew that in the way of his people, if he failed and Modocs did die, he in turn would probably be killed.

Slightly beyond where he sat was a medicine flag he'd stuck into a pile of stones. It was a four-foot crooked limb from a juniper tree. Upon it were tail feathers of a hawk and a mink's skin. A small white medicine bead completed his creation. He would make a few more flags, he decided, to place around the Stronghold. There could never be too much medicine. The doctor thought about the flag he had so painstakingly pieced together. His face hardened for a moment as he mentally saw the scalp of one of the enemy being added to the flag. What power that would give.

The flag also evoked memories of the white flag that Wright had carried so many years ago. He felt the wave of hate flood over him again. Perhaps the battle that the Modocs now faced would provide the revenge that would allow him to live the rest of his life out of the shadow that constantly plagued him.

The smoke of the fire touched his nostrils. It was time to join the Modoc people at the medicine fire to throw in sacrifices of roots and meat.

It was time for the Modocs to feel his presence.

* * * * * *

Warm Springs Indian Scouts
Replaced Klamath Indian Scouts after first battle for the Stronghold.

Warm Springs Scout
Not in typical Modoc War attire. Clothing worn by scouts is shown above.

Chapter 7
Begin the Body Count

We will be prepared to make short work of this
impudent and enterprising savage.
I feel confident the guns will astonish and terrify the Modocs.[99]

Lt. Colonel Frank Wheaton to Gen. Canby, Dec. 26, 1872

The battle to take the Stronghold and force the surrender of the Modocs took place on January 17, 1873. It pitted approximately 300 regular military men, volunteers, and Klamath scouts who had been recruited for this battle, against the small band of 50 to 60 Modocs. Troop camps were located at area ranches, primarily those of Dan Van Brimmer, John Fairchild, and Pressley Dorris to the west of the lava flow. The Louis Land and Jesse Applegate ranches were military camps for eastern troops.

The distance from Van Brimmer's to the high bluff overlooking the Stronghold was approximately eight miles. From Fairchild's it was thirteen miles to the bluff. It was rough country, and in the dead of winter, the march to the battlefield was a hard one.[100]

At the time of the conflict, the military did not know how many Modocs they were battling, and no one saw a Modoc during the fight. After the battle, Wheaton placed the number conservatively at 150. The *Yreka Union* announced 200 warriors.[101]

Lt. Col. Frank Wheaton was the commander in this battle. He was an officer of great experience and highly respected by his officers and men. The military strategy for the upcoming confrontation was "gradual compression" or squeeze them out. Troops would move in and "compress" from the east of the Stronghold under the command of

Lt. Col. Frank Wheaton

Capt. Reuben Bernard

Capt. Reuben Bernard and from the west under Maj. John Green. To the north was Tule Lake and to the south was the inhospitable no-man's land, both natural barriers. The military saw no possible escape for the Modocs.[102]

When Captain Jack first heard that the soldiers were indeed marching toward him in the Stronghold, his nerve faltered, and he was ready to surrender before the battle even began. Scarfaced Charley was almost persuaded the same way. The Indians who had killed the settlers knew that surrender would probably be death for them, and they argued for war. Curley Headed Doctor wanted a chance to work his magic, and that could happen only if war put his red tule fiber rope to the test. His reputation was at stake. He was committed to war. A bitter debate broke out. Finally, in the way that Modocs had always settled differences, a consensus was reached. The majority of Modocs still supported war.[103]

On the military side, the army entered the war with complete confidence, or if truth be told, overconfidence. There was a sense of an easy fight ahead. Wheaton wrote to Gen. Canby on Jan. 15, 1873: "I don't understand how the Modocs can think of attempting any serious resistance, though of course we are prepared for their fight or flight." Boasts were heard among the troops talking about, "Modoc steak for breakfast," and "My men will eat the Modocs raw if I let 'em go."[104]

The day before the Stronghold battle, Wheaton again wrote to Canby. "If the Modocs will only try to make good their boast to whip 1,000 soldiers, all will be satisfied." Prophetic words these were to be.[105]

Quite clearly, the soldiers expected to kill or capture every Modoc who had moved into the lava bed. But military personnel had little experience fighting in terrain like this war presented. The biggest contingency of troops was artillery soldiers, trained to handle mortars and howitzers.

Troops—Advance!

We leave for Captain Jack's Gibraltar... a more enthusiastic, jolly

set of regulars and volunteers
I never had the pleasure to command.[106]

Lt. Col. Frank Wheaton, Jan. 15, 1873

The plan was to move in early on the morning of January 17 and take the Stronghold. But as with many of the best-laid plans of men, a strange incident occurred the night before on the eastern front that signaled a bad start. The incident not only tipped off the Modocs as to what was happening, but it also resulted in three soldiers being wounded before the battle was even officially launched.

Bernard moved his troops closer to the Stronghold for the morning attack. As he moved through the thick fog, he suddenly realized that he had lost direction. Lt. William H. Boyle, who had been recruited in December from Vancouver, Washington, was stationed on the east side of the Stronghold. Boyle wrote on his experiences in the war. He described the blunder:

> Bernard, who had relied on his own judgment [rather] than upon the man employed as guide, marched into the center of the Lava Beds or, rather, into the caves occupied by Captain Jack. A sharp engagement ensued, causing troops to fall back... behind a ledge of rocks where they remained all night....

> He gained nothing from this movement and only discouraged the troops who were all night engaged in attending the wounded when they should have been getting into a good position for the coming attack.[107]

Soldiers involved were so close they could actually hear women and children crying. It is a toss-up as to whether the Modocs or the soldiers were the most surprised by this unorthodox attack.

The next morning dawned cold, dismal, and foggy. Troops were readied, and the order was given to advance. Soldiers soon discovered that to obey this command was not the same task as it had been in other wars. Skirmish lines—a row of men marching forward in unison—were quickly found to be virtually impossible in the lava bed. Wheaton described the area as "being very broken and difficult to operate in...among rocks and boulders varying in size from a match-box to a church."

Not only were there rocks to be skirted, but a seemingly level stretch of land would suddenly break into a yawning chasm. Fog had settled in and overhung the lava bed like a quiet sea. Sound was muffled and distorted.[108]

Capt. David Perry, fighting under Bernard on the west, wrote about the advance of troops on that January 16 day:

> A mist of fog hung over it [the lava bed], so dense that nothing transpiring therein was visible, while about us on the top of the bluff all was clear. To see the column go half way down and then disappear from view entirely was to say the least, uncanny

and might have suggested the words of Dante's 'Inferno,' 'All hope abandon, ye who enter here.'[109]

Capt. David Perry

What advancing troops saw as they dove down into that sea of fog did not encourage hope. The problem was they could not see. The *Yreka Journal* observed that, "It was impossible in broad daylight to see further than forty yards at most, and a person was liable to get lost unless thoroughly acquainted with the country." It was a disheartening beginning for men who were going to "eat Modocs raw."

It was not only difficult to know where the Modocs were, but determining the positions of their own units became a problem. In the confusion, the strategically placed Modocs were able to fire their rifles without revealing their positions. At one point Wheaton noted, "There was nothing to fire at but a puff of smoke issuing from cracks in the rock." Soldiers were no longer looking for Modoc beefsteak for breakfast. They were fighting for survival.[110]

Large fissures and cracks cut down into the lava. The Modocs' knowledge of these enabled them to shuttle quickly back and forth over the battlefield, baffling the U. S. troops, who were never certain exactly where the Indians were. Two or three Indians could successfully hold off large numbers of soldiers by making use of these trenches. Wheaton reported that, "The enemy was perfectly shielded from view, firing only through small holes and crevices in his inaccessible rocks and caves."[111]

Understanding the brutal threat the terrain held, the Modocs stripped off their clothing and bound themselves in rawhide bandages to protect exposed limbs. They tied bunches of sagebrush to their heads and shoulders, the camouflage blending perfectly with the surrounding landscape. Wheaton reported that, "One of our men was wounded twice during the day but he did not see an Indian at all."[112] It was like fighting phantoms. Perry asserted that, "During all this day's fighting I did not see an Indian, and I don't recall that any one else did, though they called to us frequently, applying to us all sorts of derisive epithets."[113]

One volunteer officer told of a very young soldier who had lost his way and ended up in the volunteer army ranks. The boy soldier was totally terrorized by the fighting. When the man next to him was shot and blood spurted out, the young man staggered back, retched violently, and then deliberately pointed his own carbine at his foot and pulled the trigger. He was through with soldiering for that day.[114]

When the troops did get close to the Modocs, the Indians taunted them in an attempt to make them show themselves for a clearer shot. At one point, Perry, who had raised himself on his left elbow to look at a man who had just been killed, was hit by a bullet passing through his left arm and into his side. An involuntary cry of pain shot from his lips. Immediately, jeers arose from the Modocs, and falsetto cries of "Oh, I'm shot! I'm shot!" rang out. Seriously wounded, Perry was out of the fight.[115]

Bogus Charley

Bogus Charley, who spoke excellent English, yelled out at one point, "Don't shoot this way, you are firing on your own men." Bernard actually called a halt to the firing before Boutelle informed his commander of the hoax. Several times during the campaign soldiers were thrown into confusion listening to the well-modulated voice of Bogus Charley.[116]

Howitzers, canons that fired projectiles in a curved trajectory, had been shipped to the lava bed specifically for this battle. They proved of no value when the enemy's position was hidden from view as it was in this battle. No one could tell where the rounds were landing. Afraid of hitting their own troops, leaders ordered the guns silenced. In Boyle's words, soldiers were afraid they "would do more harm to our troops than to the enemy." It was back to rifles.[117]

Maj. Green gave an insight into what the military faced:

> It was impossible to make the proposed charge, the nature of the rocky ground preventing men moving faster than at the slowest pace, and sometimes having to crawl on their hands and feet. It is utterly impossible to give a description of the place occupied by the enemy as their stronghold.[118]

The fortitude and spirit of government troops and volunteers dropped as they pressed on through the soupy fog blanket.

* * * * * *

— Forward, March —

Green felt like he was fighting phantoms in the damnable fog. It didn't help that the Modoc positions shifted so rapidly that no one knew exactly where the enemy was crouched. As for the men he was commanding, their reluctance to fight, bordering on downright cowardliness, was becoming ridiculous. The men were moving forward like a herd of cows at pasture.

My God, he was tired. How had this simple removal of a band of Indians turned into a war? He had felt so secure and confident in his order, given what seemed centuries ago, to bring the Modocs back from Lost River country to the Klamath Reservation.

Admittedly he had worked around protocol with that order and bent the rules a bit. Sometimes a man did what he knew had to be done. But the attempt to move the Modocs from Lost River had backfired, no doubt about it. Sitting in the misty cold of this forsaken lava hell reminded him of just how badly things had gone off course.

Squatting behind a pile of lava, Green ruefully thought back to how different things had been when he had taken command of Ft. Klamath last summer. He had wanted so much to do his job right, to understand the way Modocs thought, and to get to know the geography of the country.

With that in mind he had made a trip to Lost River in September to meet Captain Jack. It was a wasted trip, since Jack had refused to talk to Green. Commenting that white men talk too much, Jack had said that because his mother was ill, he couldn't meet with Green.

With a shake of his head, Green realized that Captain Jack was now just a short distance away, and it was time to do something about it. Once again Green urged his men forward. This time was worse than the last time he'd yelled a battle cry. Now they refused to move at all. What was he commanding? Men or dogs with tails between their legs?

He felt the anger build. "Forward!" he screamed. Not a movement. It was too much for the enraged Green. Disregarding the heavy fire, he leaped on a rock in plain view of both soldiers and Indians and began a profane tirade on the character and ancestry of his men and their probable future.

The Modocs were thrown off guard and absolutely

*astonished. Out of the fog and gunfire, a figure in blue
had risen above the rest, screaming and yelling in
the tongue of the invader. As Green leaped from rock
to rock, hurdled gullies, and ran from one cluster of
soldiers to another, the Modocs tried without success
to bring him down with gunshot. Wherever they put
a bullet, Green managed not to be there. He was
seemingly impenetrable.*

*Green snatched off his military glove and as he
danced his mad dance among the lava rocks, he
pounded the glove into his other hand, punctuating his
tongue-lashing with blows of his hand.*

* * * * * *

For years to follow the Modocs spoke of the magical properties
of John Green's glove that protected him during the Modoc War.
As for Green, "Uncle Johnnie" to his men, he was awarded the
Congressional Medal of Honor in 1897 for his personal bravery in
the Modoc War. This was a great irony in that this was the same
man who had been instrumental in starting the war.[119]

Modoc Victory

After ten hours of battle, the U. S. Army returned to its base
camp, bruised, completely demoralized, and having suffered
twenty-five wounded and twelve killed. Some three hundred
men had been unable to make even a dent in the powerful shield
provided by Indian skills and the treacherous lava terrain. The
soldiers' clothing was in shreds from crawling among the rocks;
their shoes were worn off their feet. A month in the field would not
have brought them to such a state.[120]

Maj. Edwin C. Mason, commanding a battalion on the western
side of the stronghold, wrote in a January 21 report to Green:

> The command having been in motion since 4 a.m., and in
> engagement with the enemy since 8 a.m., being without
> overcoats, blankets, or rations, were suffering greatly from
> exhaustion, hunger, and cold...I was obliged to carry part of
> our own wounded...in blankets and on stretchers.[121]

Boyle on the east said that as the wounded were carried
out, "The groans of the poor fellows as they were jostled against
the rocks was quite horrible." He recounted the experience of a
California volunteer named Crook whose leg had been broken.
Crook preferred to ride on the back of a pony, but his leg hung
loose and would strike against the sharp rocks and sagebrush.
Noticing his predicament, some of his comrades tied a rope to
his leg so he could lift it when he encountered a barrier. The pain
must have been excruciating.[122]

The soldiers on the eastern front retreated to the Land Ranch, some twelve miles east of Tule Lake. Boyle was one of the men on that difficult, disheartening march:

> The men and officers were so thoroughly worn out by the two days' marching and fighting that, as soon as the order "Halt!" was given, they at once fell asleep and I saw many riding and walking in their sleep that morning. And it was a great relief to all to arrive at Land's Ranch in safety, for had the Indians attacked the small party, fagged out as they were, they would have fallen easy prey to the two-legged wolves that hung on their trail.

Even unwounded soldiers, who had crawled over the treacherous lava rocks all day, became minor casualties. Many staggered to camp with scratches, bruises, cut hands, and blood oozing from torn shoes. The land, as well as the Modocs, had taken its toll. Food had been lost or discarded during the long, hard day. When soldiers stopped for the night in a temporary camp, they were not only hungry, but the best bedding facilities for even the wounded were a blanket or two apiece on the frozen ground. Soldier morale had dropped to a low that was indescribable.[123]

The twenty Klamath Indian scouts did not serve the army well. Reports were that they fired their guns into the air, rather than at the Modocs, and kept the Modocs informed of all that transpired among the troops. It was rumored that they even managed to supply ammunition to the Modocs, although there was no proof of that. It goes without saying that the U. S. Army did not again hire Klamath scouts for service in the Modoc War. Instead, Wheaton chose Warm Springs Indian scouts, under the leadership of Donald McKay, who was half Indian, for all subsequent military encounters.[124]

Here Come the Ladies

Harry De Witt Moore, in letters to his aunt and uncle, talked about the "continual confab" between Klamaths and Modocs during the battle for the Stronghold.

> The principal operator on the Modoc's side was a squaw who made herself conspicuous by the flaming red dress she had on. She is the sister of Captain Jack and can speak fluent English. By those who have had a close look at her, she is described as being very good looking and dresses in the latest Indian style, wears high-heeled, brass tipped boots such as you see on the feet of actresses. She was too far off to permit a close inspection of her personal appearance, but I am convinced that whatever her other attractions, she has a most powerful voice.[125]

The woman of the compelling voice was Princess Mary, sometimes known as Queen Mary. In addition to hollering from the walls of the Stronghold to army troops, she was prominent throughout the war using her translator skills in military and government meetings. Mary was devoted to her brother Captain Jack. Because

Jack did not speak English, she served as a translator for him on many occasions and often handled negotiations. It might be said that but for the accident of being born a woman, and an Indian woman at that, Princess Mary might have been an acknowledged and commanding leader of the Modocs. [126]

Although armed women were reported on many occasions, there is only one account, by Alfred Meacham, of a Modoc woman actually engaging in fighting:

> On the occasion of the first battle in the lava beds, 'Madam Shacknasty' had commanded an important position and held it against the assaults of U. S. soldiers. The attacking party heard her repeatedly cheering her men, and on one occasion they saw her pass, under fire, from one cliff of rocks to another.[127]

Madam Shacknasty became known after the Modoc War as Sallie Clark. She was the mother of Hot Creek leader Shacknasty Jim, who himself was one of the crack shots among the Modocs. His archery differed so much from ordinary shooting, that he was an exception even to Indians.[128]

One of the more colorful stories to emerge from the Modoc War regarded Madame Shacknasty's wartime exploits. How much of the account is truth and how much is a spoof satirizing the ineptness of the Oregon volunteers in the lava bed will never be known. But this is what a March 17, 1873, *San Francisco Chronicle* article had to say about the woman warrior:

> The battle in which Kelley [Captain Harrison Kelley, "A" Company, Oregon Volunteers] distinguished himself has more of the ludicrous than most Indian conflicts. If it were not for the melancholy fact that he lost several men killed and wounded, it would seem to have been more of farce than tragedy.
>
> Hooker Jim, aided by the squaw Shacknasty, could alone hold bay from morn to night [against] sixty-six redoubtable Oregon warriors....The squaw loaded the guns, and Hooker Jim vollied [sic] and thundered, and Kelley bullied and blundered, till Hooker Jim went to dinner and the squaw all alone bore the brunt of the battle.
>
> The story goes that Hooker Jim staying away too long, the squaw brought him back with a manzanito [sic] stick, and made the tired warrior fight on till night.

The story of Madame Shacknasty is one of the few written references to Modoc women fighting. But it was known that they did have the task of combing the battlefield after a skirmish, looking for whatever could be of value.[129] Alfred Meacham wrote many years later about the aftermath of a battle:

> Their dead bodies [the soldiers] lie stark and cold among the rocks. The Modoc men disdain to hunt up victims of the fight. The squaws are permitted to do this work....Look now in the Modoc camp when the squaws come in, bearing the arms and clothing of the fallen United States soldiers. See them parade

these before the Indian braves.[130]

* * * * * *

— Stronghold Duties —

The early morning sun was breaking through the fog of the lava bed. The silence of yesterday's battlefield was broken only by the call of a bird. To Jennie Clinton's ears it was one of the loneliest, most eerie sounds she had ever heard. But she knew that this was because of the contrast to the day before, which had been filled with the most frightening noises she had ever heard in her young life—guns, yells, screams.

Her mother had held Jennie and her sister Lillie close, covering their ears as best she could while the battle raged around those huddled in the Stronghold. But that had not helped, and Jennie's ears still rang long after the guns were silent.

Jennie knew her mother was as terrified as she was, but she had tried to hide it from the girls. Jennie's mother was one of the great storytellers among the Modocs, and Jennie had no doubt that one day her mother would tell the story of the Modocs' battle to all who would listen. That is, if any of them ever walked out alive from this stone fortress.

The cave in the Stronghold that provided shelter for the family was horribly cold, cramped, and smelled of damp mold. Jennie was born in 1859 and had spent all of her fourteen years, until now, in the Lost River wickiup where she had been born. Winters there had been a time of warmth, family closeness, and storytelling.

This excuse for a home in the Stronghold was not only physically uncomfortable, but there was also a constant feeling of uneasiness and dread among her family and the other Modocs living in similar dank caves. Jennie felt especially sorry for the Hot Creek woman who was in the cave near Jennie's. The woman was very much with child. Jennie wondered where that child would eventually be born—would they still be in the Stronghold?—and what would happen to the mother and baby in this world of chaos and uncertainty?

Jennie was practicing what she often did when she had an assigned task that she didn't want to do. She would daydream. But the task today wasn't cleaning the wickiup floor or pounding wocus seeds. Guns, ammunition, and clothing from the fallen soldiers had to be collected by the Modocs for future use. Jennie was plenty old enough to do what needed to be done. The men had done their jobs. Now she would do hers. She was Modoc and would not flinch at her responsibility.

A soldier lay some distance from the Stronghold on the other side of a small chasm. She could see no other bodies, although the fog had not completely lifted. It had taken her a while, scouting from different areas along the main trench that ran through the Stronghold, to spot this one dead soldier. Jennie slipped down the rock on which she sat and moved toward the body, trying to avoid the sharp lava rocks as much as possible.

She felt a drop of sweat run down her back, and her breath had suddenly gone out of control as she realized that her hands would have to touch the body, search for weapons, and pull off clothes. Her stomach rolled, and she cursed the day this crazy, sick war had started.

* * * * * *

Charles Putnam recorded the death of Greasy Boots on the east side of the lava flow immediately following the first battle for the Stronghold. A group of Modocs attacked a detail of military men escorting wagons full of barley. In the skirmish that followed, in which several civilians including Putnam joined in, some Modocs were cut off. Greasy Boots was running on foot when the exhausted Modoc was brought to the ground, shot, and killed.[131]

Assessing the loss of the Stronghold battle to determine what had caused the downfall of U. S. military troops, two officers directly involved in the battle felt that one major cause of the military defeat was food—the lack of it. Boyle wrote that "the troops had only three day's rations and no way of cooking; it was impossible for them to hold their positions in the lava bed."[132]

Moore, reviewing what happened in the battle for the Stronghold, agreed with Boyle. "The result was that we were to all intents and purposes beaten, although we thought at the time, and continued to think ... that if we had had another day's rations we could have cleaned them out."[133]

There is an old saying: for the want of a nail, a shoe was lost; for want of a shoe, a horse was lost; for want of a horse, a battle was lost. In the case of the Modoc War, could it be that for want of beans and hardtack, the January battle for the Stronghold was lost?

The Modocs suffered no battle casualties. In collecting rifles and ammunition dropped by the fleeing soldiers or taken from the dead, they actually gained possession of better armaments than they originally had. Deciding that Curley Headed Doctor had been right, many of the Modocs became convinced that they were invincible. This was a most unfortunate assumption for the Modocs, because that thinking precluded surrender, and it prolonged the war.

A *New York Herald* editorial took the military to task:

> This result shows that Captain Jack, and his Lieutenants, Scar-Faced Charley and Shack-Nasty Jim, not only mean to fight, but have the power to do it with effect. And yet it seems strange that, after all these weeks of preparation, involving, as it has, thousands of dollars of expense, our troops should have been so shamefully beaten. The howitzers, upon which so much reliance was placed, were of no service, on account of a heavy fog, and the reinforcements which have almost daily swelled Colonel Wheaton's force seem to have only gone there to be shot down like sheep by the unerring rifles in the practiced hands of the savages.[134]

The official report of the first campaign against the Modocs stated that, in the opinion of commanding officer Frank Wheaton, "one thousand men would be required to dislodge them [the Modocs] from their almost impregnable position." His prophetic words at the beginning of the battle, spoken almost in jest, had come true.[135]

Wheaton Punished for "Blunder"

The U. S. Army needed a scapegoat for their defeat. The end of January brought the end of Lt. Col. Wheaton—or at least his command of the troops in the Modoc country. "I am greatly disappointed and pained," said Wheaton. "I am perfectly familiar with the situation and confident that we can easily kill or capture every hostile Indian."[136]

Wheaton pleaded with Gen. Canby to retain him, but the request was denied. The *Army and Navy Journal* decried the decision to sack Wheaton:

> Time will fully vindicate Lt. Colonel Wheaton....Those who have cried 'blunder!'...will realize the fact of having done a brave officer a cruel injustice.[137]

Alfred Meacham also came to the defense of Wheaton:

> Political power is triumphant, and this worthy man is humbled because he could not perform impossibility. He had raw recruits that were unskilled in Indian wars, and he was attacking with this force the strongest natural fortress on the continent.[138]

Col. Alvan C. Gillem, a Tennessee-born West Point graduate, was given command of the Modoc War troops on January 23, 1873. Gillem was a personal friend of former President Andrew Johnson. Much of Gillem's rise in the army had been because of this personal tie. When Johnson went out of office, Gillem's star sank. But life is always full of opportunity, and the Modoc War offered a chance for Gillem to shine after the terrible defeat in the battle for the Stronghold. He arrived on February

Col. Alvan C. Gillem

7 to physically take command of the troops. Not only would Gillem fail to excel, the months ahead would prove him to be a most unpopular officer with troops and civilians alike. The *Army and Navy Journal's* comment on Wheaton became a prophecy: he would be vindicated and his replacement scorned.

Matilda Whittle
Modoc woman who often served as interpreter during the war.

**Princess Mary, Captain Jack's sister;
Artena Chockus; and One-eyed Dixie**
*These Modoc women served as interpreters and negotiators
throughout the Modoc War.*

Chapter 8
Words, Words, and More Words

Kill with bullets don't hurt much;
Starve to death hurt a heap.[139]
Captain Jack to Elijah Steele, commenting on reservation life, 1873

You sent me word that no more preparation for war
would be made by you, and that I must not go on preparing.[140]
Captain Jack to Alfred Meacham, April 5, 1873

During the next three months, no major battle took place. A peace commission was officially established shortly after the battle for the Stronghold. Secretary of the Interior Columbus Delano appointed Alfred Meacham chaiman of the peace commission on January 29, 1873. The first mission of the commission was to try to establish communication with the Modocs. The membership of the commission fluctuated greatly, and over the next few months changed on a regular basis. Only Meacham remained constant. A major goal for Meacham, once communication was resumed with the Modocs, would be to establish an armistice.[141]

No full report of negotiations exists, but over the course of time, several proposals went back and forth, not always sensible or workable. It is reported that complete amnesty was offered to the Modocs if they agreed to surrender, with surrendered Modocs to be placed on Angel Island in the San Francisco Bay until a permanent home could be found. They would be fed and clothed. Captain Jack and his headmen would be allowed to visit Washington, D.C.

Captain Jack made a counter-proposal. Forgive the Modocs and leave them in the northern California lava flow where they were. Captain Jack's Stronghold had become home to the Modocs who continued to live there. It was an odd sort of armistice, as Modocs came and went at will, slipping in and out of the Stronghold and back to the Klamath Reservation to visit relatives and friends.[142]

Not everyone felt that peace talks were appropriate. A stinging editorial in the *Yreka Journal* on March 12, 1873, argued:

> From the very first we have considered the Peace Commission a grand humbug and useless expense....Should peace be established while moving the murderers with the other Indians, to another reservation, it may not be long before the treacherous devils may be sneaking back to murder more good citizens.[143]

One surprising support for a peace commission and serious consideration of a reservation for the Modocs came from Elijah Applegate, son of Lindsay, the Klamath Reservation's first Indian agent (or, technically, sub-agent). Elijah was a writer, politician, and speaker. Along with Lindsay's other two sons, Ivan and Oliver, the Applegate clan was a prominent community family at the time of the Modoc War.

Against the wishes of most of the rest of the Applegate family—his uncle Jesse had repudiated the commission as an expensive and useless farce—Elijah, while on a speaking tour in Washington, D. C., presented a letter to Secretary of the Interior Delano supporting a peace commission and a serious search for a reservation for the Modocs. In his own words, "Jaw-bone is cheaper than ammunition." His request carried much weight.[144]

Modoc women figured prominently throughout the war by serving as messengers and interpreters. As a first step in communicating with Captain Jack, Meacham requested that Artena Choakus and One-eyed Dixie, who lived at the Fairchild Ranch, and Matilda Whittle, who had married a white ferryman named Bob Whittle, go into the Stronghold to meet with Jack. Since no one knew how the Modocs were feeling at that time, Matilda left her rings and jewelry with her husband in case she met with an unfavorable reception. Meacham commented on the undertaking by saying, "all of them expressed doubt about ever returning....Talk of heroism being confined to race, color, or sex! nonsense."[145]

The women fulfilled their mission. Artena told a *San Francisco Call* reporter that Jack still insisted upon a Lost River reservation. Matilda paraphrased Jack's words:

> We want no more war....We were pitched into it [at Lost River] by the military and citizens when we were asleep. We did not intend to trouble the citizens. We wanted to fight soldiers. The citizens should not have troubled us.

Jack also stated that he was "against using women as couriers," observing that "women do not understand when men lie."[146]

Paparazzi of the Modoc War

The Modoc War generated immense publicity. A nation of appalled Americans followed the process of this unbelievable war.

Alex McKay, San Francisco Call Reporter
One of many reporters who flocked to cover the Modoc War.

This was the first Indian campaign in the West to be extensively covered by a number of reporters, each competing with the other to be the first in print. A rag-tail group of Modocs were challenging the mighty U. S. military. The story was a hot one and generated guaranteed newspaper sales. Reporters were regulars in the army camps, as fresh-faced reporters and experienced journalists alike sought the latest news.[147]

Often the paper breaking the story first was the winner of a horse race between couriers carrying the reporters' stories over mountains and through wilderness to the newspaper offices. Lively writing, personal in style, appeared in newspapers in 1873 across the United States:

> Toby Riddle returned with Boston Charley....The hungry cuss was fed.—*San Francisco Chronicle*, April 5, 1873

> He has been stuffing the Indians' bellies so full that the brown skin is drawn over them as taunt as a drumhead.—*San Francisco Chronicle*, March 1, 1873

> The Warm Springs (scouts) shot the squaws by mistake. There is no doubt as squaws are of more value than ponies under any circumstances—especially Modoc squaws.....

> Curly-headed Jack when last seen was apparently booked for the happy hunting grounds.—*Yreka Union*, May 24, 1873

> Uncle Jesse looked at his soiled shirt...went down to a grocery store and bought a clean woolen shirt....This was over a week ago and he still has on the same shirt....He never wears underclothes, so he was not bothered with traps of that kind.—*San Francisco Chronicle*, March 2, 1873

Editorializing—offering personal opinions or views—could be

found. Obviously, libel suits were not common in 1873. An article in the *San Francisco Chronicle* on March 16 comments on two major government figures:

> T.B. Odeneal, the Oregon superintendent of Indian affairs, is a small, one-horse lawyer...pompous and overbearing, vaccilating [sic] and easily swayed where political considerations present themselves.

> L.S. Dyar... is totally unfit for the position he now holds and should be removed to give place to a man of nerve and decision of character....He is a Christian, one of the howling kind, and is ardent in getting up revivals and saving souls.

But even with the journalistic pitfalls of the era, newspapers provided valuable records and insights into the events of the Modoc War. Frequently, the only clear records to be found, and the only record of the Modoc view, were those provided by the investigative verve and interviews of the reporters who dared the frontier. Journalists often were sympathetic to certain areas of the Modoc plight. By the time of the peace negotiations, there were a half a dozen war correspondents covering the Modoc War.[148]

Oliver Knight's *Following the Indian Wars* makes it clear that newsgathering for the Indian wars required that journalists endure the hardships of campaigns and take part in any combat that might develop. "Covering an Indian expedition called for a rudimentary acquaintance with a horse, a stomach for campaign cuisine...and a willingness to camp out."[149]

Edward Fox of the *New York Herald* was a seemingly unlikely choice to cover the Modoc War. He was the *Herald's* yachting editor. But he was a former British military officer and not unaccustomed to handling firearms. Time showed that this Englishman was a sharp newshound. In an era of journalistic hearsay, he wrote a very credible account of the Stronghold battle using original Army orders and interviews with survivors.[150]

Fox asked Alfred Meacham for permission to join a delegation of negotiators and interpreters going into the Stronghold on February 24. Meacham ordered Bob Whittle, whom he had put in charge, to keep Fox away. Fox did not take "no" as an order. Instead he made his desired visit to the Modoc fortress on his own at first. The resulting story, which appeared in the *New York Herald* on February 28, 1873, to his credit, was a great one.

* * * * * *

— Reporting from the Stronghold —

The negative answer to Fox's request to go with Fairchild, Artena, and Matilda and Bob Whittle seemed pretty final, as Fox had no desire to travel on his own. He realized that he would probably fail since all he knew of the Stronghold was that it lay about twenty miles to the east.

Then Fox's big break came. In the newly fallen snow he saw the clear tracks of the four horses as they headed east. "It suddenly flashed across my mind," he later wrote in his newspaper article on the Stronghold quest, "that those tracks would lead me to the lava bed, and the Commissioners could throw no blame on Whittle."

For quite some distance he was careful to keep out of the sight of the party in front of him. When he felt certain he was in Indian country, he hurried to close the gap. Although annoyed, Bob Whittle agreed to take Fox along, just as Fox had hoped. Fox was jubilant.

The negotiating delegation came upon a scouting party of six Modocs seated around a fire. Fox took note of the fact that they were all painted. "The entire lower part of the face was smeared with a brownish red or black composition of a greasy nature." Fox used the term "hideous" to describe the Modocs, and their decorated faces reinforced for him the fact that his party was not out on a pleasurable day hike.

Half a mile farther was a camp of about fifty men, women and children. Fox especially noticed the clothing. Most of the men had on soldiers' overcoats. But it was the women who caused him to do a double take. Red petticoats! Modoc fashion at the moment for women showed them to be very partial to the bright petticoats.

The party moved forward once more over more treacherous terrain. Fox was beginning to understand how fifty or so Indians had triumphed over the white soldiers who greatly outnumbered them. Fox noted how hard it was for his horse to move. He wrote, "my quadruped required considerable persuasion in order to induce him to move forward."

The group stopped, dismounted, and leading their horses, started walking. Fox was beginning to wonder where the bulk of the Modocs were to be found. He wanted more desperately to see the fabled Captain Jack than anything he had ever wanted to see in his entire journalistic career. Then suddenly, looming before him was a dark cave that seemed to go straight down. Fox had a ridiculous moment of remembering

Alice in Wonderland tumbling down a rabbit hole.

He hesitated at the entrance, and Matilda gave him a nudge toward the lava tube. Fox put on his suave, man-of-the-world newsman face and stepped into the darkness of the lava cave. Once down in the cave, the fire burning in the center allowed Fox to see some fifty or sixty Modocs sitting in circles four or five deep. Fox already knew what words he would put down to describe this scene: "No troop of Italian bandits could have made a wilder or more picturesque picture."

He drew a startled breath—there not five feet from him sat Captain Jack. He knew him by descriptions he had heard. But Jack was obviously ill, wrapped in a blanket and supporting himself by resting his hands on the handle of a Modoc root-digger, which was stuck in the ground before him.

Bogus Charley served as translator with Steamboat Frank's help. The firelight flickering off foreign looking faces and words spoken in a strange, guttural language created a scene Fox would remember forever. Fairchild presented instructions from the peace commissioners. Discussion followed of what had happened at the Lost River Battle and where things stood now. Fairchild let everyone know that Fox was a paper man from the big city by the sea. Fox was henceforth known as "Paper Man."

When the council broke until morning, Fox met on his own with Schonchin John, Scarfaced Charley, Bogus Charley, and several others. They talked of life on the reservation. The group said that they were moved three times, were only given half a blanket, and the squaws none at all. It was the winter season. They were given no food and had to dig in the hard, frosty ground for camus roots. They killed their horses for meat.

Fox also had an opportunity to talk with Captain Jack that evening. Fox could not believe his luck. For years he had fantasized about the scoop of all scoops. In the light of a sputtering, dying fire, pen flying over paper, Fox took down the historic words of Captain Jack as translated by Bogus Charley. These things Jack knew he wanted: "...no more shoot...want same law for white and Indian."

It turned out that one dilemma for Fox was where

to sleep for the night. Fox ended up spending the night in Captain Jack's sister's cave. Fox was offered a bed in Wild Gal's cave with four men and three women on a matting eight feet wide. Pulling off his boots he crowded into bed with the Modocs. Even with all the warmth coming from seven other people, Fox reports that he was so cold he couldn't sleep all night.

The council continued the next day, mostly with a debate as to how the peace conference would be held and who could come. One conclusion Fox reached regarding the Modocs—they were not hesitant at all when it came to talking. One thing he would remember about his Stronghold visit was the writer's cramp he had developed as he wrote frantically to keep up with racing Modoc tongues. At the conclusion of the council, Fox and the negotiating party rode back to what would be great acclaim for "Paper Man."

* * * * * *

In the 1870s, the first two pages of the *New York Herald* were always devoted to advertisements. But Fox's February 28, 1873, story covered all of page three. It cost the *Herald* between five and six hundred dollars in telegraph tolls alone to pass Fox's scoop on to a hungry reading audience. The *Yreka Union* put Fox's accomplishment in journalistic perspective. "This feat of Fox has placed the *[New York] Herald* in the van, and distanced all competitors in the race for news!...It shall rank only second to Stanley's search for Livingstone in Central Africa."[151]

Fox was held in awe by many, and in disgust by others, for printing Modoc interviews and thoughts unfiltered by government or military. Despite the political thoughts on Fox, his gutsy ways appealed to a certain segment of the population. When he returned to Yreka, the ladies of that town feted him.

Stealing Horses

One little known aspect of negotiations had a profound impact on events that were to transpire over the next few months. John Fairchild met with the Modocs on behalf of the peace commission to negotiate an armistice between the Modocs and the government. The term "armistice" was defined by the peace commission: *no act of war would be committed by us, or permitted by them, while negotiations for peace were going on.*[152]

Jack responded to Fairchild and the commission by saying:

> I understand you about not fighting, or killing cattle, or stealing horses. Tell your people they need not be afraid to go over the country while we are making peace. My boys will stay in the

rocks while it is being settled; we will not fire the first shot.

An armistice was declared.

In the latter part of February, Capt. James Biddle and K Troop were dispatched on patrol by Canby. Fate stepped in and placed a massive stumbling block to peace. Biddle came upon two Modocs guarding a horse herd. The Modocs, on seeing the patrol, ran off, wanting to avoid a confrontation.

Sgt. Maurice Fitzgerald, who in much later years wrote about his Modoc War experiences, rode with Troop K that day. "It was difficult to restrain some of the boys from pursuing them, but our orders not to fire or attack, unless fired upon, were imperative." Less clear, however, was how to deal with booty, in this case, the horses.[153]

A March 14, 1873, letter from Canby to Secretary of War W. T. Sherman explains how the booty was handled:

> The party found and brought in thirty-three horses and mules, which is all, or nearly all, that was left of the Modocs' band. The Indians guarding it were not molested, and ran off into the lava beds.
>
> I wish them to see that we are fully prepared for anything they may attempt, and this may incline them to keep their promises in future.[154]

Meacham vehemently condemned what had happened. The peace commission was his baby. His understanding was that the military would act in the role of advisor to the commission, not define terms or set precedent as Canby had done. The terms of armistice, which he had established, had been violated. Meacham; Scarfaced Charley; Captain Jack's sister, Princess Mary; and his wife, Lizzie, went to Canby asking for a return of the horses. They were denied. Through them, Captain Jack requested that at the very least, his own riding horse be returned. Canby coolly answered, "When peace is made you shall get your horse."[155]

Meacham, in his verbose and flowery writing style, described the scene at the horse corral:

> You are accustomed to think of the Indians as unfeeling brutes. In this you are mistaken....Next to her child the Indian woman loves her horse. The scene which ensued when Mary and Lizzie sprang into the corral and called the names of their horses was one calculated to move the hardest heart. The ponies with uplifted heads came running to meet them, and gave proof of attachment by rubbing against the women who caressed them...
>
> They [the two women] beheld the finest horses of the band under blankets, already appropriated by army officers...
>
> Here was the beginning of the awful ending of the Peace Commission.[156]

"Stock Rancho" Garners Opposition

With the war launched, the land acquisition plan of Jesse Carr and Jesse Applegate looked to be on track. The removal of the Modocs would open up land. The Carr and Applegate names cropped up frequently in newspapers, especially the *San Francisco Chronicle*. Correspondent Robert Bogart often took the two to task. However, even the *Chronicle* had no idea of the scope of the two Jesses' "stock rancho" plan—a massive take-over of land. In the March 2, 1873, edition, the *Chronicle* took a stand against the alleged land grabbing of Carr and Applegate under the headline "Violation of the Homestead Act:"

> If the land had already been taken up by actual settlers, it might be advanced as a good reason why the Indians should not be permitted to regain possession of it. But it is not true.... Dennis Crawley lives on land taken up by Jesse Carr of San Francisco and is employed to live upon it and hold it for five years and when he has acquired title to turn it over to Carr— a direct violation of the Homestead Act. In fact, if the truth were known, every piece of ground in that section in Lost River is being held by the settlers for the two Jesses—Carr and Applegate.

Although the treaty placing the Modocs on the Klamath Reservation was drawn up and signed in 1864, it was not ready for signatures to ratify it until 1869, with some changes made to the original treaty. Bogart stated that the treaty giving title to the Modoc Lost River land was faulty:

> When the treaty... went to Washington [D.C.] to be ratified and then came back to the Indians to be ratified, [Captain] Jack refused to do it. He had learned in the interim that the Indians were to be swindled in the exchange of their fertile Lost river [sic] section for the bleak, barren hills of Yainox [sic], and he refused to become a party to it. But the treaty was enforced, the Indians removed, and Carr and Applegate had the land surveyed, took possession of it, and are now trying to hold it by bogus settlers.

The Modocs did not knowingly ratify a treaty or yield the Lost River country, with its fine system of waterways, for a new and different home among their northern adversaries.[157]

Even military personnel had thoughts on what was happening with the land. Moore said in a letter home to relatives that "too much Applegate, too much steal."

A Permanent Home for the Troops

The distance and rough terrain between the temporary military camps established at the Van Brimmer and Fairchild Ranches to the battlefield was a problem. Canby was ready to move troops into a more permanent setting. In addition to the need to be closer to the Stronghold, Canby figured it was good for the Modocs to see the military on the move toward them. Another major reason for moving was that Canby wanted to get as far away from camp followers as possible.

Camp followers congregated around any encampment the military established. But this was different—the lack of combat and drill left a void to be filled. Every payday was the occasion for a gambling and drinking spree. Drinking was out of hand. As a final resort, military men were limited to two drinks a day with an hour's interval in between.

Civilians caused the biggest problems. Professional gamblers were always around on payday to clean out soldiers' pockets. There were at least two hundred teamsters, packers, scouts, stockmen, "sutlers" or sellers, newspapermen, world travelers, and sightseeing settlers. Then there were the "laundresses," women who did not do laundry. When money was exhausted, the "laundresses" traded their bed-time for ammunition. One group of fun-loving civilians cooked up a scheme where they helped Bogus Charley steal a can of gunpowder almost under the noses of the soldiers.[158]

On Monday, March 31, troops moved out of Van Brimmer's and camped that night on the long bluff—some 400 - 600 feet high—overlooking the lava flow and the Stronghold. The next morning troops moved down to the base of the bluff, and the elaborate bivouac Gillem's Camp was born. Situated at the northern end of the bluff, the camp was right next to Tule Lake, at the very edge of the lava flow, and only three miles west of the Stronghold. Directly above the camp was an outcropping of boulders called "Signal Rock," that would be used by signalmen to communicate to Hospital Rock.

Hospital Rock, on the southeast corner of Tule Lake, across the lava flow from Gillem's Camp, provided a natural shelter and was used as a camp and field hospital. This was the location where the signalmen to the east were stationed. Not only were messages sent regularly across the lava flow from east to west, but signalmen would carry their signal flags on patrols so they could signal back to either Gillem's Camp or Hospital Rock.

Gillem's Camp in time added a horse corral, a cemetery, and a hospital. Conical bell tents were erected to house officers, while enlisted men were placed in smaller, standard wall tents. A general field hospital was set up with bed sacks filled with hay. Separate tents served as hospital kitchen and convalescent mess tent. Tule Lake was shallow along the camp's shore. It provided both drinking water and bathing facilities, although how those two needs were separated in the lake is not known—the knowledge has drifted off in the mists of time.[159]

One of the most ubiquitous residents in any military camp settlement was the sutler, a merchant of that era who followed the army selling merchandise to the soldiers. *New York Herald* correspondent Edward Fox reported that trading of all sorts was going on. "The squaws also brought in several bags of feathers the other day, which they traded to the sutler for provisions and clothing." Irishman Pat McManus was the sutler in Gillem's Camp. McManus inadvertently became a part of the action in the war itself.

Captain Jack's Cave
Photo taken after the Modocs had evacuated the Stronghold.
Note the defensive rock walls built by Modocs.

Gillem's Camp - 1873

Major military camp during the Modoc War, located three miles west of Captain Jack's Stronghold. The conical tents were those of the officers, the small tents were housing for enlisted men.

Chapter 9
To Kill or Not to Kill—
That is the Question

I am your chief. I will kill Canby. But hear me, my people.
This day's work will cost the life of every Modoc brave.
We will not live to see it ended.[160]

Captain Jack in protest of Peace Commission killings, 1873

A marriage had taken place in 1869 between a Modoc woman and a miner by the name of Frank Riddle. At the time Oregon Superintendent of Indian Affairs Alfred Meacham had issued an edict that no white man could live with an Indian woman without benefit of marriage. So it was that Toby Riddle—or Winema as she was dubbed by Meacham following the Modoc War—became a lawfully wedded wife. For this she was grateful to Meacham and became his friend.

Toby had taught her husband the Modoc language, and he in turn had taught her English. With their dexterity of language and Toby's close relationship to Meacham, they became major interpreters during negotiations between the military and the Modoc.[161]

Toby was a woman torn between loyalties. Cousin to Captain Jack, she had great sympathy for the Modocs and understood the pain they suffered in being forced from their homeland, coerced onto a reservation, and eventually fighting a bitter battle with the military. But Toby was married to a white man and lived in Frank's world, too. She had high hopes for peace as she and Frank were asked to serve as interpreters for the peace conference. Time and again

Toby Riddle (Winema)

103

throughout the negotiations they had served as interpreters, at times even putting themselves at risk.

Peace Conference Countdown

The four peace commission members were Alfred Meacham; Gen. E.R.S. Canby; Rev. Eleazar Thomas, a Methodist minister from Petaluma, California; and Leroy S. Dyar, Indian agent at the Klamath Agency. A preliminary planning conference between the commissioners and Modoc leaders was held on April 2, 1873, midway between the Stronghold and Gillem's camp. Nothing close to an agreement was reached—except on one issue. A bitter wind had sprung up, and it had started to rain. Canby asked that further meetings have a tent available. Captain Jack boasted that Modocs did not mind bad weather—did Canby think he would melt like snow in the spring thaw? The storm increased in violence and as both parties broke for their camps, they agreed to meet again on the third. Jack told Canby to bring the tent.[162]

When they returned to Gillem's Camp, Toby Riddle told Meacham that she thought the Modocs were playing for time, and treachery was in the air. Meacham passed the woman's thoughts on to Canby, who gave little or no credence to her warning.

The tent went up on April 3, but the Modocs didn't show. They did not come the next day, either, but later in the day Hooker Jim and Boston Charley rode into Gillem's Camp. They asked to speak to Meacham and Fairchild to try to work something out.

After speaking to Meacham, the two Modocs were allowed by Canby to look around the newly established Gillem's Camp. It was hoped that the two would see the gun emplacements, the sentry posts, and numbers of men and advise their fellow Modocs to surrender.

What most captured the attention of the Modocs was the men sending messages from Signal Rock above the camp to the troops on the east side of the lava flow at Hospital Rock. They asked what the men were doing, and when they were told that this is the way the military communicated—a form of talking—they were very upset. How unfair, they complained, to talk over the heads of the Modocs hunkered down in the Stronghold.[163]

There were accounts during the rest of the war of Modocs springing up on the sides of the Stronghold frantically waving petticoats or shirts, mocking the military signalmen and the unfair way that the U. S. Army had of communicating.[164]

A Yellow Dog

The Modocs appeared at the tent on April 5. Although talk went in a lot of circles, Captain Jack did express an interest in living in the lava flow permanently. Canby was greatly encouraged over

Jack's willingness to concede the Lost River reservation in favor of a permanent encampment in the Stronghold.

Clarification seemed necessary so the decision was made to send Toby to the Stronghold two days later. She was instructed to offer army protection for any Modoc who wished to surrender. Captain Jack seemed willing to surrender. But the rest of the Modocs would not consider surrender.

Toby came back from the Stronghold obviously distressed. She sat on her horse for a long time before dismounting. She would speak only to her husband, Frank. He coaxed out of her the cause of her anguish. A Modoc named Weuim, or William, Faithful had followed her out of the Stronghold and advised her and the commission members not to go to the tent again. From the tone of talk in the Stronghold, he felt bloodshed was likely. Riddle went immediately to Gillem and Canby, who discussed it with commission members. Gillem emphatically did not believe it, but Meacham and Dyar did.[165]

A few days later, Captain Jack sent three Modocs with the message that he would meet with the commission. It was at this point that a wagging, careless tongue caused a serious problem. Rev. Thomas took Bogus Charley, one of the Modoc messengers, aside and asked him, in a hurt tone, why the Modocs wanted to kill the commissioners. Bogus Charley jumped on that statement instantly, and demanded to know who had said that. Rev. Thomas was not coy or subtle. He eventually blurted out that it was Toby.

Frank Riddle was furious with Rev. Thomas. The minister had compromised Toby and put her at risk. Shortly thereafter a single Modoc appeared saying it was vital that Toby return to the Stronghold. The issue was talked over by the commissioners who agreed that Toby would most likely be safe. For the Modocs to kill her would only bring them grief and no advantage. They would not be so stupid as to start a war over a woman.

Reluctantly, Toby went. Frank let Thomas know that he was a yellow dog and that if anything happened to Toby, he would personally kill him. That turned out to be unnecessary as Toby returned. Although the Modocs questioned her at length, they finally allowed her to leave. Negotiations continued on setting up a peace conference.[166]

Finally, despite Toby's dire warnings, despite Meacham's and Dyar's feeling that only tragedy could result, an official peace conference date was set for Good Friday, April 11. It was done.

A council of war was held in the Stronghold the night before the conference. The Modocs met to determine what they would do the next day. The magnitude and unusual circumstances of the war had shattered the traditional Modoc three-way division of leadership—civil, religious, and military. Captain Jack was forced to take both the role of civil leader (*la`qi*), who conducted the assembly of people, and war leader.

The outside world may have seen Jack as a totalitarian leader, but in the age-old manner of the Modoc, consensus would rule in a gathering of the assembly. What the people decided as a group was what would be done.

* * * * * *

— The People Rule —

The lava cave was always clammy and damp. But it did offer protection. Captain Jack sat near the entrance on a tule mat that his wives, Lizzie and Rebecca, had woven. Jack wiggled the toe of his boot into the weaving of the mat. He thought to himself that if someone didn't really know this was a cave, it might have been the floor of a wickiup—except for the smell, of course.

Rosie, Jack's small daughter, slept not far from him. Occasionally the little girl would emit whimpering noises and small whooshs of air, which caused him to smile. She was the love of his life. He would not trade this one small girl for anything in life. At night sometimes Jack would feel self-doubt creep in and would wonder if he was giving her a better or a worse life with the decisions he was making. He was profoundly aware of how his judgments were affecting the lives of the youngest to the most elderly Modoc.

Glancing back into the cave's dark depths, he found it incredible to believe that his people had been driven to living in caves, although he wondered if the military men were any more comfortable living in tents. He also had to admit that since he and his two wives were forced to live in a hole in the rocks, at least being war leader gave him one of the nicer caves. This one had a southern exposure, a real boon through the hard winter.

It was a quiet, windless night. On this night, he had needed to think. But he knew that the silence of the night was about to be broken.

Flames from the fire in the council grounds circling Jack's cave shot high into the air. Already Jack heard footsteps coming toward his cave and could see shadows moving toward him. Men, women, and the

Captain Jack's younger wife, Lizzie; his sister, Princess Mary; his older wife, Rebecca; and daughter, Rosie.

older children would seat themselves inside the rock wall on the gentle slope above the rostrum rock in front of Jack's cave.

It was the night of decision. The Modocs would resolve on this night how to handle the negotiations with the peace commission. As was the custom in Modoc society, all, even women, had a right to speak. Ultimately, it was the consensus of those gathered who would determine the course that every Modoc would follow. Each Modoc wishing to speak stepped forward, standing on the natural rock platform in front of Jack's cave.

Many spoke in anger. Schonchin John and Curley Headed Doctor were vehement in their feelings about killing the peace commissioners. Jack knew that much of that desire to kill stemmed from their narrow escape from Ben Wright when he had taken so many Modoc lives during the massacre twenty years ago.

Jack also knew that many of the Hot Creeks were still bitter. Their attempt to move in peace to the Klamath Reservation had instead resulted in the band being driven by the actions of inflamed settlers into the Stronghold and war. The Hot Creeks were very young men. Shacknasty Jim was only twenty-two. Bogus Charley was twenty-four. They listened and were swayed by the words of the older men, Schonchin John and Curley Headed Doctor.

There were other Modocs who anticipated that the army would leave if their leaders at the peace conference were killed. The feeling of invincibility that Curley Headed Doctor had instilled ran high.

Jack listened patiently to the people who spoke. He then moved forward to the rostrum to address the waiting Modocs. He could feel his heart thud rapidly as he looked around at these people, whose lives hung in the balance between amity and combat, life and death.

He began to feel his way with words. He felt his confidence build as he offered an impassioned plea for peace. His voice gathered strength, purpose, and power. Then suddenly, from behind the fire, a shadowy figure leaped through the air and landed on the rock next to him. To Jack's surprise he felt a shawl encircle his shoulders and a woman's basket hat pushed roughly onto his head. "You are a fish-hearted woman," the Modoc beside him yelled.

He knew then the choice that was before him. He would follow the will of the majority of his people and move against the peace commission—or cease to lead. At that moment, in the depths of his soul, Jack knew he had lost. The fate of the Modocs would be tossed to the winds like a handful of seeds.

* * * * * *

Captain Jack was cast by fate onto the horns of a dilemma. Should he keep faith with the societal mores of the Modoc people and fight numerically superior odds to defend them and their customs? Or should he yield his people's homeland and independence to the ever-encroaching trespassers and join Old Schonchin on the Klamath Reservation?[167]

Captain Jack repeatedly spoke for peace, both at the beginning of the war and throughout the campaign. But he was not destined to live in peace, for at each turning point in his life, he was thrust into combat, sometimes by his own actions, sometimes by his stubborn pride, sometimes by the acts of non-Indians, and sometimes by the will of his own people. Only a handful of Modocs sided with Captain Jack for peace that night. They were strongly opposed by the others, who voted to kill the members of the peace commission. Many Modocs still believed that the magic of Curley Headed Doctor made them invincible.

A Good Friday That Wasn't So Good

The peace conference was set for Good Friday, April 11, 1873. Knowing that the Modocs had voted to attack the peace commissioners, Toby and Frank Riddle tried to warn the commissioners once again not to meet with the Modocs.

Omens of bad will on the part of the Modocs had been reported since late February from several different sources. Meacham had felt enough alarm to wire Secretary Delano that a meeting with the Modocs would result in death to the commissioners. The mission he said, "was a failure."

In an astonishing, insulting answer, the secretary on March 5 replied, "The mission should not be a failure. I think I understand now their [the Modocs] unwillingness to confide in you. Continue negotiations." General of the Army William T. Sherman further pushed the issue by wiring Canby that "All parties here have absolute faith in you but mistrust the commissioners."[168]

Good Friday dawned unclouded. The snow had melted from the hillsides to be replaced with wild flowers. Visibility was so clear that several soldiers had scrambled up Gillem's Bluff to watch the activities. Even without field glasses, they could clearly see the tent erected for the conference. The four peace commissioners, with Toby and Frank Riddle, left on horses from Gillem's Camp for the short ride to the conference site.

Any misgivings Captain Jack and his men had about killing the peace commissioners on that day were swept away by their memories of Ben Wright, who killed over thirty Modocs in 1852 under a white flag of truce. The ghosts of Wright and his Modoc victims had found their way to the wind-swept, desolate conference site.

* * * * * *

— A White Flag of Truce —

It was a nightmare doused in blood.

In tears, Toby Riddle had tried to drag Meacham off his horse as he'd ridden out of camp that morning. And still, he and the others were going. As the peace commissioners prepared to ride out, Oliver Applegate slipped a small derringer into Dyar's pocket. Meacham, seeing this, put a derringer in his own coat pocket.

In a short note penciled to his wife, Orpha, Meacham said, "You may be a widow tonight. You shall not be a coward's wife....The chances are all against us. I have done my best to prevent this meeting. I am in no way to blame." He had left $650 with John Fairchild for his wife.

Canby wrote to his wife, Louisa, "Don't be discouraged or gloomy, darling. I will take good care of myself and come home as soon as possible."

Rev. Thomas, recruited for the peace commission shortly before the conference, was known to be a man of peace, especially compassionate toward the Modocs. He was brought on board, to some extent, to placate the militant humanitarians back East, who had deluged President Grant with petitions and grants to end the war. Fifty-nine years old and totally bald, the dome-headed minister was heard to say just before leaving for the conference, "God almighty would not let any such body of men be hurt that was on as good a mission as I am." Yet he was also heard to say, "I am in the hands of God. If He requires my life, I am ready for the sacrifice."

Thomas, like Meacham, was always a formal dresser and had dressed carefully in a light gray tweed suit. In the event that he did not return, he had paid his bill at the sutler's store so there would be no accounts unpaid.

Gen. Canby had no trepidation about going to the peace conference. He had been contemptuous of the Riddles' warnings and said field glasses would be adequate protection. Any suspicious moves on the part of the Modoc delegation would bring instant action from the soldiers watching from the bluff. Canby refused to entertain the thought of double-dealing by the Indians.

The Good Friday peace conference began in the late morning. All sat in a semicircular group about a smoky sagebrush campfire: the peace commissioners, the Riddles, and eight Modocs—Captain Jack, Schonchin John, Boston Charley, Black Jim, Ellen's Man George, Shacknasty Jim, Hooker Jim, and Bogus Charley.

Canby was dressed in full dress uniform topped by his high black felt hat with gold cord, his saber scabbard empty. He opened the conference by offering his own brand of peace pipe: he passed out cigars. Everyone but Rev. Thomas lit their cigars, and they all shook hands.

Gen. E. R. S. Canby

Rev. Eleazer Thomas

The men then turned to the task at hand and talk flowed back and forth, with the Riddles interpreting. Gen. Canby opened the conference by relating how he had worked with two other tribes who had moved to new homes and were now quite prosperous and happy. Rev. Thomas at one point fell to his knees, arms raised to the heavens, saying that, "God wishes us all to be at peace so that no more blood will be shed."

But tension was now in the air and there was a sense of unrest. Some Indians were on their feet moving about. Hooker Jim got up and removed Meacham's overcoat from the pommel of Meacham's saddle and put it on. He grabbed Meacham's hat off his head, put it on, and began to imitate Meacham's waddling walk, saying to Bogus Charley, "You think I look like old man Meacham?"

Dyar was jittery and ill at ease. He walked over to his horse, ostensibly to check a stirrup. Frank Riddle had moved behind Toby Riddle's horse. Toby herself had slipped from sitting in front of Meacham to lying prone on the ground.

Suddenly Jack jumped to his feet and announced he had to answer a call of nature. No one was embarrassed as all were used to the forthright and blunt ways of the Modocs. But the call of nature was really a signal for action. Jack returned, and yelled out the Modoc words for "all ready." Two hidden, fully armed Modocs, Slolux and Barncho, who were minor warriors and little known, appeared. At exactly twelve minutes after noon, Captain Jack raised his gun from a distance of five feet, pointed it at Canby's head, and fired. Toby Riddle screamed.

Toby could not believe what she saw. The gun had misfired. Why did Canby not run? Why didn't he fight back? He sat, perhaps in shock. Jack re-cocked the gun and fired again, delivering a death shot below the left eye. Then to everyone's disbelief, Canby struggled to his feet and ran some forty yards before thudding to the ground dead. Ellen's Man George followed and shot Canby again as he lay on the ground. He then reached down and took the general's watch, slipping it into his pocket.

Toby had been close enough to Canby to hear his last words as the fighting had broken out. "Jack, what does this mean?" Toby remembered that just the night before Canby had told her that he did not think that Jack intended to harm him. Himself a man of honor, Canby firmly believed that his reputation as having dealt fairly with Indians would protect him.

Even as Toby stood locked in horror at the sight

of Canby's futile death run, a movement nearby drew her eyes to another scene of impending death. Boston Charley shot Rev. Thomas in the chest. "Don't shoot again, Boston, I shall die anyway," Thomas stammered as he rose to his feet and began staggering away. It is not clear who it was, but someone then shot Thomas in the head.

The smell of blood, the yells of men, the screams of horses were all part of the nightmare. Dyar ran at first gunfire. Hooker Jim began pursuing and shooting at him. Dyar pulled the derringer hidden in his pocket and turned upon his pursuer. Hooker Jim abruptly stopped, turned, and ran the other way. Dyar escaped unhurt.

At Jack's "get ready" signal, Schonchin John turned on Meacham with a gun. Alarmed, Meacham drew his concealed derringer and pulled the trigger, but in his haste, he failed to cock the gun. Still, the derringer did buy Meacham some time, stopping Schonchin in his tracks. Meacham turned and ran. Schonchin began shooting at him, joined in the melee by Shacknasty Jim, Slolux, and Barncho. Meacham tripped and fell unconscious as a bullet creased his forehead leaving him stretched out on the ground unconscious and seriously wounded. A finger on one hand hung by a shred.

Shacknasty Jim was on him in a flash, removing his clothes, which he obviously wanted. Slolux placed a rifle at Meacham's head but Shacknasty impatiently pushed it away, probably because he didn't want the clothes bloodied or dirtied. Toby heard Boston Charley say he was going to scalp Meacham and watched him begin the gruesome task. As Meacham was bald, Charley made a slice in Meacham's forehead, cut around one ear, and began to tug at the skin.

Toby was a legitimate wife only because of Meacham. Memories of the good times she and her husband had shared with this man boiled through her brain, and she shouted with all her energy, "Shû'ldhăsh gépka!" which translated to, "The soldiers are coming!" It worked, she saw with relief. The Modocs instantly turned and took flight. Toby moved to the aid of the unconscious Alfred Meacham, bloodied and clothed only in his red flannel long johns.

Peace Conference Tent

When soldiers arrived a half-hour later, they found
Toby sitting beside Meacham. The naked bodies of
Thomas and Canby lay where they had fallen. As a
light snow began to fall, a portion of the canvas tent
erected for the peace conference was cut into strips as
shrouds for the bodies.

Dr. Thomas Cabaniss, a civilian contract surgeon,
had ridden out from Gillem's Camp at the first
sound of gunfire. He was one of the first to reach
Meacham. Finding Meacham still breathing, he
offered the standard army remedy for shock—a stiff
shot of brandy. Meacham was near death, but as he
regained consciousness, he remembered that he was a
temperance man opposed to alcohol. He tried to push
the brandy away.

"Down with it!" snapped Cabaniss. "Stop your
nonsense," and with that he ordered his assistants to
pry Meacham's teeth apart.

When Canby's young orderly, Scott, saw the naked, bullet-riddled body of Canby he threw himself on the body, moaning with grief and screaming with rage.

* * * * * *

Meanwhile, on the east side of the lava flow at Hospital Rock, a scenario was unfolding that was also part of the Modoc strategy for undermining the peace conference. Miller's Charley, Curley Headed Jack, and an unidentified Modoc had approached with a white flag of truce. Maj. Edwin C. Mason asked lieutenants William Boyle and William Sherwood to go out to meet them. The lieutenants went beyond the picket lines, where Mason did not mean for them to go. Curley Headed Jack wanted to know if Boyle was the "tyee" or "leader" of the Hospital Rock military force. Boyle told the Modocs he was not, that Mason was the leader, and the military men turned away to return to Hospital Rock.[169]

Lt. William Sherwood

Second Lt. Harry De Witt Moore was the Hospital Rock signalman and adjunct to Mason at the time of the attack. Moore "could see the whole thing from the signal station with the glass." He wrote in his letters home to relatives:

> The Indians picked up their guns, which they had concealed, and fired four shots, two of which took affect in Lt. Sherwood's body, one in the arm and one in the thigh shattering the bone....Boyle escaped unhurt... The troops put Sherwood on a stretcher, perfectly conscious and equally cool....While he was left to himself, he took out his handkerchief and tied it around his arm....He suffered terribly and died at 1:00 a.m. on April 14th.

When the first shot was fired on the eastern side, Moore instantly flagged this message to Signal Rock: "We are attacked. Boyle and Sherwood are probably killed. Get General Canby back as soon as possible."[170]

Moore's letters, unpublished and sitting in a relative's box for 130 years, continue in honesty and utter frustration:

> What I am going to say to you is for your ears. If it were to get out it might get me in serious difficulty. I think this murder ought to be investigated....If the troops had been sent out immediately upon receipt of my dispatch, General Canby ...would have been saved.

Moore continued by saying that Signal Rock signalman Lt.

John Adams received his message.

> This is the attempt that was made—several commandants of companies were at the signal station when the message was read. They were told by Lt. Adams that they better get their companies out.

> Adams rushed down immediately to General Gillem and gave him my dispatch. The latter acted like the stupid man he is... and after considerable delay...fumbled around and commenced writing down my message. He had gotten half of it written when the firing was heard—when the troops were sent out it was all over.

Moore rode over to Gillem's Camp that evening and saw, heard about, and recorded in writing the aftermath of the killings. His comment that "we felt terrible when the tragedy occurred," probably doesn't even start to express what he must have been feeling.

At the end of his writing on the peace commission killings, Moore comments again on Gillem:

> I don't blame General [sic] Gillem for being shocked when he heard the news, but I do contend that he has no right to control troops when his wits desert him in an emergency. If it had been a corporal who had done what he has, he would be Court [sic] marshaled and dismissed, but he is not a corporal and that's what saves him.[171]

The questions are huge. Would the Peace Commission have even met if Secretary of the Interior Delano, General of the Army Sherman, and Canby heeded the dire warnings of Meacham and others? What would have happened had there been prompt action in alerting the peace commissioners, who were only a quarter of a mile from Gillem's Camp, to the attack?

Peace Conference Aftermath

In the frontier town of Yreka, Delano was hanged in effigy for his insistence on the appointment of a peace commission.[172]

Meacham recovered, but he would bear the scar on his head from the attempted scalping. Also, the *New York Herald* on April 14, 1873, stated that "...his finger will have to be amputated."[173]

Canby's body was laid in state in Yreka. A thousand people filed by the remains. Two hundred children were dismissed from classes, marching two by two past the body. His funeral was held in Portland, Oregon, with at least nine ministers participating in the ceremony. The honors paid to Canby were almost equal to those paid to Lincoln. Canby had little money in savings. The citizens of Portland raised $5,000 for his widow, Louisa Hawkins Canby. Canby's body was then transported to Indianapolis for burial.[174]

Six thousand people viewed Rev. Thomas' remains. His San

Francisco funeral was attended by the governor of California, the mayor of San Francisco, many prestigious military officers, and some forty ministers.

The minister had been eager to join the peace commission. Rev. Thomas had a deep compassion for the Modocs. His thinking was reflected in actions taken by his son. A letter written by E. C. Thomas, the minister's son, to U. S. Senator A. A. Sargent from California was picked up and published by the media. Thomas asked for punishment for the guilty but asked that the uninvolved Modocs be treated with justice, peace, and security. He stated that, "It was the white man's and not the Modocs' fault that my Father [sic] lost his life." That statement met with mixed reviews. The May 21, 1873, *Yreka Journal* stated that, "such sentimentality as that shown by young Thomas will not be appreciated."[175]

Sherwood, in the words of Moore, "was buried that day in a rough box behind the camp, a bleak place for one to rest."

Perhaps the greatest tragedy in the taking of Canby's life was that he was a man who could have dealt with Modoc issues most fairly. He might even have been instrumental in arriving at a just peace settlement. The potential existed to improve the course of Modoc history. Canby's record of dealing with the Modocs tended to be a benevolent one. Certainly it was a relationship worth further exploration.

The army's general order on Canby's death said: "Thus perished one of the kindest and best gentlemen of this or any other country, whose social values equaled his military virtues."[176]

Gen. Canby was the only general killed in an Indian war.[177] With the peace conference killings, the Modocs had set themselves on a path of no return. All hope of peace was lost, and their fate was sealed.

What would have happend if Canby, Thomas, and the peace commission had not been attacked or killed? Where would Modoc be today? These are haunting questions. [178]

Jefferson in Command, Gillem in Trouble

Col. Jefferson C. Davis was appointed as Canby's replacement in charge of the entire military Department of the Columbia, which included the Klamath-Modoc region in its District of the Lakes. Davis was a veteran of both the Mexican and Civil Wars (on the Union side), and had no fondness for the Confederacy. He was resentful that his name was exactly the same as the president of the Confederate States of America.

While fighting in Georgia, Davis had accumulated several former slave non-combatants whose numbers grew to the point that Davis felt they were an encumbrance. To maintain his fighting

Col. Jefferson C. Davis

efficiency, he ordered the former slaves to leave. When they refused to leave, Davis ordered a bridge destroyed, stranding them on the wrong side of a wide stream. As a result, many of the former slaves were killed by Confederate cavalry. Others drowned trying to swim across the river. The furor throughout the North following this incident caused Davis to be relieved of his post. Davis drifted through obscure posts until General of the Army Sherman decided to give Davis a second chance by selecting him to serve in the Modoc War.[179]

Davis did not arrive at Gillem's Camp until May 2. Until then, Gillem continued to command the troops. Dislike of Gillem by his officers, men, and settlers in the area had continued to grow. Just prior to the peace conference, he had met with majors Mason and Green. Rashly and with dripping sarcasm, he told them that "half a dozen men could take the Stronghold." It was a slap in the face to the majors for their planning and military judgment.[180]

Gillem once asked rancher John Fairchild for a comparison of certain elements in Gillem's command to Wheaton's command. Fairchild's response was not favorable to Gillem, and the two men maintained a frosty relationship after that.[181]

When Gillem first took command, Boyle had said, "Gillem never asked any information or allowed Wheaton to give any, but blustered around the camp for a few days bragging about what he would do, and how he would capture and kill the Modocs had he the opportunity."[182]

Chapter 10
Second Battle for the Stronghold

Make the attack so strong and persistent that the Modoc fate may
be commensurate with their crime.
You will be fully justified in their utter extinction.[183]

General of the Army W. T. Sherman, April 12, 1873

The shock and horror of the peace commission killings had U. S. army troops ready to make Modocs pay sorely for what they had done. The military men had been quiet and inactive much too long. Now they truly wanted "to eat Modocs raw."

From April 15 through 17, 1873, within days of the peace conference meeting, the second battle for the Stronghold took place. Troops, numbering approximately 650 men, were under the command of Gillem. Donald McKay and his seventy-two Warm Springs Indian scouts had arrived the day of the peace conference killings. They, too, were primed for battle. "Gradual compression" was still the plan. Green commanded the troops to the west, as he had done in the first battle for the Stronghold, and Mason took the eastern troops.

The night of April 14 was clear. The nightmare fog of the first battle in January was just a bad memory. Sgt. Maurice Fitzgerald was part of the ghost-like troops on the eastern side of the Stronghold who moved under the cover of darkness:

> It was a beautiful and balmy night; not a breath of air was stirring....There was no moonlight; but a star-bespangled sky afforded enough light to enable us to pick our footsteps over the jagged rocks.

But the serene night did not fool anyone. The soldiers would not again underestimate the harshness of the terrain. They also understood that a pile of rocks or an innocent looking clump of sagebrush might suddenly spout fire—or a bunch of sagebrush could be a Modoc's camouflaged head. They knew that when the sun came up, the enemy would still be unseen. Once again the prone bodies of Modoc marksmen would blend perfectly into the rough terrain.

But the military had a trick or two of their own this time. Four Coehorn mortars were ready for use. This heavy artillery allowed a ball to be lifted up into the air and deposited in the trenches of the Stronghold. It worked as if it had been designed just for the army assault on the natural lava fortress.[184]

Dr. Cabaniss, who had come out with the western troops, reported that, "At dawn a bombshell from Mason's side of the stronghold [sic] was dropped into the Modoc camp, followed by a long and prolonged Indian war cry." The battle was on.[185]

Wheaton, before his dismissal after the January battle, had planned to acquire boats so a water attack would be possible. Gillem initially didn't think much of the idea, but eventually put two or three boats on the lake. Although used for transporting supplies, not battle purposes, the boats shortened the distance from Gillem's Camp to Hospital Rock. A fifty-mile trip by land shrank to a paltry five miles by water.[186]

The harshness of the lava flow and the inhospitable terrain once again punished the U. S. soldiers as they moved forward. But this time the march to the Stronghold was much more deliberate. The army troops advanced very slowly and methodically. Boyle was one of those military men who crept forward and slept under the stars:

> The soldiers were instructed to build stone breastworks sufficient to hold five or six men and at no time to allow themselves to be surprised. So they managed to allow two or three to sleep while the others watched, and you could see all the soldiers sleeping as soundly with their heads pillowed on a rock, as if they had been in their camp.[187]

The Modocs had a different set of challenges in forming their war plan. It must be remembered that somewhere around a hundred women and children were also in the Stronghold. Not only did the Modocs have to formulate an aggressive battle strategy, they also had to protect families. They took efforts to fortify the interior of the Stronghold. Stones were piled in front of cave and rock shelters to deflect bullets or rolling cannon balls.[188]

One civilian almost became a battle casualty. Astonishingly, the Gillem's Camp sutler Pat McManus decided to ride out to where the soldiers were engaged and see how the battle was progressing. While carelessly riding to the south, he got too close to the Stronghold. Steamboat Frank shot his mule out from under him.

Cowering behind a rock, with Frank periodically firing a shot to keep him there, McManus had to wait until dark before he was able to sneak out and start the long walk home. When he did get back, he was nearly shot by Gillem Camp sentries, who did not recognize him in the dark. "Dry up there!" he screamed. "It's me! Don't you know a white man on his knees from an Indian on his belly?" So it was that McManus did not join the rolls of civilian casualties.[189]

On the Front Line

Boyle had been recruited from Vancouver, Washington, to serve as an officer in the Modoc War. The long trek to Modoc country in December, mostly on foot through winter weather, was arduous. One of the other officers who had made the long, exhausting journey with Boyle also wrote about the rigors of this unusual war. Moore was faithful in writing letters to his aunt and uncle. He had written to them on a regular basis since the day he had left Vancouver to join the troops involved in the Modoc rebellion. His letters were poignant and revealing.

A West Pointer born in Pennsylvania, Moore wanted his kinsfolk to have some idea of what this second battle of the Stronghold was like. He wrote a long letter home while camped in the lava battlefield:

> I know you cannot understand why we have not been more successful....I will try to explain why this is. This country we are in is rough beyond description. It is not regularly rough but broken up into all sorts of shapes and all solid rock, very little soil. You go up one of these gorges and suddenly you are up against a wall of solid rock—what the French call an 'impasse.'
>
> Now the Modocs know all these trails, and when we advance upon them they glide out like snakes and we see nothing of them. I have fought against Modocs for 4 days and in that time I have seen just 5 Modocs and those the first day....
>
> The Modocs in the first fight captured 8 of our rifles and quantities of ammunition. Since then they have captured more from dead men, and in the fight yesterday, I have no doubt that a great many more were taken. They can always supply themselves with ammunition by going over the ground occupied by our lines. They can shoot with great accuracy.
>
> We are very uncomfortable here. We have no tents and the men are on picket all the time. I live in a den of rocks with a canvass cover. Rattlesnakes are a plenty and scorpions abundant. It is uncomfortable on this account to sleep on the ground. It is too cold for them to come out much but I have seen several of each.
>
> I am writing by a sagebrush fire and the smoke is blowing into my eyes. It is as dark as Egypt. I want to finish this tonight as I think we will be ordered to attack tomorrow, and I want you to get this letter. I can see Indians' fires all around me.

In a January 1873 dispatch, Mason commended Moore and two other officers for their bravery in the second battle for the Stronghold. "They behaved in the most gallant manner, they led their men to the attack and imparted to them that confidence that can only be inspired by the display of the highest soldierly qualities."[190]

Disobeying Orders

Gillem's battle plan for the troops in this second battle had Mason's eastern and Green's western troops swing more south, effectively surrounding the Modocs.

But that maneuver did not work, due in part to the tenacity and skill of the Modocs. Another contributing factor was that Mason did not accept Gillem's orders and refused to move his troops to the south because of "weakening the line too much." Gillem was extremely upset with Mason, and his denunciation of him was bitter and direct. Gillem claimed a year later that Mason had said, "It was not part of *my plan* to expose *my men* unnecessarily."[191]

Agitating Gillem further was the fact that Green contacted Mason directly, and the two officers developed a second plan of their own. The two subordinates paid no attention to Gillem's orders, blatantly disobeying him. They moved north along Tule Lake and cut off the Modocs' water supply. This was a major coup and accomplished without the loss of a man.

During the night of the sixteenth, the Modocs made desperate attempts to secure water but were driven back. The Modocs also experienced the might of the Coehorn mortars. Every fifteen minutes or so, a mortar would fire. Cries of rage and pain could be heard as the balls were lobbed into the air and then bit into the rocks of the Stronghold interior.[192]

But the troops suffered, too, from the nights when artillery bombarded the Stronghold. Fitzgerald made the comment that he'd never been so exhausted in his life as after two sleepless nights and three frenzied days of scrambling over crusted lava.[193] Capt. David Perry had been wounded in the first battle for the Stonghold, but now totally recovered, he was on horseback patrolling the west side of the lava flow. His journal has this account:

> I can't write more to-night [sic] as I am very tired and have to be in the saddle at daylight. I have not washed nor combed my hair for three days. It's not pleasant to live in the rocks for three days and two nights with now and then a bite of cold food, and an incessant fire on the line all the time.[194]

Knowing that the Modocs were cut off from their water was a huge boost to the morale of the soldiers. Soldiers crossed the red tule rope that the shaman had placed as a guarantee to the Modocs that soldiers could not enter the Stronghold. Curley Headed Doctor's vow that no Modoc protected by his magic would be killed was torn to shreds. The Modocs were in trouble. But the troops to the north who had cut off the water supply and crossed the red rope had done so at a price. A huge gap to the south had been left in the army lines.[195]

The Modocs were outnumbered and outgunned. The shortage of water forced Captain Jack to evacuate the Stronghold during the night through the gap the military had left, exploding the myth that this "no-man's land" to the south posed a natural barrier.

To cover the flight of the Modocs, Captain Jack initiated a vigorous round of firing around midnight. A few Modocs were left behind shouting and firing, while the women, children, and other Modoc men slipped into the night. They used a natural land bridge, running south through the lava bed, that avoided the chasms and the worst of the jagged lava.

Although the Modocs were never more than four or five hundred yards from the troops, no one detected their movement. The Warm Springs Indian scouts later said they had heard children crying, but it was not reported to their superior officers. One soldier made the statement that the Modocs "had passed out under the line of troops as ants would pass through a sponge."[196]

The Modocs had prepared ahead in the event of evacuation of the Stronghold. The passage leading out of the Stronghold was marked by sticks and stones piled on top of one another so that the Modocs could pass out as well by night as by day.[197]

Once again, the Modocs' alliance with the land proved a mighty weapon. Time and again throughout the war, when the soldiers were convinced they had their foes cornered, the elusive Modocs would slide away.

Troops Take the Stronghold

The three-day battle ended on March 17. Orders were given to enter Captain Jack's Stronghold. A few minutes before the charge, Dr. Cabaniss and three or four other men gathered rocks to throw up a wall. They uncovered a sad and unwelcome sight. The skeleton they found half covered in rocks had his fingers cut off and was scalped. The body was that of a soldier by the name of Brennen, who had been missing since the January 17 battle.[198]

A civilian—Charles Putnam—had joined the eastern skirmish line as it was moving toward the Stronghold. His memoirs record an interesting incident:

> The officer in command of Troop G ordered a charge. Only one man obeyed the order. He started forward on all fours saying, 'Come on boys!' He crawled through the brush for about twenty steps before he discovered he was the only man in the charge, then he stopped. After that it was a common occurrence in quarters to hear some one call out, 'G Troop, charge!' Then some fellow would drop down on his hands and knees and start across the floor full speed.[199]

Both Green's and Mason's units moved forward cautiously toward the Stronghold. Gillem, who came from the west with Green, could not find any of Mason's units. He got up on the highest rock available, angrily crying, "Forward, Forward," until Mason finally appeared. The breach between Mason and Gillem was a long way from healing.[200]

Triumphant government troops entered the Stronghold, confidently expecting to accept the surrender of the Modocs. It was an empty victory as the Stronghold itself was vacated. They were astounded to find that the Modocs had miraculously escaped. One old, wounded Modoc man was found and killed—even after he had offered his surrender.[201] The soldiers scalped his entire head, even his eyebrows. His ears were taken as trophies and his locks cut into bits.

Fitzgerald tells of a particularly ghastly happening involving a Troop K lieutenant, a West Point graduate "whose name I will refrain from mentioning:"

> We found a squaw, probably eighty or ninety years old, squatted on her haunches among the rocks on the edge of the Stronghold. Her gray hair was hanging in disorder over her wizened and wrinkled countenance. As we were passing by this wretched specimen...abandoned to her fate by her own people, as being too old and feeble to be taken along, we stopped to gaze upon her, but with no thought of inflicting punishment upon such a helpless human being...

> Turning his cold blue eye upon her, Lieut. ____ said: "Is there anyone here who will put that old hag out of the way?" A Pennsylvania Dutchman stepped from the ranks and said, "I'll fix her, Lieutenant!" He then deliberately placed his carbine to her head and blew out her brains.

Fitzgerald also gave a recounting of "the head of a Modoc severed from the trunk, perhaps by some soldier...that passing troopers generally saluted with a vicious kick."[202]

The Stronghold had served as a makeshift home during the long winter months for 150 men, women, children, and babies. The stench of human over-crowding was everywhere. The walls of the caverns were black with smoke from fires built for warmth and cooking. The lack of water and the unrelenting attack of the soldiers had forced a hasty exit. Personal belongings were strewn about. The carcasses of partially consumed animals and fish in a putrid state lay where they had been left.

There was not much for the conquering troops to claim as a trophy—with one exception—a medicine flag. Three of them had been erected above the Stronghold. One in particular had stood high in the air, a symbol to troops of the defiance of the Modocs. The flag the soldiers grabbed in the Stronghold was now a symbol of defeat.[203]

There was a concern that the Modocs might decide to come back to the Stronghold, so troops moved into the Stronghold. As a defensive strategy, they built forts facing out over the lava flow.

Should the Modocs return, they would find their former fortress a Rock of Gibraltar—in control of blue-coated conquerors.[204] It is interesting to note that the first actual Modoc casualty in the lava bed, one of very few in actual combat during the war, was during the second battle for the Stronghold when Shacknasty Frank discovered a Coehorn mortar projectile that had failed to explode. His interest in the canon ball was a costly one. Cabaniss reported finding the body: "...his hands and bowels torn...having picked it (the cannon ball) up to examine it while the fuse was still burning."

The official military casualty count for the three-day battle was six killed and seventeen wounded.[205]

A Brutal Killing

After safely moving his men and families out of the Stronghold, Captain Jack decided to go on the offensive with a surprise attack the very next day. Jack had Hooker Jim and a handful of picked men double back to attack Gillem's Camp. Since few of Gillem's men were in the camp, the raid would probably have been successful, but Captain Jack hadn't counted on having to deal with the civilian members of the camp. Well-armed and experienced in combat, the civilians beat the attack back.

Corp. Charles A. Pentz kept a very careful journal of his Modoc War experiences. A signalman, he was one of the few military men in Gillem's Camp when the Modocs appeared out of nowhere on April 17:

> We took every advantage of the little time we had, and broke open boxes of ammunition and arms and made all the camp followers, sutlers, teamsters, and also all the sick and wounded that were able, take a gun and throw themselves out as pickets, to keep the enemy from firing into camp.[206]

The overpowered Modocs headed back to join Captain Jack. En route they stumbled on two reporters and a nineteen-year-old Yreka boy, Eugene Hovey, who were bringing supplies to the soldiers who had now set up camp in the Stronghold. In one of the war's horrible moments, Hooker Jim shot Hovey while the reporters ran for their lives. Hovey was stripped of his clothes, his body was mutilated, and his head smashed until it was "as thick as a man's hand."[207]

After the Modoc War, soldiers and others are photographed in Captain Jack's Stronghold. Harry De Witt Moore is front row, third from the left, in white hat.

Chapter 11
Thomas-Wright Battle

The sufferings of that night's march made
many a young man old.[208]

Lt. William Boyle, April 1873

They who stood to the fight filled true soldiers' graves.
The cowards who ran away
disgraced themselves and the service.[209]

Colonel Jefferson C. Davis, Nov. 1, 1873 Annual Report

Where were the Modocs? That question plagued Gillem. Maybe they had moved completely out of the lava flow or perhaps they were on their way back to Tule Lake. On April 20, Boyle had seen a party of Modocs at the lake. He was taken by surprise when he saw that, "in plain sight of General [sic] Gillem's camp, they poured water and some of them had the audacity to bathe themselves in the Lake.... Only a feeble attempt was made to get them or attack them."[210]

In an attempt to pin-point the whereabouts of the illusive Modocs, a patrol of sixty-four soldiers, a guide, a packer with two assistants, and Dr. Bernard Semig, a civilian physician, set forth on April 26, 1873, from Gillem's Camp. The patrol was under the leadership of Capt. Evan Thomas, who had missed most of the fighting in the Stronghold. Along with Thomas were five other commissioned officers, including Lt. Thomas Wright. These officers were not only very young but were from prominent military families.[211]

Before leaving, those men who had written to friends and relatives gave their letters to other soldiers to mail. Wright had written to his wife the evening before "to amuse her." No one was particularly concerned about coming back as this was a routine scouting patrol.

Pat McManus, the camp sutler who had almost lost his life in the second battle for the Stronghold, was determined again to

Capt. Evan Thomas

Lt. Thomas F. Wright

check out the military action and go with the patrol. While he was back at his tent preparing to leave, Toby Riddle unbridled his horse and drove it away. McManus was enraged, but Toby calmly let him know that she had done it for his wife.[212]

At noon, in the shadow of a small, 200-feet-high knoll known today as Hardin Butte, the men stopped to eat, some even removing their shoes to rest weary feet. One man even began to trim his toenails. They were not alone. A short distance away, a small band of Modocs, under the leadership of Scarfaced Charley, watched the extraordinary sight of shoeless soldiers. As the army patrol prepared to eat lunch, the Modocs attacked.[213]

As the orange flashes of gunfire blazed down on them, many soldiers panicked, some running in bare feet with weapons and rations being tossed aside. Pandemonium took over for much of the patrol. Many soldiers, trying to solve the dilemma of flight or fight, coward or hero, simply threw away their rifles and started on a wild dash cross the lava flow for Gillem's Camp. Rarely had army history recorded such contrasts in bravery and cowardice. Those who remained stood by each other, often dying for each other.[214]

It was a military triumph for the Modocs—a battle that left nearly two-thirds of the patrol dead on the battlefield or so severely wounded that they would not survive. Scarfaced Charley's force numbered only slightly over twenty. His entrapment of this military scouting patrol could be said to be one of the most perfectly carried out ambushes in Indian military history.[215]

This battle, strategically well planned and executed by the Modoc, is known in history as the "Thomas-Wright Battle," named after the officers in command.

One of the first to fall was Wright.

* * * * * *

— Reluctant Warrior —

Scarfaced Charley was not a born warrior, he decided, as he watched the bloody scene below him. Not twenty yards away, pinned down by crossfire from ridges on both sides, the young lieutenant, Thomas Wright, struggled to breathe as blood poured from a bullet wound in his groin. While on a rest stop only minutes before the Modoc attack on the government troops, Wright had commented to Evan Thomas that "when no one sees any Indians, it is time to start looking for them."

Wright never had the chance to look because the Modocs found him. As soon as the Modocs opened fire, he charged them. Scarfaced Charley had watched and been amazed at this white soldier's bravery and selflessness in attempting to defend his men. Charley had also seen that some of the soldiers accompanying the young officer had turned and run away, true deserters, leaving him to fight as best he could.

Scarfaced Charley watched the badly wounded soldier and instinctively knew that it was only a matter of time before the soldier drew breath no more. The ground beneath Wright was soaked with blood.

The young soldier's eyes were blue and full of tears. Blue eyes, white skin—brown eyes, brown skin. No great differences when surely the fallen officer had a mother who would grieve for him as much as Scarfaced Charley's mother would grieve if he died.

The dying officer raised himself onto his elbow and reached down to his waist where he struggled to pull something out of his pocket—a knife perhaps as a last defense? As Charley watched in amazement, the wounded man pulled out a gold pocket watch, exhausted with the effort. For a moment he held it to his cheek as his body convulsed in pain.

Painstakingly Wright began to dig in the sand with his fingers until he had hollowed out a small hole. With a final effort, he placed his father's watch in the depression and began to scratch the sand back into place. Blood was now pouring from his mouth, and the red flow mixed with the sand beneath his blue uniform. Then another bullet ripped into his body, this time through his heart. His head sunk to the ground and he moved no more.

Charley covered his eyes and his stomach heaved. Senseless war, he thought. Charley was stretched out flat on his stomach, with his men to the left and right of him. That fateful day, less than five months ago, when soldiers had first ridden into his Lost River camp had finally come down to this: a blue-eyed boy who died alone in the sand, Modocs hunting people instead of game, and Modoc children crying in hunger as their mothers wearily followed in the footsteps of their men.

The day was still young, and Charley fought on. There were more charges to be made, more men to be killed. But his heart was not in this battle. Three hours it had been going on.

Years later he would remember this day, this moment, and not be able to recall whether his mind had guided his legs or his legs led him to his actions. A blinding light seemed to erupt in his brain. His legs coiled under him, and he shot upright. He stood high on a rock, and his voice carried to the military men crouched below him and fighting for their lives, almost certain of their deaths. "All you fellows that ain't dead had better go home. We don't want to kill you all in one day."

Then he signaled his men to withdraw.

* * * * * *

Thomas had fought a losing battle. He and some thirty-five remaining men had turned north and scattered in an attempt to outrun the Modocs. Finally Thomas realized that he could not get away from the Modocs. So selecting a hollow filled with small rocks and sagebrush, he had ordered his small command, which had dwindled to twenty men, to shelter themselves as best they could. He was reported by a survivor to have said, "I will not retreat a step farther. This is as good a place to die as any." The Indians above rained deadly bullets into the mass of poorly concealed soldiers until the voice of Scarfaced Charley broke off the attack.

Most of the men huddled with Thomas died. Dr. Semig, although badly wounded, managed through great odds to pull through. Despite his pain and discomfort—he later had a leg amputated—he was engaged in cheering other wounded men around him. Not one of the five young military officers on the Thomas-Wright patrol survived that deadly day.[216]

A Trail of Terror

A bitter storm of sleet and rain came down in torrents,
freezing as it fell. In a short time
an overcoat would stand alone... .
The night was as black as a wolf's mouth.[217]

Second Lt. Frazier A. Boutelle, U. S. Army

Darkness settled over a scene of unbelievable pain for those left on the battlefield. Most of the surviving soldiers had been severely injured. They were also intensely afraid the Modocs might return.

A rescue patrol finally arrived but, incredibly, there were no doctors among the rescuers, and they brought no water. It would be thirty-two hours before the first of the wounded reached Gillem's Camp. Most of the survivors of Scarfaced Charley's raid had to be carried back. Those who were still walking and unwounded had to do the carrying.[218]

Boutelle, who had fired the first shot of the Modoc War at the Lost River Battle, was on the rescue patrol:

> We came upon the most heartbreaking sight it has been my fate to behold... The sight of dead men was not new to me. In my service during the Civil War I had seen them by the acre, but the sight of the poor fellows lying under the sagebrush dead or dying and known to have been uselessly slaughtered was simply revolting... The fearful ordeal through which these poor fellows had passed—shot down in the morning, lying all day without food, water, attention or protection from the cold...[219]

Capt. Joel Trimble, also on the rescue patrol, described the dead as "presenting different forms of anguish and distortion, some in the position of desperate defense, others prostrate in figures of dire helplessness." The dead and wounded were in confused heaps and almost all had been shot several times. The Modocs had stripped many naked.[220]

For the soldiers, the trail back to Gillem's Camp was one of tears, terror, and blood. The sun faded and the weather turned blustery. Sleet and freezing rain fell constantly. The biting wind tortured both those on stretchers and those carrying stretchers over the jagged lava. The total, consuming darkness that followed was so intense that each man had to touch the shoulder of the man in front as they struggled through the bitter night. They felt they had entered Hell.

Boyle was overwhelmed. He later said, "The elements at that

time seemed to be trying to cover this awful scene by one of the most awful storms I ever beheld... Never did men suffer as did the officers and soldiers on that night, hearing the wails of the dying and with the fearful spectacle of dead men packed on the backs of mules."[221]

Of the sixty-four soldiers who had set out in search of Modocs, twenty-seven were killed and seventeen injured in the Thomas-Wright Battle. The only Modoc casualty was a young warrior shot to death while plundering the not quite dead.[222]

The only known eyewitness account of the battle, unknown until recently, was that of Corp. Charles A. Pentz, who had been ordered to take his flag signal equipment and accompany the Thomas-Wright patrol. He reported that he was told to bring "a haversack with lunch only as the party would return at sunset the same day." His journal entry on April 26, 1873, recounts his experience. It is an incredible story of survival:

> Now and then Lt. Wright would call the attention of Maj.[sic] Thomas to a cave or deep chasm where any number of men could be concealed, and...[he would give] a curse [to] the Modocs for causing him to be brought into such a S- of a b- of a country. ...

> As soon as we halted at the base of the black knoll, Maj. [sic] Thomas asked me to come with him...then proceeded to ascent [sic] the black knoll....Half way to the top of the knoll...firing began on the left, which proved to be the enemy....Maj. [sic] Thomas at this time told me to signal to camp that we were attacked...Maj. [sic] Thomas stood on the side of the knoll in a very exposed position and gave his orders in a clear and distinct manner....

> The indians [sic] saw my signal flag as soon as I began to use it and opened a severe fire upon us....Maj. [sic] Thomas finding it getting rather warm ordered me to get back to the rear with the flag...as my flag was drawing the fire of the enemy. I then started on the double quick with my flag in one hand and a remington [sic] pistol in the other...

> The indians [sic] came after me as they could see the white signal flag wherever I went....I got into the ledge....Lt. Wright was standing up at this time. He turned to me and said, 'do away with that flag.' I replied, "What do I do with it? Eat it?"

> I started [running] with my flag in hand and some of the indians [sic] followed me on the double quick....I threw myself down on my back and took the signal flag off of the staff and put it in my bosom so that they could not see me. Then I arose to my feet and started on the run again, the indians [sic] after me with a yell....I finally elided [sic] the Devils.

On Pentz's return to Gillem's camp, Pentz reported to Maj. Green:

> I told him it was the most demoralized affair that I ever saw in my life. I told him wherever I went with my signal flag...both officers and men...kept away from me as if I had the Cholera.

After his escape, Pentz actually turned around and went back with the rescue patrol—another horrifying experience:

> We had to lay on our arms during the night. I had neither blanket or overcoat, and I suffered very much from the cold.... This was the hardest night that ever I put in in my life. Did not have any water, food or sleep for nearly forty-eight hours.[223]

Thirteen bodies were buried where they fell, but the rest were brought back to the Gillem's Camp Cemetery. Some time later, all the bodies were disinterred and sent to Ft. Klamath. Eventually, some of the Modoc War fatalities came to rest at the Presidio in San Francisco, California. Other bodies were sent home for burial. The shocking loss of life was felt throughout the troops. Hardened soldiers who had been in service for much of their lives wept like children.[224]

Alfred Meacham, recovering from his wounds received at the peace conference, looked out the tent flap from his Gillem Camp hospital bed and saw two soldiers bury a small, straight box in the cemetery. Meacham was puzzled by this until he was told that Sgt. Gude, a good friend of Pentz's, had asked to have his amputated leg put to rest.[225]

Once again Gillem received the brunt of blame and criticism for a military action gone wrong. The *Army and Navy Journal* offered a harsh reprimand: "This latest expedition against the Modocs, which has resulted so disastrously...need[s] a fuller explanation than is contained in the report of General [sic] Gillem." Boutelle felt that "General [sic] Gillem has been justly blamed for sending an inexperienced man in command of such an expedition. The experience of the past few weeks should have indicated to him that it was not proper to send any small party anywhere in the lava beds."[226]

Boyle, ever critical of Gillem, recalls troops being ready to ride out in support of the downed Thomas-Wright patrol. "But Gillem, as usual, lost all control of himself and would not act nor let others, and before the troops left camp under Green, darkness had settled and the weather which had been unusually pleasant soon turned blustery, stormy and disagreeable." Meacham concurred with Boyle, asserting that Gillem waited a full three hours before sending out a rescue patrol.[227]

Shortly after the Thomas-Wright Battle, Gillem was relieved of command. Lt. Colonel Frank Wheaton, who had originally been in Gillem's position, was reinstated.

Canby's replacement, Col. Davis, in his official report on the battle, stated that a "well-direct fire...from the Indians caused a large number, probably two-thirds, of the enlisted men to break and run away in the most cowardly manner." He continued by saying that an error was made by the officer in command by not pushing his skirmish line further to the front and on the flanks before halting. But he said this mistake could have been easily and quickly remedied had troops stood by the officers and obeyed their commands:

> This they did not do. The result was conspicuous cowardice on the part of the men who ran away....The lesson taught by this affair is that a great many of the enlisted men here are utterly unfit for Indian fighting of this kind, being only cowardly beef-eaters [English ceremonial guards who served the royal family]. My recommendation is, however, that they be kept here, trained, and made to fight.[228]

The military was in such disarray after the Thomas-Wright Battle that Davis did not think he could send a detail out to find the bodies of fallen soldiers. He also wanted to get a fix on the position of the Modocs before sending troops back to the Thomas-Wright site. So he called on two Modoc women who had proved time and again to be a capable team at tracking, negotiating, and whatever else needed to be done.

Lt. Arthur Cranston

One-eyed Dixie and Artena Choakus left Gillem's Camp on May 6, riding, they claimed, eighteen hours without water. When they returned a couple days later, they reported that they had found the bodies of Lt. Arthur Cranston, one of the officers with the Thomas-Wright patrol, and those who had died with him. Military troops had combed the area where the bodies were found, but the geology in the lava flows had so many twists and turns that the bodies had not been found. Since they had seen no Modocs, the area was considered safe for soldiers and the Warm Springs Indian scouts. On hearing this report, Davis sent a detail to ride out to recover the missing bodies.[229]

Gillem's Camp was a sorrowful place in the days following the Thomas-Wright Battle.

* * * * * *

— A Mother's Love —

A long dreary winter! And for what? Those thoughts were keen on the mind of Capt. Trimble. To drive a couple hundred miserable aborigines from a desolate natural shelter in the wilderness so that a few thieving cattlemen might ranch their wild steers on an isolated stretch of land, the dimensions of

several reasonable-sized counties.

Trimble was on duty near Gillem's Camp and found himself with plenty of time to think. The last few nightmare days, seeing the defeat and sufferings of troops involved in the Thomas-Wright Battle, had caused a sense of hopelessness and anxiety. What, he wondered as he took in the stark desolation of the land, was it all about?

As his mind wandered, so did his eyes. Suddenly he was startled to see a strange object traveling down the trail. As the object came closer, starkly outlined against the black lava rock, Trimble realized it was a woman with a long, gray lace veil streaming from her hat.

As she drew nearer he saw she was beyond her middle years. The mother of Lt. George M. Harris had journeyed day and night from Philadelphia to the bedside of her dying son, wounded in the Thomas-Wright Battle. Twenty-five year old Harris had received rifle balls through the lung, back, and ribs. When the casualty notice reached her, Mrs. Harris, totally on her own initiative, with no permission from anyone, began her journey by train, continued by stagecoach, hired a supply wagon to get her within reach of her son, and finally came into the army camp on the back of a

Lt. George M. Harris

mule she had borrowed from a packer. She now stood before Trimble asking for her son.

Harris was a brave man, uncomplaining of the pain of his severe injury as the patrol had struggled through the sleet and snow that terrible night following the battle. Trimble knew that Harris's back wound, although serious, would not have killed him but for the careless and rough way he had been transported back to camp. Trimble once again felt the helplessness and anger he had experienced over the last few days. But what peace it would bring Harris, Trimble knew, to have his mother near. Harris's brother, too, had come to be with him.

Harris's men fairly idolized him. They often repeated the last words they heard him say in battle: 'Men, we are surrounded. We must fight and die like men and soldiers.'

Through the last twenty-four hours of Harris's life, the son was with his mother, lucid and able to know she was there. Lt. George M. Harris died in the arms of his mother sixteen days after he was shot.

* * * * * *

Oliver C. Applegate, Toby and Frank Riddle.
Note the traditional tule basket hats woven and worn by Modoc women.

Chapter 12
The Beginning of the End

There are some Modocs fifteen miles from here. They all want to return to the fold and live in peace with the whites.

Artena, Modoc negotiator, *Yreka Union*, May 24, 1873

Time was running out for the Modocs. They found living in the cracks of a lava flow difficult at best. Some 150 men, women, and children had to be provided for, and water was becoming a severe need. At first, ice from the numerous ice caves in the lava supplied water. The Modocs moved from ice cave to ice cave until the caves were depleted of ice. It usually took a year for ice to reform in significant quantities.[230]

Jeff Riddle, the son of Toby and Frank Riddle, described, many years after the war, the situation of the Modocs at that time:

> Some had young children that had to be carried, children from seven years old and up had to walk the best they could. The real old men and women was [sic] more bother to the middle-aged people than the children. Some of them was [sic] partly blind. They could not see to travel through the rocks and brush.[231]

Then came the incident that marked the downward spiral of the Modocs. At a skirmish in an area near the extreme southeast of the lava flow known as Sorass Lake, the Modocs felt their first real defeat.

Captain Jack knew that another fight was inevitable and had prepared for another battle like the Thomas-Wright encounter. Davis, on his end, selected a newcomer to move troops out to confront the Modocs. Capt. Henry Hasbrouck was a good choice, more than ready to mount the battle. Among the troops was the ever-present Second Lt. Boutelle and the Warm Springs scouts. After arriving at Sorass Lake—an undrinkable puddle of alkali water surrounded by smelly mud—and finding the lake without the liberal supply of water expected, Hasbrouck, on a whim, renamed it Dry Lake. The name stuck, and that is what it is called today. It was on this strange lake that Hasbrouck set up camp.[232]

Captain Jack had decided to take the offensive with a surprise attack on Hasbrouck's camp modeled after Scarfaced Charley's successful attack less than a month earlier. Dressed in Canby's uniform, Captain Jack at the crack of dawn on May 10, 1873, moved against Hasbrouk's troops with a blaze of gunfire. But the real surprise of the surprise attack was reserved for Captain Jack.

The first warning that the Modocs were approaching was when a dog belonging to the boss of the pack train began to growl. When the dog continued to growl, the pack train boss went to the officer of the guard and insisted that Hasbrouck be awakened. The man's obvious alarm caused the guard to awaken Hasbrouck, who quickly rallied his sleeping men to the cause. Private Charles Hardin recalled the scene: "Men rolled over behind saddles and bundles of blanket. No covering however small being ignored, they fastened on belts and pulled on boots under a hail of bullets." These soldiers were ready to fight. They charged when they needed to, the bluecoats moving forward. After battling for months against an enemy they couldn't see, the troops fought with a vengeance.[233]

Now the second shock of the morning hit Captain Jack. Suddenly Donald McKay and his Warm Springs scouts appeared, having outflanked the Modocs. The scouts were now working to cut them off at the rear. They were unable to do so, but Captain Jack and his men having had enough, turned and fled.[234]

Captain Jack's surprise attack was a calamity. Although Hasbrouck lost five soldiers and scouts, Captain Jack knew that the tide had turned.

Another event turned the tide even more. Ellen's Man George, a Hot Creek Modoc and cousin to Shacknasty Jim,[235] was wounded in battle and later died in a large crack in the lava. The body of Ellen's Man George was taken about three and a half miles away from the battlefield. In a clearing there, a pit was hollowed out and the body placed on top of a pile of brush and logs. In the age-old tradition of the Modocs, the body was cremated. In times of war, it was Modoc custom to cremate a warrior's body on or near the battlefield. As flames licked at the body, those watching saw General Canby's watch and three hundred and fifty dollars in gold that had been in George's pocket slip into the fire. It was allowed to burn along with the man who had helped kill Canby.[236]

The friction that had been brewing between bands for some time surged to the surface. Claiming that Captain Jack had exposed the Hot Creeks to front-line positions to protect his own band, the Hot Creek warriors and men from other bands who sided with them, split from Jack's band, leaving Jack with only about thirty warriors.

A Congressional Medal of Honor

The Sorass Lake Battle provided the background for a great story of valor. It showed that not only soldiers are battle heroes. Dr. John O. Skinner, a contract surgeon assigned to Harbrouck's troops, worked under constant fire to save lives:

Dr. John O. Skinner
Congressional Medal of Honor

Immediately after the firing started, and the first men were hit, the resourceful surgeon established a rough field hospital at the only spot affording any kind of shelter on the dry lake bed. A man lying prone behind this cover would be protected from flying lead, even though the men attending him would not.

When Trooper Hardin brought his wounded comrade to this spot, he found Surgeon Skinner working all alone, with several badly wounded men on his hands. As Hardin started back, the surgeon shouted, "There's plenty of you fellows up front already; you can do more here." Hardin stayed, although in later life he confessed that with bullets flying in all directions, for a few moments he was in about the hottest spot he had ever encounttered [sic] in his entire Army career. Under Surgeon Skinner's directions, shouted to him while the doctor himself was tending other wounded, young Hardin saved a soldier's life when he stopped the flow of blood gushing from the wounded man's arm.[237]

Skinner received the Congressional Medal of Honor, "via a special act of Congress because at the time he was a civilian contract surgeon serving with the Army."[238]

Betrayers or Betrayed?

"The Hot Creeks had a fuss with Captain Jack."

San Francisco Chronicle, May 24, 1873

After the Sorass Lake encounter, the army troops decided to scout the area thoroughly. They surprised a party of Modocs, taking five women and five children prisoner. From these women the soldiers learned of a huge break in the Modoc ranks. This dissent brought the Modoc War to a hasty conclusion.

The Modoc War occurred in an era when communication was limited. There was no one to tell the Modoc side of the story. Many Modocs did not speak English, had no written language, and little voice among non-Indians. It is understandable why much of Modoc reasoning and emotions surrounding the war are lost in silence.

Much of Modoc history is derived from military records and government documents. Newspapers managed to carry some of Modoc thought, but much of what happened on the Modoc side and their feelings about the events that occurred are murky or unknown. The information coming from the captured women indicating a break in the Modoc ranks was mentioned briefly in newspapers and letters but was considered insignificant. Details of this revelation were mostly unrecorded. Yet momentous events were to transpire as a result. Conclusions were drawn about individual Modocs.

Four Modoc "bloodhounds," from the Hot Creek band of Modocs, agreed to aid the military in bringing about Captain Jack's surrender. The general conclusion was, and still is, that they were traitors. Many books and writings freely use this term. Yet this deduction is reached without an understanding of Modoc societal and military life. The agreement by the "bloodhounds" to track Captain Jack is a direct result of the splitting apart of Modoc bands.

A significant number of Modocs had indicated they were ready to surrender. They would no longer follow Captain Jack, declaring a longer battle useless and claiming Captain Jack now had no ability to fight except in self-defense. Women's and children's lives were at stake. In Col. Davis's Nov. 1, 1873, official report on the Modoc War to the U. S. War Department, the rift is addressed:

> The chief [Captain Jack] could no longer keep his warriors up to the work required of them, lying on their arms night and day and watching for an attack. These exactions were so great, and the conduct of the leader so tyrannical, that insubordination sprang up, which led to dissenusions [sic], and the final separation of this band into two parties; they left the lava beds bitter enemies.[239]

Historian Hubert Howe Bancroft in *History of Oregon, Volume II*, talks about the confrontation:

> At the last stormy conference among the Modocs, Jack had reluctantly consented to a cessation of hostilities, and the Modoc advocates of peace [Hot Creek Modocs] had retired to their beds among the rocks satisfied; but when morning came they found their captain gone, with his adherents and all the best horses and arms.[240]

The May 24, 1873, *Yreka Journal* provides more detail:

> Lt. Boutelle tells us the Modocs had a row among themselves the day after the battle near Sorass Lake. Two thirds of the warriors decided there was no use in continuing the contest.

Then in the journalistic style of that era, comes the *Journal's* elaborate description of Captain Jack's response:

> Jack waxed wroth at the disaffection and threatened to warm the recreant warriors....This resolution led to Jack's clandestine departure with the finest accontrements [sic] in the armorial cleft and the finest steeds in the stable.

The irony stands out. The very Modocs, many of them Hot Creeks, who had opted for war, now spoke for peace. Captain Jack, who had stood defiantly for peace throughout most of the war, now chose to continue fighting.

It was just after the Dry Lake Battle that there was a curious happening involving the mysticism of Modoc prophecy.[241] The *San Francisco Call*, May 21, 1873, carried the story, written from the Fairchild Ranch:

> Last evening, Artena, One-eyed Dixie and five Modoc matrons, all residents at this ranch, interviewed the five Hot Creek squaws captured by Captain Hasbrouck's command.... The cause of disaffection among the Modocs after the Sorass Lake fight is as novel as it is interesting. The redoubtable Jack had consulted a stolen chronometer [a timepiece designed to keep time with great accuracy, an instrument unknown to the Modocs] and, after sundry gestures and explanations, promised his followers that they should shed rifle bullets as a duck does water and escape unharmed. The confidence this statement inspired was rudely dispelled by the Hasbrouck encounter at Sorass Lake, where several Modocs were killed and others wounded. The result was that indignation reigned supreme in Jack's household and the Hot Creeks decided to fight no more.

It all perhaps seems a little convoluted and strange to modern thinking, but it should be acknowledged that mysticism and religions from many cultures and eras have made prophecies and offered hope. Other than the newspaper article, there is little known or written about this incident. It is a good example of how difficult it is to trace the Modoc side of history.

Steamboat Frank

More importantly, the Hot Creek Modocs were truly angered by Captain Jack's desertion in the dead of night, leaving the Hot Creek men to care for their women and children as best they could. They felt betrayed and victimized. In the days ahead, Shacknasty Jim, Steamboat Frank, Bogus Charley, and Hooker Jim volunteered to hunt Captain Jack down for the U. S. Army. History has cast them as traitors, turning against their leader, but Captain Jack had been their leader only in time of war. To the Hot Creeks, it was Captain Jack who had betrayed them rather than the other way around. Captain Jack was now endangering innocent lives.

The traditional moral war code of the Modoc, foreign to the non-

Hooker Jim

Indian, allowed complete freedom to join or to resign from a war party. As author Erwin Thompson says, "In the individual-oriented tribal organization of the American West, it was an easy matter for the Hot Creeks to decide to go their own way." It was at this point the Hot Creeks must have felt the futility of what Captain Jack was doing in continuing to fight and the danger to which he was continuing to expose Modoc men and their families. They were through.[242]

But in trying to understand Captain Jack's motivation, it must be remembered that these were among the same men who had so vehemently voted for war and cast Jack's appeals for peace aside. Over Captain Jack's objections, they had voted to kill Canby and the other peace commissioners. As their leader, Jack had been expected to kill Canby even though he had voted against the killings. He did his job, with the result he anticipated. Jack may have felt that these men, who had pressured him so insistently to turn against peace and to fight, now were not prepared to face the consequences of their actions.

Now they wanted peace. But Captain Jack knew a line had been crossed when Canby was killed. An honorable peace was no longer possible. Perhaps Jack felt he could no longer negotiate with the Hot Creeks. It may not have mattered to him anymore what he did in terms of the Hot Creeks. He knew that if he fell into the hands of the military, he was doomed to certain death for killing Canby. His only chance of survival was to escape.

It is unreasonable to draw conclusions based on incomplete information or lack of knowledge of another group, especially one from a different culture. There was little or no opportunity for the Modocs to explain their actions or alter the public's perception of the events. What we do know is that this was very much an internal Modoc problem.

It would be faulty thinking to assume that the Hot Creeks who volunteered to track Captain Jack were "traitors." That perception is based on the limited communication of the times and an inadequate understanding of the Modoc culture. It seems equally faulty to cast Jack as a wanton murderer for responding to the wishes of his people, to the complexity of the Modoc War, and to events that preceded the war, primarily the Ben Wright massacre.

Time to Quit

The trusty Modoc twosome, One-eyed Dixie and Artena, had ridden out earlier in the day of May 22, 1873. As army emissaries, they were commissioned to meet with the Hot Creeks and try to persuade them to come to the Fairchild Ranch to surrender. Artena had no confidence that the Modocs would surrender because of their fear that the soldiers would be on them and kill them. Davis convinced her that he could control his men. Through the two women, the Hot Creeks were offered safe conduct to ride in and surrender.[243]

The May 24, 1873, *San Francisco Call* reported that One-eyed Dixie had returned "her horse completely blown. She...at once let her tongue loose." Full of excitement, she told Fairchild that the Modocs would surrender but only if their trusted friend Fairchild would go out to meet them. Artena arrived shortly thereafter, her horse flecked with foam, and verified that it was all true. The Hot Creeks were coming. Sixty-two Modocs, which included a dozen men, were ready to surrender.[244]

* * * * * *

— Sorrowful Surrender —

Shacknasty Jim was exhausted. He had trouble staying awake as his miserable excuse for a horse swayed back and forth. The short, slender Modoc's face, with its slanted eyes and high, sharp cheekbones, was smeared with tree pitch in the traditional Modoc way of mourning. His wife, Anna, rode with the women bringing up the rear of the cavalcade. She had their tiny baby tied securely to her back. His heart lurched every time he thought about his wife and the infant. Born only a few

Shacknasty Jim
Leader of the Hot Creek band of Modocs and great-grandfather of Cheewa James. James is an elongation of Jim.

months earlier, the birth had been bitter sweet. To have his first-born son was the greatest thing that had happened to him in his twenty-two years. But why, oh why, did it have to happen now—in the midst of pain, mental anguish, and physical deprivation? It wasn't a fitting environment for a first-born son.

Malnutrition had robbed Anna of the sweet, round face he remembered from not so very long ago. The boy had been born in the Stronghold at the height of the war, and the birth had taken its toll on Anna. As for the child, Jim wondered if he would even survive.

The sun was dipping into the surrounding hills, and John Fairchild, riding in front of Shacknasty Jim, was silhouetted against the golden haze. Fairchild had been Jim's friend, mentor, and boss for several years prior to this insane situation they were all in now. Fairchild was one of the few men Jim trusted—emphatically and with no reservations. He and Fairchild were now riding home, or at least to what had once been home to Jim. He had worked many long hours and days on this ranch. Leading the procession today was Charles Blair, Fairchild's ranch manager. Charles, Shacknasty Jim, and his brother Shacknasty Frank had worked closely together, mending fences, putting up hay, and searching for a stray steer now and then. It didn't seem possible that Frank was dead now, and Charlie was rounding up Modocs instead of steers.

Jim and his band had come back to the Fairchild Ranch to surrender. It was the same war they had tried to avoid in the first place.

Shacknasty Jim's eyes moved through the dusk into the distance. He sat bolt upright, no longer tired, as he saw an astounding sight spread out before him. A sea of blue stretched from the outer corrals of the Fairchild Ranch, past the ranch house, and halfway up the hill in back. Five hundred soldiers had ridden in from military camps and posts all over the area to witness the surrender of the Hot Creeks.

What a spectacle the military men were seeing as the grimy band of Modocs rode in. The early shouts of "They're here, the Modocs are here!" died down, then faded out. An eerie, unnatural silence followed, uncustomary for the soldiers. The twelve men, twenty women, and thirty children riding in were destitute. Jim was aware that his band presented a sorry, undignified sight, repelling to the soldiers. But he no longer cared. The horses were skinny nags, men were wearing parts of U. S. Army uniforms stripped from bodies of the dead, and women were clothed in tattered dresses, crudely patched, taken months ago from the homes of settlers. Both men and women had daubed their faces with pitch, which to many of the soldiers was a particularly unpleasant, even hideous sight.

Women and children were literally piled upon a few gaunt ponies, which fairly staggered under them. This was perhaps a result of Captain Jack's night raid of their horses. There were half-naked children and aged women who could scarcely hobble. A more squalid, foot-sore, and hungry rabble could not be imagined.

A slight spring breeze touched Jim's cheek. The world was beginning to renew itself just at the time when the Modocs faced the final death knell of the life they had known for centuries. The Modocs were confronting the greatest unknown they had ever experienced.

Although the breeze was not that cold, Jim's bony body trembled. He was worn out, exhausted from lack of food and the constant struggle to survive. But the shivering was caused by more than wind. It was his thoughts that troubled Jim as he contemplated the fate of the fragile, emaciated piece of flesh that was his son. Always before, time and tradition had moved hand in hand with the Modocs to bring a boy to adulthood, when he would take his place among his band. What was this child's destiny to be? With a sadness so intense it took his breath, Jim had to admit he did not know.

Jim had no way of knowing that this tiny boy, who would become known as Clark James, would grow to adulthood in a place far away from the ancestral Modoc lands and in a way that would bear little resemblance to the age-old Modoc culture.

The surrender went smoothly. For all the sorrow of defeat, Shacknasty Jim was glad to be done with war.

* * * * * *

The emotional distress of the Modocs, especially children, can only be imagined. History does not record the stress Modocs experienced—the constant presence of suffering and death, the din of battle, families pulled apart, hunger and thirst, and hurried retreats in the night. A strange incident occurred immediately following the surrender of the Hot Creeks. Davis had accepted the surrender of the Hot Creeks on behalf of the U.S military. As the Hot Creek leaders, now prisoners, stood talking inside Davis's tent, there was a commotion outside, the flap of the tent flew in violently, and an Indian threw himself to the tent floor. The face that looked up at Davis was that of Hooker Jim. The military man had earlier questioned the prisoners as to the whereabouts of Hooker Jim because he had not shown for the surrender.

When Davis, in astonishment, asked him why he had not come in with the rest, Hooker told him that he held back waiting to see if his fellow Modocs would be murdered. Seeing that the Hot Creeks had come to no harm, and not trusting the soldiers outside the tent, Hooker Jim had bolted at top speed past the soldiers, plowed into Davis's tent, and threw himself upon the mercy of the army leader.[245]

Davis recruited and made good use of four Modoc scouts. or "bloodhounds" as they became known. The scouts were fairly certain they knew where Captain Jack was hiding, and they were ready to assist in his capture.

Canby's Cross
Early cross placed at site where Gen. E. R. S. Canby was killed on April 11, 1873. Permanent monument can be seen today in Lava Beds National Monument.

Chapter 13
Jack's Legs Give Out

Even in defeat and at the moment of surrender, the great Modoc chief was self-possessed and acted a manly part.[246]

Samuel Clarke, Oregon newspaperman, June 1, 1873

Following the surrender of the Hot Creeks, Captain Jack now faced a military force ten times the size of his own band. The army found Jack and his band on the summit of a distinctive pumice butte, devoid of brush or timber, today known as Big Sand Butte. Confident that they had Jack's band of warriors in their grasp, the troopers camped for the night near the butte. But to their dismay, the troopers discovered in the morning that Captain Jack, encumbered as he was with women and children, had silently moved his warriors off the butte during the night. The Modocs moved into the lava flows nearby and eventually vanished.[247]

A sense of futility seized the soldiers. Once again Captain Jack had managed to escape them. His elusiveness and ability to survive were amazing. Yet this was not a major victory for Jack. His band had almost no water, food supplies were low, clothes were worn to threads, and their weapons were in deplorable condition.

The land was an enemy to all. Both sides had to battle thirst and rugged terrain. Indians and soldiers alike asked themselves, would it ever end? Eventually, it did end. The war should have ended on May 12, 1873, but it lasted for three extra weeks. And all because of a horse.

May 11: Most of the remaining Modocs were discovered in a canyon on Willow Creek east and slightly north of the lava bed. When the army scouts and troops arrived, Captain Jack agreed to allow the four Modocs with them, now scouts for the army, to spend the night in his camp and to talk. The scouts told Jack and the other Modocs present at the council that they had been well treated after surrendering. They urged Jack and the remaining Modoc men and families to surrender as they had.

It infuriated Captain Jack that these men were still seeking his surrender after they had continually urged him to fight in earlier days. He told them to go live with the whites if they wished, but said that if they ever came back within gunshot of him, he would shoot them like dogs. Scarfaced Charley spoke up at this moment and asked to talk to the scouts privately, even though Jack had earlier forbidden it.

Charley's defiance of Jack indicated that the two friends, under the stress of hunger and the humiliation of defeat, must have quarreled. Charley then told the four men that most of the twenty-four men with Jack were tired of hunger and living like animals. They wanted to quit and would do so the next day.[248]

May 12: The troops were ready to accept the surrender of the Modocs. John Fairchild, Bogus Charley, and Shacknasty Jim stepped forward and urged the Modocs to come out. In response, Boston Charley moved into sight and placed his gun in front of them. The three men put their guns down also, and the usual handshaking ceremony took place. It looked as if it was going to be a shoo-in.

At that moment, Steamboat Frank's nervous horse moved away from him. The hammer of Frank's gun caught on a shrub. The gun fired with a loud explosion. Modocs scattered in every direction. The surrender-that-might-have-been was over. For the next few weeks troops doggedly chased the Modocs.[249]

Dr. Thomas Cabaniss

May 29 - 30: The Modocs were tracked to Langell Valley farther to the north. On the ridge above the valley, Maj. John Green (of the "magic glove") and soldiers lined the bluff. *San Francisco Evening Bulletin* correspondent William Bunker described the impressive sight:

Along the crest of the bluff and down the steep trail on its side charged the entire force of 230 men. Never had I seen a more beautiful military movement.

Scarfaced Charley, who had shouted out for the soldiers on the Thomas-Wright battlefield who were still alive to go home, now started a shouting conversation with the troops.

Here a most surprising negotiator entered the picture—Dr. Thomas Cabaniss, the same contract surgeon who poured brandy down the injured Alfred Meacham's throat. Cabaniss had ridden with the troops in the event his services were needed.

Cabaniss yelled back at Scarfaced Charley. Eventually Charley put down his weapon and moved down the bluff to meet with Cabaniss face to face. Charley told Cabaniss that the Modocs were thirsty, ravenously hungry, very tired, and wanted to quit.

Cabaniss walked back with Charley to the Modoc camp to talk with Captain Jack, whom he found wrapped in a white blanket and sitting on a rock. Jack and Cabaniss had good history. Six years prior Cabaniss had set Jack's badly broken arm. Jack had referred to him since then as "Yreka Doctor." Jack shook hands with Cabaniss and agreed that the Modocs had gone as far as they could. Tomorrow they would surrender. Today they were hungry.[250]

Cabaniss came back up the bluff to the soldiers. When he explained the situation, he was given supplies and encouragement, although there were those that felt the physician had overstepped his duties. Cabaniss returned with food and clothing for the Modocs. He was invited to spend the night in the Modoc camp, which he did.

The next morning Captain Jack, three of his men, and their families had vanished. Although the press labeled Jack's flight "emotional insanity," Scarfaced Charley perhaps described it more accurately: "His heart failed him."

With the rest of the Modocs ready to give up, Charley was the first to surrender. Because he had done all his fighting in the open, Charley was considered by many of his opponents to be the true Modoc hero of the war. Schonchin John, one of the oldest Modoc warriors, was next to surrender. Vociferous, fighting with vengeance, and never espousing peace, Schonchin John finally ended his days as a warrior.[251]

June 1: Capt. Jack and the remnants of his band were trailed by Captain Perry and his men and were again found in a deep ravine at Willow Creek. Perry looked down into the gorge in front of him:

> They [Jack and his band] had with them the infant daughter of the chief, by whose tiny footprints, pattered on the earth, the trailers made sure of their game....One poor deformed henchman, with devoted loyalty, stood guard....A small white cloth on which was spread some freshly cured camas root, drying, claimed his attention for a moment and he was surprised and captured....Trembling with fright and unspeakable anguish, he was made to disclose the proximity of his master....
>
> I saw on the opposite bank...an Indian dog suddenly appear at the top of the ravine, and just as suddenly an arm appeared and snatched the dog out of sight. I then knew that the coveted

prize was mine....

Jack and his family were secreted in a little cave near the top of the ravine and within point blank range of the ledge on which I stood. I told my scouts to ask Jack if he would surrender, and to come out if he desired and give himself up. He replied that he would surrender, but requested time to put on a clean shirt.[252]

Jack first sent out two women, probably his wives Rebecca and Lizzie (Spe-ach-is and Whe-cha), and then a couple boys. Finally Jack himself emerged, clutching his daughter, Rosie, to his chest. Humpy Joe, Captain Jack's hunchbacked half-brother, cowered nearby.[253]

Although Perry's account has been widely accepted, Charles Putnam gave a different account of Jack's surrender and claimed to be directly involved, along with the Warm Springs scouts. *Sacramento Record* correspondent, H. Wallace Atwell, backed him up.[254]

According to Putnam, he and two scouts walked to the rim of the canyon, where Captain Jack, below them, had earlier been seen with a gun poked over the rocks. At this time, Jack had laid down his gun, and one of the scouts went down to Jack and shook hands with him. The two then came up to where Putnam was, and the rest of the scouts joined them. The scouts gathered about Jack in a circle, laid down their guns, and each scout in turn shook Jack's hand. Jack's first question to Putnam was asking where John Fairchild and his sister Mary were. Putnam in turn asked Jack how many of his men had been killed altogether. He counted on his fingers, naming different ones, then said, "but ten."[255]

History has clouded the exact happenings and sequence of events in the surrender, and perhaps parts of both stories are true. But Jack's surrender words were recorded. Dirty and weak with hunger and fatigue, this Modoc leader, who had so confounded military strategists, said only, "Jack's legs give out."

Coming to an End

The Modoc War was officially ended. It was an extremely expensive campaign. Direct costs by the end of the war were estimated in the neighborhood of $500,000 for supplies, transportation, pay for Oregon and California volunteers, and other services. But this estimate did not include pay and pension for regular army forces. Much of the bill was due to large scale profiteering. The volunteer forces billed the government much more than regular army men were paid. Exorbitant rates were paid for transporting men and supplies from various locations into the battle area.

Even leaving out the huge expense of paying soldiers, some estimates are that it cost $10,000 per Modoc—in 1873 money—to subdue these Indians in battle. If the cost were to be calculated in

2008 money, it would amount to $289,170 per Modoc.[256]

All Modoc prisoners were transferred and held at Boyle's Camp (or Peninsula Camp as it was sometimes known), the new military site that Davis had established on the east side of Tule Lake.

As the captives began to adjust to their new surroundings, they were surprised and definitely concerned to see a gallows being built. There didn't seem much doubt as to who would be mounting those gallows steps. Davis had actually taken it upon himself to set an execution date of June 6 for selected Modocs. Davis gathered lumber, rope, chains, and tackle and had started to build the gallows when an order from Washington, D. C. countermanding Davis's plan was received—the prisoners were to be held until further orders.

Davis defended his actions by saying, "I thought to avoid an unnecessary expense and the farce of a trial by doing the work myself. I had no doubt of my authority...to thus execute a band of outlaws, robbers, and murderers like these....Delay will destroy the moral effect which their prompt execution would have upon other tribes." Upset at having his plans overthrown, he was heard to say, "If I had any way of making a living for my family outside of the army, I would resign today."[257]

The Modoc War was unique in that it was heavily photographed. Edward Muybridge, "father" of the motion picture, and Yreka photographer Louis Heller, a native of Switzerland, were the photographers. Boyle's Camp served as the site for many of the posed portraits of the Modocs.

The June 28, 1873, edition of the *Yreka Journal* announced the establishment of Heller's headquarters at the Yosemite Gallery in San Francisco, where readers were invited to get the "counterfeit presentation" of Captain Jack and other Modoc warriors.[258]

One week after Jack's surrender, on June 8, 1873, four Modocs who were still at large gave themselves up at John Fairchild's. They—along with their women and children, bringing the number to eighteen—were loaded into a large ranch wagon. Driven by John Fairchld's brother James, the wagon headed toward Boyle's Camp, where the Modocs were to be housed. But revenge was in the air. Two unidentified white men stopped the wagon and fired point-blank at the Modocs, killing Little John, Tee-Hee Jack, Pony, and Mooch. Little John's wife was severely injured. The four men were literally blasted to pieces, and blood poured out of the wagon and ran in the ruts fifty feet down the road.

It was later proven that the only crime of these particular warriors was that of fighting soldiers and armed volunteers in open combat. Tee-Hee Jack was one of the survivors of the Ben Wright massacre. He escaped from one bloody slaughter, only to die in another one nineteen years later.[259]

Fairchild and the army itself maintained Oregon volunteers were responsible for the killings. However, despite protests from indignant friends of the Indians in Philadelphia and New York, there was no investigation or search for the murderers.[260]

To avoid further problems, Davis decided to send all Modoc prisoners, under heavy guard, to Ft. Klamath on June 13. Seven large freight wagons were used to transport the Modocs.

The responsibility of transporting the prisoners from Boyle's Camp to the fort fell on Maj. E .C. Mason, whom Davis had put in command. Mason, known as an efficient, capable officer, had commanded the troops on the east side of the lava flow during the second battle for the Stronghold.[261]

* * * * * *

— Move 'Em Out! —

The wagons lurched and swayed with the crowd of Modocs and their belongings stacked aboard. Captain Jack and Schonchin John, both in shackles, rode in the front wagon, along with a few other Modoc men in chains and several women.

Captain Jack made a striking sight and could easily be seen from any point along the road, although considering the isolation of the road and the unannounced transporting of the Modocs, there weren't many people to see him. He was wearing a bright red blanket, and on his head was a clean white handkerchief. Even as a prisoner Jack clung to his dignity. In spirit he was respected by his immediate followers as the man who had the right to command and be obeyed.

Maj. Mason had received orders from Col. Davis about noon on Friday to break camp and "move 'em out." The Modocs he was seeing now were very different from the elusive, battle-wise Modocs he had dealt with in the first few months of the war. The Modocs he was escorting were quiet and feeling the pain of leaving the Lost River country.

The short and heavily bearded Mason, in his usual no-nonsense, get-it-done way, had pulled his escort troops together, loaded the Modoc prisoners, and per orders, "moved 'em out" within an hour of the order. Guards rode behind each wagon.

Because of the roughness of the terrain through

which the road passed and the fact that the prisoners had to be watched and attended to, Mason and his troops were constantly on guard. Mason, riding on horseback next to one of the wagons, shifted in his saddle and sighed deeply as he thought about the bad blood which had developed between Captain Jack's men and the Hot Creeks following the Sorass Lake episode. It was hard enough to transport prisoners without having to worry about them being at each other's throats.

Maj. Edwin Mason

It had been the custom at Boyle's Camp to post sentinels between the two factions as well as around them on account of the threatening language by Captain Jack's group toward the Hot Creeks. Mason still had to keep them apart.

A woman's scream penetrated Mason's thoughts and instantly he whirled his horse around to see one of the wagons tilted sideways on two wheels. A large ledge of rocks had created an almost impassable barrier, and this wagon just hadn't made it through.

The wagon was filled with Hot Creek women and children, and almost instantly the men whose families were in that wagon rushed to support the collapsed side. They held the wagon up by sheer strength.

"Get over there," Mason yelled to his men as the wagon tilted farther on its side, threatening to crush the Modocs trying to support it. Although these two groups of men had fought against each other with abandon during the Modoc War, they now worked as a team to upright the wagon, spurred on by women's and children's shrieks and sobbing.

When the wagon was back on four wheels, Mason called a halt while the riders in the wagon poured over the sides into the arms of relatives and friends. Mason had to admit to himself that he was hugely relieved that there had been no tragedy here, and everyone seemed to be all right. After all his strategic planning and military acumen during the war, it would have been disastrous to lose people in his care because a wagon overturned.

But the troubles for that day were not over. Later that night after camp was set, and most Modocs and troops were sleeping, Curley Headed Doctor and Black Jim, who were shackled together, tried to escape. The attempt was short-lived. Almost immediately, the chain between them caught on sagebrush and tripped them up. Black Jim nursed a bloody nose. They both spewed obscenities in Modoc and English as they nursed their bruises and bumps.

But bigger problems faced Mason. On Sunday morning of the trip, prisoners and soldiers took a break and were at rest beside the clear and rapidly running Lost River near the Natural Bridge. It was there that Curley Headed Jack of the Hot Creeks shot himself in the side of the head with a concealed army revolver, leaving a fist-sized hole. Curley Headed Jack had been involved in the Peace Conference killing of Lt. William Sherwood near Hospital Rock. Bogus Charley said, after the suicide, that Curley Headed Jack had talked of knowing he would die and that he wanted to die in his homeland by Lost River, but no one suspected Jack would take his own life to accomplish that.

Mason was truly shocked by Curley Headed Jack's suicide. He watched as Jack's mother and female friends began a dismal howling. Jack was unconscious and fading fast, and so they smeared blood from his wound on themselves and used other Modoc customs to try to save his life. Jack's mother held his head in her lap, trying to scrape the blood from his ear. Another woman placed her hand upon his heart, and a third blew in his face. The sight of those poor women huddled over Curley Headed Jack was terrible in its sadness, and Mason was deeply distressed.

Shacknasty Jim, Bogus Charley, Steamboat Frank, and other Hot Creeks were openly crying. Captain Jack's faction behaved as if nothing had happened. Indeed, the bitterness between the bands ran deep, and bad blood still existed.

Capt. E. M. Camp, officer of the day, took charge of the burial detail. No historical accounts exist of what the Modocs thought of this break from their custom of cremation. But Curley Headed Jack was buried with the revolver across his heart. All his trinkets and a half-dollar were tumbled into the grave upon him.

Within an hour of Jack's interment, the wagon caravan was back on the road, but when camp was established that night at the hot sulphur springs near Linkville, the moans and howls of grieving could be heard into the night. This was the way of mourning that Modocs had practiced for centuries.

The fourth day brought more troubles. Mason pulled his coat tightly around him against the intense wind and rain that had hit the wagons. He could see a Modoc woman in the wagon next to him huddled over her two little ones looking like a mother bird protecting her chicks.

Worse than the weather was a six-mile stretch of road around Modoc Point and along the shore of Klamath Lake that was barely navigable. As the first wagon was wrecked, the swearing of the teamsters mixed with the shrieks of the Modoc. Mason ordered six of his men to help those inside the wrecked wagon into another wagon. He rode up and down along the line throughout the day as one wagon after another ran into trouble. Finally Mason managed to get troops, captives, and baggage past Modoc Point and to open ground. With five wagons disabled, the disorderly caravan camped through the night in a gale of wind from the mountains above.

At three o'clock the next afternoon, the motley looking procession rolled into Ft. Klamath. Mason, mounted on his horse, watched as the patched-up wagons, exhausted troops, and thoroughly disheartened Modocs moved past him.

Mason realized he was dog-tired—physically, mentally, and emotionally. He was not sure whether a bath or sleep would come first.

* * * * * *

Once Again, Another Home

Davis had directed that a stockade be built at Ft. Klamath to house the captives—forty-four men, forty-nine women and sixty-two children. This would be home for the Modocs until October 12. Nearly four months would be spent within this 150-foot by

50-foot pine stockade. Sleeping, eating, cooking, and visiting took place in this small space, and all toilet and sewage facilities were located here. The space allotted to each person averaged four feet by eight feet. This was indeed a concentration camp.

The stockade was divided into two rooms, each with its own door leading out. The two rooms were constructed to separate the two factions of Modocs, those associated with Captain Jack and those who belonged to or were associated with the Hot Creek band. The animosity between these two groups was more intense than ever. Twenty-four-hour guards paced back and forth in front of the doors and along raised platforms at the stockade corners. No one went in or out without permission.[262]

Athough living under artificial and constricting situations, life moved fairly easily on a daily basis for Modoc families. A July 5, 1873, official dispatch from Ft. Klamath commented on the unity of Modoc families:

> The harmony existing in these Modoc families is wonderful to behold. Never have I seen its equal in any other country or among any other people. The woman has things her own way all the time. She can get up first in the morning, build the fire, clean up the premises, bring all the rations from the commissary, bring the wood and water with which she cooks breakfast, do the cooking, wrap the rags about the children, and never be interfered with once....The male Modoc never gets under foot....He seldom if ever trifles or interferes with the domestic arrangements of the family as long as he gets enough to eat.[263]

The four Modoc scouts who had assisted in the capture of Captain Jack were housed separately in tents as a reward for their service as scouts. Scarfaced Charley was also given his freedom, probably out of respect for what the military considered his fair and square way of fighting. Bogus Charley and Steamboat Frank, both of whom spoke English, gathered from fragments of conversation from the troops that Modocs not scheduled for execution would be transferred to an island near San Francisco. Building on this unreliable information, Frank began the manufacture of moccasins that he said he intended to sell in the new San Francisco market. His wife could be seen sewing moccasins.[264]

Eleven heavily shackled prisoners were placed in wooden cells in the guardhouse. Whitewashed inside and out, the guardhouse was about forty feet square and had a porch in front, adding to the impression that there was a small family inside.

A small family of sorts did live inside. Captain Jack and Schonchin John resided in one cell, with the others spread between two other cells. There were grates in the rear of the cells to allow air and light, and the windowless doors all emptied into a main room. Two or three times each week they were marched to the stockade and allowed to see their families. It was reported that the Modocs huddled together, and no noise could be heard two feet from the door. The prisoners looked dejected, and some onlookers concluded from seeing them that death in any form would be welcome relief.[265]

Captain Jack and Schonchin John
Photographed as prisoners of war after their capture.

Curley Headed Jack, Weium, and Buckskin Doctor in chains.

Chapter 14
A Trial, a Hanging, and an Exile

I hardly know how to talk here. I don't know how white people talk in such a place as this.[266]

Captain Jack, testifying at trial, July 8, 1873

Captain Jack, Schonchin John, Black Jim, Boston Charley, and two minor warriors, Slolux and Barncho, were put on trial at Ft. Klamath for war crimes involving the slaying of General Canby and Reverend Thomas at the peace conference under a white truce flag. The first official day of the four-day trial was July 5, 1873. The trial was highly unusual and, by today's standards, bordered on the bizarre. One can only imagine what a trial of this magnitude would be like today. Even in its time the trial drew great attention.

There were huge lapses of legal protocol. Slolux and Barncho often sat or reclined on the floor, Slolux on occasion even dropping to the floor to sleep. Barncho refused to sit with the others and said not a word during the entire trial. Because these Modocs on trial spoke little English or their knowledge of English was sparse, Toby and Frank Riddle were hired as interpreters. Much of what transpired was lost on the Modocs. They were without legal counsel. All six Modocs were judged together, without benefit of separate hearings. What constituted a "war crime" was open to question.[267]

Another aspect of the trial that would likely raise eyebrows in today's legal system is that the five-man military commission appointed to decide the fate of the Modocs on trial included three military officers who had been under attack by the same men they judged: Capt. John Mendenhall, Lt. George Kingsbury, and Capt. Henry Hasbrouck. Hasbrouck had led the successful Sorass Lake Battle in May against the Modocs.[268]

The trial centered on events at the peace conference. Many legal questions that could have been addressed were not. For example, testimony showed that the terms of the agreement stipulated "unarmed" participants, but it was not just the Modocs who violated that provision. Meacham and Dyar carried derringers and pulled them out of their pockets at the peace conference.

Further complicating the ethics of the trial was the fact that the armistice agreement negotiated between Captain Jack and the original peace commission, under the chairmanship of Meacham, had been violated in the eyes of Meacham and Jack by the capture of Modoc horses in February.[269]

Despite the lack of formality and the awkwardness of the trial, the verdict was little surprise to anyone. All six defendants were found guilty and sentenced to hang on the morning of October 3, 1873. The other Modoc prisoners of war—men, women and children—were to be exiled.

President Ulysses S. Grant wanted more than just tribal exile. He felt that the exiled families should be scattered among other tribes of Indians as an example to Indian tribes across the United States. But his thinking did not prevail, and the Modoc prisoners of war would eventually be exiled as a tribe.[270]

The storm of disapproval that was bound to arise on all sides was not long in unleashing its fury. Some felt that although justice had been dealt to those on trial, other Modoc murderers should have been brought to justice. Oregon Governor Lafayette Grover wrote and spoke about the injustice of letting murderers run free.

Other Americans took the side of the Modocs. A barrage of letters and petitions poured in from people across the country who objected to the way the trial had been conducted and its outcome. Elijah Steele, the Yreka lawyer, contended that "this war was brought about by designing men for selfish purposes...."I cannot...avoid the feeling that a great wrong has been committed and should be investigated." He petitioned Secretary of the Interior Delano to delay the execution.[271]

At a meeting of citizens in Philadelphia, a resolution was passed asking President Grant to commute the Modocs' sentences. Members of the Society of Friends asked for clemency for the Modocs.[272]

The American Indian Aid Association, in a statement in the *New York Star* on July 23, 1873, objected to "any execution by virtue of any trial in which the original causes of the war and the death of Canby and Thomas are ignored." The gallows Davis had erected did not escape their attention. They talked about "the ridiculous farce of administering justice by erecting the gallows of General [sic] Davis before the trial begins."[273]

Writing under the name "Bill Dadd, the Scribe," H. Wallace Atwell was a war correspondent throughout the Modoc War for the *Sacramento Record* and later the *New York Herald*. Atwell was at first shocked at reports of Canby's death. He originally called for extermination of the Modocs. But after thinking about the incident for some time, Atwell changed his opinion. In a July 30 letter to Secretary of the Interior Delano, he asked Delano "to defer action on the finding of the commission appointed to try Captain Jack and other Modoc prisoners until a full and fair investigation of the causes leading to that sad affair...can be had." He asked that a commission "compel the attendance of witnesses, who, otherwise, would keep very clear of an investigating committee. We know that those prisoners were tried without counsel."[274]

Some who protested the outcome of the Modoc trial referred to a letter written on June 17 by J. K. Luttrell, member of Congress, Third Congressional District, California, who said, "Humanity demands a thorough investigation of the causes of the late war.... Such investigation...will convince the public that fraud and speculation was the cause of the war....The war was caused by the wrongful acts of bad white men."

Although favoring the hanging of those who actually participated in the murders, Luttrell also said, "Let us have both sides of the question; let us have the sworn statement of the Indians which will, I am credibly informed, be corroborated by the testimonial of responsible white men." Luttrell offered to take on the task of organizing the investigation.[275]

There were several other calls for clemency, but they were ignored.

The day before the execution the *San Francisco Call* reported on Captain Jack's condition. "Poor fellow! His hand shook like an aspen, and his body trembled as if shaken with the palsy. He looks twenty years older than he did a year since, and is without doubt badly shattered, both mentally and physically."

* * * * *

— The Night Before —

Throughout the night of October 2, 1873, Captain Jack could hear the arrival of visitors to Fort Klamath. They were coming, he thought with bitterness, to watch him dangle in the air. His chest tightened once again as he thought of hanging to death. His soul would suffocate within his body, preventing its escape to immortality. Death he did not fear. Hanging he did.

His naturally nervous nature had always manifested itself in stomach and digestion disorders. His Indian name, Kientpoos, "Having-the-Waterbrash," referred to stomach problems, and tonight Jack was living up to his name. He was truly in terror, and his stomach rolled. *For days he had observed his hands shaking when once they had been steady.*

During the last few months, Jack's face had become thin and haggard. His fingers trembled, barely obeying him as he reached up and touched his high, sharp cheekbones, nose, and chin. It was like touching the face of a stranger.

Jack rolled his stocky, 5'8" frame over on the hard floor and once again a recurring pain surged through his hip and left arm. He had injured his arm years ago while hunting, but lately it had started to cause trouble again. Dr. Cabaniss had set his arm. He had also diagnosed Jack's hip problem as neuralgia. Jack grimaced in the dark. Tomorrow all that pain would not exist, he realized, because he would not exist.

Jack decided not to sleep, to be completely conscious for the few hours he had left. But he dozed off from time to time, twitching uncomfortably on the guardhouse floor. Near morning he woke from a dream that had brought to him the gentle, laughing face of his daughter, Rosie.

Yesterday he had been taken to the stockade to see her and his wives, Rebecca and Lizzie. It had been a strange time. No one spoke a word. He had sat on a box covered with a shawl Lizzie had spread over it. The silence was broken by Rosie rushing towards him with frantic screams and throwing her arms around his neck. He extended his arms to her and then held her close to him for several minutes.

As Captain Jack remembered that moment, he felt intense agony, knowing that he would never again see her intent little face as she played at his feet—nor have her jump with glee into his arms when he returned home. She would probably grow to womanhood and have children he would never know. What was her destiny? Jack felt some comfort from the thought that it surely was better than his.

Anger surged through his body at the thought of not seeing Rosie's children, his grandchildren, someday. Jack's bitterness had many targets. He recoiled in pain at the thought of the non-Indian invaders who came onto the Modocs' land. They were a part of the whole problem. They had no understanding of the Modocs and no sense of equity.

Jack's animosity included many of the Modocs who slept in temporary dwellings not far from the guardhouse. "For a long time," he thought, "I was a good man and willing to forgive the injuries of the white man. I was in favor of peace but other Modocs were not."

But the anger moved from him as he acknowledged that he had not handled everything well, despite his good intentions. "How I would like to undo it all and have it forgotten," he thought.

* * * * * *

The *San Francisco Call* carried the voices of the condemned. Slolux said, "My child died yesterday, and I am here in the guardhouse and unable to be with the mourners."

Black Jim told the *Call* that "my heart is very good. I always was on hand in the war to do my part in the first fight." Boston Charley said that he was "not afraid to die."

The Hangman Calls
*You do me a great wrong
in taking my life.
War is a terrible thing.
All must suffer, the best horses, the
best cattle and the best men.*[276]

Schonchin John, Oct. 2, 1873

Black Jim

Of all the statements made by the Modocs in the immediate days before their hanging, Boston Charley's comments were most lucid when it came to defining the Modoc cultural concepts of war and why the Modocs killed the peace commissioners:

> They [the Modocs] suspected Canby and the commissioners of treachery and their hearts were wild....The young warriors thought that Canby, Thomas, Meacham and Gillem were powerful men and that the death of these Tyees would avoid all further troubles. I am telling what I know to be the truth, nothing more.[277]

President Ulysses S. Grant, on September 10, 1873, had issued this order regarding two Modocs deemed to be merely tools in the hands of older and more able men:

> The executive order dated August 22, 1873, approving the sentence of death of certain Modoc Indian prisoners, is hereby modified in the cases of Barncho, alias One-eyed Jim, and

of Slolux, alias Cok; and the sentences in the said cases is commuted to imprisonment for life on Alcatras Island, harbor of San Francisco, California.

A U. S. War Department communication followed two day later with specific orders regarding the reprieve of the two Modocs:

The President [U. S. Grant] directs me to instruct you not to promulgate the order until shortly before the time of executing the death sentence upon Captain Jack and the other three [Modoc prisoners] named in general court-martial orders.[278]

The officer of the day told Slolux and Barncho of their reprieve at 1:00 a.m. the morning of their scheduled executions. Scarfaced Charley was there to interpret. At first the two men did not understand that their lives were spared. But it was true. For almost a month the noose had been removed from their necks without them even knowing it.[279]

A *San Francisco Chronicle* article on October, 12, 1873, carries this comment:

About an hour before the execution an officer visited Captain Jack in his cell and procured about a dozen autographs from the condemned Chief, which consisted of 'his X mark.' The officer guided Jack's hand while he held the pen. Jack sat on the floor, his habitual position. After Jack had finished his autographs, he asked the officer to bring in Boston Charley. The latter was brought in, when Jack asked him what those papers were for, referring to the autographs. Boston interpreted Jack's question, when Jack was told that they were only to be preserved in remembrance of him. Jack probably thought they had some connection to a reprieve.[280]

The gallows at Ft. Klamath were enormous, 20 feet in height and 30 feet in length. The mountain roads from Jacksonville and Ashland were packed with Oregonians coming to watch the sight. It is said that one school in Ashland released its pupils so they could experience the appalling scene. A big turnout from Yreka was not anticipated for the hanging spectacle because there was a conflicting event—the Siskiyou County Fair was beginning that week!

There were about 300 military men at the hanging. All surviving Modocs—men, women, and children—were required to attend. The Klamath Indians, whose reservation was situated four miles south of this station, were also required to attend. The government wanted to make sure the Indians saw what happened to those who did not cooperate. In all, some 2,000 people were present.[281]

A covered wagon had a special place on the grounds in front of the scaffold. In the wagon sat Lost River settler Louisa Boddy. The Modocs had killed four members of her family right after the Lost River Battle. She sat with what remained of her family.

Captain Jack, wearing a striped cotton shirt opened at the breast and revealing a red-flannel undershirt, was very weak. He had to be helped into the wagon taking the condemned men from the guardhouse to the gallows. He pulled his blanket up nearly to his ears as the wagon rolled toward the gallows. The army band played the Death March with muffled drums. The wagon stopped, and the four men were ordered to approach the gallows, under which four or five dogs belonging to the garrison had sought shade.

A blacksmith removed each man's shackles from his ankles as he prepared to climb the ladder to the scaffold. A metal chain joined Jack's leg irons to those of Schonchin John. They had been chained together much of the time since Captain Jack's surrender some months before. But now the two men were separated. Boston Charley and Black Jim went up first, with Charley chewing on a quid of tobacco and spitting it out forcefully as he climbed the steps. The hangman settled a noose around Jack's neck, after trimming some hair so that the rope fit better.[282]

As the four condemned men stood on the scaffold awaiting death, a settler from Goose Lake took the opportunity to call out, "Jack! What would you give me to take your place?"

As quick as the question had been asked, Captain Jack fired back an answer. "Five hundred ponies and both my wives."[283]

The trade was not made, and at 10:10 a.m., official Ft. Klamath time, October 3, 1873, a white handkerchief was lifted and dropped by one of the military officers. Four black-hooded prisoners dropped to their deaths on the gallows.

At the drop, a long and continuous wail of anguish ripped through the air from the watching Modoc prisoners. The intense moaning continued as the bodies swung round and round. The Modoc people were grieving in their own way for their hanged leaders. Captain Jack and Black Jim apparently died instantly and easily. Boston Charley and Schonchin John suffered great convulsions. The watching Modocs continued to moan and weep. The bodies hung from the gallows for thirty minutes before being cut down.[284]

The crowd stayed until the bodies came down. Strands of rope that had executed the prisoners sold for $5 a strand. Hair clipped from around Captain Jack's neck went to the highest bidder. Dr. Cabaniss claimed the hangman's knots from Jack's and Schonchin's necks.[285]

Shift to a New Home

Twelve days after the hanging, thirty-nine Modoc men, fifty-four women, and sixty children were sent by wagon to Redding, California, then by railroad to Oklahoma Indian Territory, debarking in Baxter Springs, Kansas. Their final home was to be at the Quapaw Indian Agency in what is today Oklahoma.

Most of the Modocs had never ridden on a train. History does not record what these Modocs thought or felt as they boarded this huge mechanical beast. Depression...sorrow...uncertainty... fear—all of these powerful emotions must have been traveling companions of the Modocs on that train.

Barncho and Slolux were sent to Alcatraz Prison in San Francisco. Barncho died there in 1875 and is buried in Golden Gate National Cemetery in Colma, California. Slolux was released from Alcatraz in 1878 and joined the Modocs originally exiled to Oklahoma Indian Territory. His name can be found as George Denny on the Oklahoma Modoc census rolls. He died in 1899 and is buried in the Modoc Cemetery in Oklahoma.[286]

The final act had closed on the war in which some fifty or so Modoc warriors had been subdued. On the U. S. military side, sixty-eight soldiers, volunteers, Warm Springs scouts, and civilians lost their lives as a result of the Modoc War. Seventy-five were listed as wounded. Five Modocs died in battle, four POWs were shot in the back of a buckboard, one committed suicide, and four were hanged.[287]

At least that was the official tally. Modoc casualties and fatalities were actually higher, but official lists did not include women and children who were killed during the Modoc War. In most cases they were simply not recorded.

Although the four bodies of the executed Modocs were placed in graves near the hanging site at Fort Klamath, these men do not rest in peace. The heads of the four men were surgically removed, placed in two wooden barrels, and shipped to the Army Medical Museum in Washington, D.C. for research purposes—craniology. The four skulls eventually ended up at the Smithsonian Institution, before being returned to Modoc hands in 1984.[288]

Stories circulated for years regarding Jack's head being exhibited in a pickled condition, but there seems to be no consensus on that. However, a remarkable letter was written in 1934 by Jeff C. Riddle, the son of Toby and Frank Riddle, to Ruth Fish, a journalist in Klamath Falls, Oregon.[289]

Writing in pencil on notebook paper, with misspellings, grammar that had no regard for capital letters, and with periods scattered like fly specks throughout sentences, Jeff Riddle emotionally recounted his experience as a child while on a speaking tour with his parents:

Bonanza, Oregon, Jan. 15th, 1934

About the middle of February 1875, while in Washington D.C., one day walking up Pennsylvania avenue with a Detective. Whos name was Leslie Speed showing me the sights. in the city. I noticed a grupe of people in front of a door. others passing in and out. I asked Mr Speed what they were doing he said they were viewing a great Indian chief. he did tell me it was only a head. he paid the door keeper twenty cents. for both of us. when I passed in I expected to see a living Indian. looked for such. to my dismay, I saw Captain Jack's head in a large Jar. pickled. I knew th instant it was Jacks head the face was allmost black as a negros but I knew his features. I do not know what ever became of it.

You or others may think. it is a long time any one to Remember things and be able to tell much. which is very true in many things ordinary—the sight of the chiefs head in a big glass jar struck me with such force. so far from home. I have never forgotten it and never will as long as I live.

Modoc Grave Sites at Ft. Klamath
The original graves and headboards of the four executed Modocs.
The site was eliminated when Ft. Klamath was
abandoned and rediscovered in the early forties.
It is not known whether the bodies are in the graves.

Captain Jack's X

Found on e-bay by Modoc enthusiast Bill Johnson and purchased by the Klamath County Museum for $4000. Several copies of Jack's "X" were collected as mementos by a military officer just before Jack's execution. (Photo courtesy of Klamath County Museum)

Modoc
The Tribe That Wouldn't Die

Part Two
Modoc Post-War

Jennie Lawver Clinton, 1859-1950
Last survivor of the Modoc War.

Chapter 1
The Exile

The Modocs plow and sow and reap with the same
resistant courage with which they fought. [1]

H.W. Jones, Quapaw Indian Agency Agent, 1874

—The Land of Exile—

The constant jerking of the train had totally
intimidated the Modoc prisoners-of-war in the initial
hours of the journey east. The train had pulled out of
the Redding, California, Central Pacific station on the
evening of October 23, 1873. Just a few weeks before
that, four Modoc leaders, including war chief Captain
Jack, had been hanged at Ft. Klamath, Oregon.

Many of the children had at first huddled and
sobbed as the iron monster, with a snort of steam and
fire, pulled out of the station. But being children, they
had also been the first to adjust. After being on the
train almost a week, some of the older children were
running through the crowded cars, still exploring this
strange, new moving world. Finally, now that the fear
had died a bit and curiosity had taken over, there was
even yelling and laughter from some of the children.
But others did not respond to much of anything. Their
fear went much deeper than that caused by the new
experience of a train.

"The worst part of this war was the impact on
youngsters," thought U.S. Army Capt. Henry Hasbrouck.
He stood at the back of one of the rail cars, one booted
foot resting on a seat, his arms crossed over his chest.
Once in a while a little brown face would turn shyly
toward him. "They're cute little rascals!" he thought to
himself. These Modoc kids had been dragged around for

six months across some of the most jagged terrain and through some of the roughest fighting he'd ever seen.

It took more than a thousand troops to finally bring the fifty or so Modoc warriors under control. "The

price tag on that must be something else," Hasbrouck reflected. The troops and the Modocs, as well as the families of the Modocs, had struggled to the weary end of the war, which came on the first of June. Capt. Hasbrouck had actually commanded the troops at the May 10 battle that had turned the war in favor of the military. The Sorass (Dry) Lake Battle had been the beginning of the end for the Modocs.

Capt. Henry Hasbrouck

Hasbrouck shook his head slowly. After what he thought was a pretty well run battle, look at where he was now. Hasbrouck had managed to pull the single most unusual assignment he had ever had. He hadn't decided whether he was given the command as a reward for a job well done or as a "somebody-has-to-do-it" type duty.

Hasbrouck was commander of twenty soldiers from the Light Battery B, Fourth Artillery, and Company G, Twelfth Infantry, under orders to escort forty Modoc men, fifty-nine women, and fifty-six children, all prisoners of war, into exile. The train was headed for Ft. D. A. Russell in Wyoming Territory, although the Modocs had not been told where they were going.

The journey had started from Ft. Klamath on October 10, 1873. Twenty-seven wagons, with high sides that permitted only the heads of the Modocs to show, left under heavy guard. The wagons had wound their way from Ft. Klamath down through northern California. It had gone fairly well, Hasbrouck reflected. The Indians handled the fatigue well, and Acting Assistant Surgeon John E. Tallon had very few cases of illness or injury. It had taken twelve days to get to Redding from Ft. Klamath. Slolux and Barncho, two Modoc warriors who had been sentenced to Alcatraz, had gone on to San Francisco.

Hasbrouck turned to leave the Modoc emigrant car and return to the coach car set up for the military officers. He glanced back at the emigrant car as he left. It was a pretty basic way to haul passengers, but Hasbrouck concluded that it sure beat those wagons from Ft. Klamath to Redding. Over 150 Modocs lived and slept in three cars. Twenty military men occupied two cars directly in front and back of the Modocs' cars. An officer's coach car and the baggage car completed the caravan.

Armed soldiers stood night and day at each of the doors to the Modoc cars. Every Modoc man capable of carrying arms was in irons except for the newly appointed chief, Scarfaced Charley. Car window shutters were drawn so that none of the curious spectators along the route could peer in.

"These spectators aren't just inquisitive," Hasbrouck mused. "They are unbelievably snoopy and nosey!" He felt like he was on a vaudeville train. The Modocs were a pretty sorry looking group of performers. They were dirty, and because clothing was sparse, some were nearly naked. The Modoc custom of smearing the face and hair in mourning with pine pitch and then sprinkling on ashes had resulted in the name "tar heads" among non-Indians.

Correspondent Edward Fox, along with a few other reporters, was braving the long, tedious train trip. Fox had made the comment that the Modocs looked like they "had lain out under an ash heap all winter." Hasbrouck laughed to himself as he realized that that line would undoubtedly appear in the New York Herald.

When the train stopped at stations along the way, Hasbrouck was besieged with local deputy sheriffs, postal clerks, and just about anyone else who held a local position. When Hasbrouck told them that the Modocs could not be marched out of the cars for any purported "inspection," there was disappointment. Crowds thronged train platforms at each stop, craning necks and pushing one another in an attempt to see the once celebrated and lately notorious Modocs.

Scarfaced Charley, a slight man who spoke English well, and Princess Mary were the stars of the group, Hasbrouck decided. He had noticed that Charley had become quite sedate and dignified since the elevation *to his office. Princess Mary was a voluptuous young woman in her late teens or early twenties with long black hair. She had been called "handsome" by some reporters, but in mourning for her brother, Captain Jack, with pitch smeared on her face, she looked something less than handsome. She had sat next to Captain Jack's young wife Lizzie for most of the trip. The two of them had left an indelible impression on the escorting troops as every evening the two tarheaded women would howl and wail up to six hours at a stretch in mourning.*

That ended permanently and abruptly one evening. Someone at one of the stops had smuggled a bottle of whiskey to Princess Mary. The Modoc woman got royally drunk, and in her crowded rail car, she brought up a good part of what she had put down. Hasbrouck's vigilance increased to make sure that whiskey and other intoxicating liquors did not make another appearance in the Modoc cars.

In Truckee, a mountain town in northern California, and at other stops along the way, the Modocs were given fruit, coffee, and other luxuries. Hasbrouck was always amazed at human nature—none of the soldiers were ever offered these presents. At one stop, someone fired a shot as the train moved out, barely missing one of Hasbrouck's men.

In Ogden, Utah, a change was made to the cars of the Union Pacific. One hundred fifty Modocs needed to be moved off one train, onto another. A mob of people waiting to see the Modocs crowded the platform. Soldiers stood shoulder to shoulder with the Modocs, helping them push their way through to the waiting train.

In Cheyenne, Wyoming, a decision was made to forego Fort Russell and move the Modocs on to Fort McPherson, Nebraska. After a four-hour wait on the tracks, ten cars of cattle were hooked onto the Modoc train. Cows attached, the rail caravan was on its way to Nebraska.

The flat Nebraska landscape rushed by, and Hasbrouck realized that this nearly week-long train ride was about to end. The date was October 29, 1873. Someone should write a book about this trip, Hasbrouck thought to himself with amusement. It was that bizarre. Certainly this was a journey about which he would be telling his grandchildren some day.

Hasbrouck heard the train whistle blow, announcing the McPherson train station just ahead. Undoubtedly the crowds would be waiting again, and for the last time he would deal with another mass of humanity coming to see the circus.

Hasbrouck clapped his hat on his head and turned to the door. His nineteen-day journey from Ft. Klamath had ended.

* * * * * *

Capt. Hasbrouck officially ended his journey and turned the Modocs over to Capt. Melville C. Wilkinson, U. S. Army, Special Commissioner in Charge of Removal.[2] Hasbrouck and his men journeyed back to Klamath country. His military career continued almost three more decades, and he retired as a brigadier general.[3]

The Land of Exile

The Modocs were removed from the train and taken in six wagons to the Platte River, a short distance from the train station. The *Yreka [California] Journal* reporter, who had come on the train, found an opportunity to interview some of the Modocs as the wagons bumped along. Scarfaced Charley speculated that if there were game in this new land, he would be happy. Perhaps realizing that weapons would be necessary to hunt, he hastily added, "All my men be good. No fight with Sioux."[4]

Long Jim, who was now second in command to Scarfaced Charley, proved to be, according to the Nov. 12, 1873, *Yreka Journal*, "a good natured young fellow and expresses himself to be fully satisfied with the disposition of the tribe made by the government." Shacknasty Jim was described as "a hard looking case and though speaking English fluently, has doggedly refused to hold any conversation since they left Oregon."

The Modocs were unloaded from the wagons some five miles down the road and bundled to Brady's Isle in the middle of the river. They were furnished with wall tents and Sibley stoves. In a strange country, with no arms and totally dependent on the military for food and protection, the Modocs seemed resigned to whatever happened.[5]

What happened next was unexpected. A few days after setting up camp on the Platte River island, the Modocs were put back on wagons and placed on a train once again with Wilkinson in charge. The destination was Oklahoma Indian Territory, and this train ride was far more difficult. Scantily clad and poorly fed, the Modocs were chained together in cattle cars for the long, bitterly cold trip.[6]

Because there were no trains directly into Indian Territory, the last leg of the journey was via Kansas City to Fort Scott, Kansas, and then to the last railroad station on the line, Baxter Springs, Kansas. Baxter Springs was a typical border town. The Texas cattle trade had stimulated its growth. The town was coarse and rowdy, catering to the Texas cowboy. Saloons and dance halls lined the streets.[7]

On a bleak Sunday, November 16, 1873, the Modocs' train rolled into Baxter Springs with its dispirited and extremely hungry human cargo. Able-bodied men were loaded into wagons and transported to the Quapaw Indian Agency, some fifteen miles away, in Oklahoma Indian Territory. Their job was to build shelter. Women, children, and males unable to work remained behind, quartered at the Hyland Hotel. There they patiently waited for word that they had someplace to live.[8]

This was the home of exile.

From International Notoriety to Obscurity

Many accounts of the Modoc War have been set down, but the most succinct, and in its own way moving, was uttered by a Modoc who had endured and survived the war. Now relocated at the Quapaw Indian Agency, Bogus Charley gave his accounting of how the Modocs came to be in Oklahoma:

> We be at Tula [Tule] Lake and Lost river. Plenty game, warm country; government, he buy claim; we go to Fort Klamath, Oregon, on mountain, cold country. He say give grub. Gives beef once—no game, hungry—stay two moons. Captain Jack say, go back to Tula Lake—go there,—settler there—game gone. Settler says, 'go way.' Captain Jack say, 'No, both stay'—no grub-hungry—kill settler's cattle—soldiers come, drive us back—fight long time.[9]

Having fought a battle that created international headlines in its time and that would spawn books and writings for over a century, history then turned its back on the Modocs. This tribe now started down an obscure road of little interest to the American press or anyone else.

The exiled Modocs not only grieved for their homeland, but many had left relatives on the Klamath Reservation where the so-called "peaceable" Modocs, those who did not participate in the Modoc War, still remained. Friends and family had been cut apart when some Modocs remained in Oregon and the others were exiled to Oklahoma Indian Territory. There were now two distinct groups of Modocs, related in blood but separated by half a continent.

Chapter 2
The Greed for Modoc Land Continues

*Carr's insistence on taking over the land...
contributed to the most frightful and expensive Indian war in
American history, the Modoc War.*[10]

Paul Gates, historian, 1977

The Modoc War in 1873 had taken place because of the Modocs'
desire to remain on their ancestral Lost River, Tule Lake, and
Clear Lake lands near Yreka, California. They had lived there for
centuries. The Modocs were removed to the Klamath Reservation,
but the arrangement did not work. They left the reservation and
moved back to their home. The Modoc War was the result of the
Modocs trying to remain in their ancestral home.

With the removal of the Modocs, the fertile Modoc country
opened up. The *Yreka Journal* on Nov. 19, 1873, shortly after the
Modoc's removal to Oklahoma, reported that:

> "Everything looks prosperous and ranchers are busy attending
> to their cattle and sheep, with plenty of good pastures....The
> Boddy family [of which four men had been killed by Modocs in
> November of 1872] has returned to their house and lands....
> The whole country is being speedily gobbled up by settlers, and
> it will not be long before the Lost River and Lava Bed vicinity
> will become a prosperous and wealthy country."

The time had come for the prosperous California politician,
businessman, rancher, and developer Jesse Carr to make his move
on the land previously inhabited by the Modocs. Now it was time
to deal with the settlers. He was aided by his employee, explorer
and surveyor Jesse Applegate, who had been very active during
the Modoc War. Both men shared in land, livestock, and politics
at all levels, and were associated with issues and events up and
down the Pacific Coast.[11]

The two had formulated a "stock rancho" land and livestock
scheme before the Modoc War started. The scheme involved the

Carr's "China Wall" - 2007
(Photo courtesy of Karen Weatherby)

occupation of thousands of acres of rich grazing and cattle land in the former Modoc territory. Certainly the war that removed the Modocs from their ancestral and very fertile land was beneficial to Carr and Applegate. The next step came into play.

Sometime earlier, John P. Irish, the port collector for the City of San Francisco, had told interested cattlemen that he could put through Congress a land lease bill that would benefit them. The bill would make it possible for large cattlemen to lease huge tracts of homestead land from the government at a very small cost per acre. The leasers of this land would be given the privilege of using the land as though deeded.[12]

It was a land baron's dream. With the aid of that legislation, Carr continued his land quest and proceeded to have a complete survey made and a map drawn. This was done in part with Applegate's help. His "signed Jesse Applegate, Dep Surv" appears on the left side of the survey map along with this statement: "The purpose of the map is to truly represent the great stock farm of the Hon. Jesse D. Carr..." Historians who have studied the map have concluded that, "the enclosed areas would amount to somewhere near 150,000 acres." Many of those acres were former Modoc territory.[13]

Then Carr built what probably qualified as one of the wonders of western America. Carr's so-called "China Wall," started in 1877, took seven years to build, with 300 Chinese, Swedes, and Chileans as laborers.[14] The stone wall had a solid foundation, and on that were stacked heavy rocks to a height of five feet with strands of barbed wire along the four-foot wide top. Over one hundred miles long, it took three days to ride around the monstrous wall when it was completed. It is said that the wall cost $75,000 and "the lives of many Chinamen, the bones of whose skeletons are still bleaching alongside the scene of their labors."[15]

An 1889 *San Francisco Chronicle* article described Carr's activities:

> In his communication to the land offices Jesse D. Carr has said that the surrounding rancheros are well pleased with this wall, as it prevents stock from scattering. How well pleased they are can be judged by the following facts: This wall enclosed... public land, which by right should afford free pasturage to the stock of everybody raising cattle in those parts and also on Tule Lake. It has been so built that it encloses every spring, every meadow, every piece of swamp land on which grass grows, every mountain that furnishes timber and shade trees, and every stream and streamlet...Carr has so cleverly contrived to fence in this country that anybody attempting to rear stock on Tule Lake would have the cattle perish of thirst.[16]

The people affected were settlers completely cut off from water. Louisa Boddy, a survivor of the Modoc settler killings, was one of those settlers. She had filed on the border of Clear Lake and built a cabin. Having survived the Modocs, she was now at war with Carr. According to the *San Francisco Chronicle*, Carr repeatedly sent orders to have her barns and cabins pulled down or burned and to have her driven off the land. She was just one of many settlers whom Carr wanted away from his land.[17]

> There is not a resident on Tule Lake...[even] to the smallest landowner who has not a grievance against Carr....He has been slowly driving into bankruptcy other stockmen, delayed settlement and otherwise retarded the progress of the county.[18]

The Fall of the Wall

A *San Francisco Chronicle* headline of October 7, 1902, read "Carr Ordered Off Land."

> After a quarter century, Jesse D. Carr will have to relinquish possession of 84,335 acres of public land in Northern California and Southern Oregon. The United States Court of Appeals yesterday affirmed the judgment of the Circuit Court of Appeals in favor of the government.

The suit against Carr was filed by the U.S. government under the authority of an act of Congress of Feb. 25, 1885, to prevent the unlawful occupancy of public lands. That was twelve years after the Modoc War.

Oregon District Judge Bellinger ordered the wall torn down, and U. S. Marshal Gambell entered history by executing the judge's order. He spent nearly three months with a crew of men knocking holes in the wall so that the land might be considered open.[19]

Jesse Carr was arrested. But he died in 1903 at the age of eighty-nine before he was brought to trial. He was buried in Salinas, California. His two sons, Larkin and John Carr, and daughter, Jesse D. Seale, inherited the bulk of Carr's estate, estimated at $750,000.[20]

Jesse Applegate had his own hardships:

> The surviving Applegates are broken down and penniless. One is confined in a Southern Oregon asylum and his only memory relates to Jesse D. Carr who is popularly supposed to have been the cause of the ruin of the once flourishing Applegate family.[21]

According to Jesse Applegate's niece, Shannon, he suffered from sleeplessness and nightmares—"tonight's dark horses." Her cousin Sally, Jesse's daughter, remembered her father's distress:

> [He was] prowling about the house half the night until at last exhaustion took him. But no sooner would he shut his eyes than a regular 'haunt' commenced.

> He evidently took to wandering about the countryside, even taking the train to Linkville or Ashland without telling anyone. Once someone found him half-dazed along the roadway, muttering about one harebrained business venture or another, which he insisted was 'bound to bring money.'[22]

Shannon Applegate said that the family decided they had no choice but to "put him away." They left him first at Linkville and then up at Salem in the asylum. Jesse Applegate died in 1888.[23]

Huge portions of the wall can still be seen today stretching across former Modoc lands. The wall stands as silent testimony to a lust for land and for lives lost.

Chapter 3
The New Homeland

The Modoc only required just treatment, executed with firmness and kindness, to make them a singularly reliable people.[24]

Capt. Melville Wilkinson, U.S. Army, 1873

After their exile in 1873 to Oklahoma Indian Territory, the Modocs began a new kind of battle unheralded and vastly unknown. The age-old Modoc culture from the Lost River country of Oregon and California began a huge transformation. Modocs started anew at the Quapaw Agency, located in the very northeastern corner of what is today the state of Oklahoma.

The Modocs exiled to Oklahoma Indian Territory exemplify the fate of many American Indian tribes in having their culture, language, religion, and arts threatened with extinction. The assimilation of the Modocs into the non-Indian way of life was extremely rapid. One major reason for this was the tremendous spiritual and psychological deflation resulting from the loss of the Modoc War. The Modoc spirit was dashed. Never again would an Indian agent experience any trouble from the tribe once branded in papers from east to west as "savages" and "renegades."

But this new life carried strings from the past. "The widows of the slain still shade their sorrows beneath sable mourning," stated an account in an 1876 copy of the *Boston Beacon.* "The orphans wear saddened faces at mention of Modoc names. The remnant band of savage heroes shout back their anguish to the bleak winds of their prairie home in a land of exile. The Modoc chief lives only in the ignominious role of outlaw."

Practical considerations demanded shelter, and to this end the Modocs, unskilled carpenters that they were, with only one day's help from three local laborers, constructed a building from scrap lumber. This took them only one week. The building resembled an army barrack in that it was built so that the lumber might not be spoiled for future use. Erected for the extremely low cost of $524.40, the price included a large cook stove. The building was

Modoc Prisoners of War, November 1873
*(Back row, left to right) Steamboat Frank, Shacknasty Jim, Scarfaced
Charley, Capt. Melville Wilkinson, Bogus Charley, William (Weium)*

*Faithful, Long Jim. (Front row, left to right) Princess Mary's niece,
unidentified, Bogus Charley's wife and child, Long Jim's wife, Captain
Jack's young wife Lizzie, Captain Jack's daughter Rosie, Captain Jack's
sister Princess Mary, Samuel Clinton's wife and child.*

placed only 200 yards from Quapaw Agency headquarters so that the Modocs would be under the direct supervision of Indian Agent Hiram W. Jones.[25]

Although money had been appropriated to provide the Modocs with clothing and food, the funds did not materialize for some time. At the conclusion of the Modoc War, a small quantity of clothing had been issued, but many months later at the Quapaw Agency, the Modocs were desperate for clothing.

Agent Jones was very much aware of the fact that lack of the necessities of life and the refusal in 1870 of the Klamath Reservation agent to do anything about it had been a cause of the original Modoc rebellion. Most anxious to avoid a repetition of history, he accordingly put all hands at the agency to work making garments. A visitor to the agency stated that he saw one of Jones' daughters cut out 17 pairs of pants in one day.[26]

It was with great relief that the agency personnel greeted the $15,000 appropriation that finally arrived on September 13, 1874, almost a year after the Modocs' arrival.

A New York reporter, Claiborne A. Young, visited the agency in 1874. Young reported the Modocs to be active and liking work. One of their favorite expressions was "go quick." He also stated that the Modocs were most remarkable in their truthfulness. Agent Jones' wife said that the only case of a lie that she knew of resulted in the man being put in the guard-house, a structure made of green oak logs, heavily daubed with clay.[27]

The Modocs at the Quapaw Agency were neatly dressed in clothes similar to those of the non-Indians of the area. The women, however, still wore the round, brimless caps of their own braiding. Lacking the grasses of the Modoc homeland, the women now used shucks for their weaving. Used to fine, natural materials, they found basket weaving, the most advanced of the Modoc arts, to be an unrewarding endeavor in their strange new home. An age-old craft teetered precariously on the brink of extinction.[28]

A Culture in Transition

Despite the Modocs' effort to hang on to some old customs, the facts are indisputable. The Modocs' rebellion left them not only emotionally and physically drained but also aware that their dramatic resistance had brought them only death and exile. A massive cultural transition was beginning.

A report by Commissioner of Indian Affairs F. H. Smith was not only accurate but prophetic. Dated November 21, 1874, it stated:

> In a formal talk, for which every member of the band, male and female, assembled, on the morning of the 23rd of September, the expression of satisfaction in their present location and prospects and of their determination to go to work immediately

on their new reservation, and become like white men as rapidly as possible, was hearty and unanimous by the chiefs, and assented to by the entire band.[29]

When Smith mentioned he would be returning to the Yainax section of the Klamath Reservation, where the remaining Modocs were living, many Modocs implored him to carry messages, photographs, and gifts to loved ones they had left behind.[30]

It was at this time that the possibility of moving the remaining Klamath Reservation Modocs to Oklahoma surfaced. Although the Indian agent on the Klamath Reservation felt there would be no objection on behalf of the Oregon Modocs, he was dead wrong. The Oregon Modocs were not moving. They would live and die on their own land.[31]

One small area of friction had developed at the Quapaw Agency. This involved the persistence by some of the members of the band in gambling—even to the point, in some instances, of losing blankets and clothing. Modocs had practiced gambling for centuries, and the arrival of new blankets brought stakes for the gambling. Modoc gambling games were complex and well developed. Scarfaced Charley, declining to use his authority to stop the gaming, was deposed and a new chief emerged.[32]

Quapaw Quaker Mission School, 1880

In this manner Bogus Charley became the leader of the Modocs in 1874. This short, stocky man, twenty-five years old when he became chief, had considerable contact with non-Indians because of his above-average command of English. He was to remain in authority until 1880 when formal Modoc tribal government in Oklahoma came to an end, not to be resumed for almost one hundred years.[33]

The formation of an Indian school was instrumental in the Modoc assimilation into the surrounding white culture. The Quapaw Quaker Mission School, formed in 1872, operated according to contract between the Federal government and the Associated Executive Committee of Friends of Indian Affairs. The government paid for land, a building, and money to pay for teachers. In addition to academic and religious curriculum, boys received practical experience in farming procedures, animal husbandry, and carpentry. The mission school planted fruit trees, raised vegetables, and maintained livestock for the needs of the school. The excess stock and crops were sold. Girls received basic instruction in cooking and sewing.[34]

Twenty-five Modoc children were welcomed into the school and another teacher, Asa Tuttle, husband of the current teacher, Emaline, was hired as the second teacher. The children did well in school, and some adults were learning to read and write. The conversion of the Modocs to Quakerism also started as great emphasis was placed on religion and moral training.[35]

A few Modocs retained the names by which they were known during the war: Scarfaced Charley, Shacknasty Jim, Bogus Charley, and Curley Headed Doctor. But most Modocs adopted names that fit better into the society around them. Some new names were a rearrangement of old names: Miller's Charley became Charley Miller, Faithful William changed to William Faithful, and Long Jim became James Long. Other Modocs selected names of people they knew or had heard of and obviously liked. Henry Hudson, Ben Lawver, and Ulysses S. Grant had all carried Modoc names at one time. Whus-sum-kpel, Ha-kar-gar-ush, and A-ke-kis, although alive in body, were dead in name. Slolux, sentenced to Alcatraz Prison in San Francisco for his role in the 1873 peace conference killings, became George Denny. After five years of serving his term, he joined the Modocs at the Quapaw Agency. In this transition, the names by which many Modocs were known during the Modoc War were not recorded and many lost.[36]

At this point, the Modocs' names blended in with names indistinguishable from those of non-Indians of that time. The Modoc rolls included names like Robin Hood, Clark James, Peter McCarty, Minnie Snyder, Martha Lawver, Daniel Clinton, and Sallie Clark. Asa Tuttle named himself after the teacher at the Friends school. Amos Kist took his name from an Indian agent who administered the Modocs shortly before 1880. U. S. Grant, with no attempt at modesty, named himself after the president of the United States.

Quaker Pastor Jeremiah (Jerry) Hubbard one day met a Modoc who had named himself after him. Pastor Hubbard was most astonished and flattered, although he commented, "He was the homliest [sic] Indian I ever saw." In order to differentiate himself from the minister, the Indian tacked "Modoc" on the end of the name. Because Pastor Hubbard noted that his namesake was a hunchback, it seems likely that this Modoc fought in the war as Humpy Joe, Captain Jack's half-brother. Jeff Riddle claimed that the Modoc captured at the same time as Jack adopted the name Jerry Hubbard.[37] Much later, in the year 1890, Pastor Hubbard had the pleasure of marrying Jerry Hubbard Modoc and Jennie Modoc. [38]

By the end of 1875, with only twenty able-bodied men, the Modocs had built twelve log houses, with most having two bedrooms. They had harvested fifty acres of corn, cut trees, and made 17,000 fence rails. They had fenced 160 acres of the 200 acres that Agent Jones had plowed for them.[39]

The agent stated that the Modocs were regarded as the best of the Quapaw Agency's tribes. They were diligent and worked with more initiative than he had expected. Anthropologist Lucille J. Martin wrote in a 1968 research study:

> Official agents' reports and records indicate this small band of people made more progress with less land than any other group under the jurisdiction of the Quapaw Agency....From reports, records and conversations with residents of the area, the Modoc appear to have been very industrious. Both men and women worked in the fields, and the men continued to hunt and fish to supplement their food supply....To supplement their meager cash income, fifty of the Modoc men and boys took jobs in nearby towns.[40]

The men worked at anything that brought in an income. They hauled materials. They cut timber and sold it to builders in nearby Seneca, Missouri, and Baxter Springs. The women supplemented the family income by selling beadwork and trinkets to nearby residents and people passing through the area.

But for all their hard work and all the positive reports, the Modocs were in trouble. Families had a constant struggle to provide food and clothing. There was never enough quantity or quality of food. Everything from basic necessities to medicine was in short supply.

The biggest challenge to the Modoc people was one of staggering proportions. There had been much illness and death since arriving at the Quapaw Agency. The infant mortality rate was extremely high. Tuberculosis and other respiratory diseases were killing adults, too. Simply put, the Modocs were dying at an alarming rate. In six short years the Modoc population dropped from over 150 to 99.[41]

Modoc Men at Quapaw Agency
Scarfaced Charley, Bogus Charley, Steamboat Frank,
Long Jim, and Shacknasty Jim

Chapter 4
The Jones Family Indian Ring

I have told him my people are sick...are going to die.
He told me 'I've got no medicine for you.'[42]

Bogus Charley, Modoc Chief, 1878

This corrupt administration dominated Modoc life for five years, a
time when the Modoc population was reduced by one third.[43]

Dr. Albert L. Hurtado, Historian, 1981

One of the great ironies of the Modoc War was that these Modocs, once touted coast to coast as "savages" and "bloodthirsty murderers," became Quakers, people of peace. Almost every Modoc man, woman, and child shipped back to Oklahoma Indian Territory was converted by missionaries on the Quapaw Agency to the Society of Friends

A second huge irony is that some of these same Quakers scammed the Modoc people out of resources and goods allotted to them by the United States government through what was known as an Indian ring. The impact of this planned deprivation of the Modocs was devastating. As historian Albert Hurtado says, "It is ironic that this unfortunate state of affairs developed under the auspices of a group long known for its humanitarian principles with regard to Indian-white relations."[44]

President Ulysses S. Grant had initiated the "Quaker Policy" in 1869. The idea was to assign Quakers and other protestant denominations to administration posts at Indian agencies and reservations throughout the west. The Office of Indian Affairs prior to this had been rife with graft and corruption. The thinking was that Quakers and other religious people would more fairly and honestly administer to Native peoples. Their strong ethics would keep them away from graft and opportunism.[45]

Indian rings were common in nineteenth century Indian reservation administration. The classic Indian ring operated in more remote areas where public scrutiny wasn't as close.

The conspiracy was between a politician, an Indian agent, and tradesmen. This wicked triangle was dependant on each of its members to succeed. The Indian rings were able to swindle Indian people out of their resources and annuities like a well-oiled machine.

The Quapaw Agency Indian ring was a family group who were related by blood and marriage. Enoch Hoag, one of the original proponents of the "Quaker Policy," was appointed by President Grant to be superintendent of the Central Indian Superintendency, overseeing three reservations in Kansas and seven in Oklahoma Indian Territory. Hiram W. Jones was the Indian agent at the Quapaw Indian agency. The initial link in the Quapaw Agency Indian ring was the fact that Hoag's and Jones's wives were first cousins. Jones hired his and Hoag's relatives to fill positions on the Quapaw. Eleven of the twelve employees of the agency were related.[46]

The Modocs were set up from the beginning by the Indian ring. Six tribes, other than the Modoc, resided on Quapaw Agency land: Peoria, Ottawa, Quapaw, Eastern Shawnee, Wyandotte, and Seneca. Capt. Wilkinson, who escorted the Modocs to the Quapaw Agency from Ft. McPherson, Nebraska, in December, 1873, suggested housing the Modocs away from the Quapaw Indians. He felt the Quapaws would be a bad influence. He further felt that they should not be near Baxter Springs, "a notorious place for corrupting Indians." The Modocs also needed to be under the care of a reliable man.[47]

Indian Agent Jones stepped in with the perfect answer—allow the Modocs to build temporary housing near the Jones home. This way the Modocs could receive the personal attention of the agent.[48] Another irony: in avoiding "bad Indians" and a "notorious town," the Modocs were placed in one of the most detrimental, horrendous situations in all of the centuries-long history of the Modoc people. In proverbial thinking, the chickens climbed in a coop with a fox.

The following year, Jones installed his son Endsley Jones as sub-agent for the Modocs at $600 a year. The son remained on the payroll until March 1876, although his duties were vague, appearing, through correspondence of the time, to be performing general administrative tasks. At the time of Endsley Jones's hiring, negotiations with the Interior Department placed the Modocs on a 4,000-acre section on the northeast corner of Shawnee land. It was to become their permanent home.[49]

One of the big money drains was the Quapaw Quaker Mission School. Jones contracted his brother-in-law Asa Tuttle and Asa's wife, Emaline, to run the school at two dollars per student per week. The Modocs had a deep interest in educating their children. So the mission school system was easy to justify, even though money for education had not been stipulated by the government at this time. This mission school system operated throughout Jones's tenure.[50] The Modocs paid dearly for that education. Over a two-year period the Tuttles had received a sum of $6,787.40, called exorbitant by investigations conducted later. The mission Indian school system was characterized as "a giant concern" run by the Jones family.[51]

Jones restricted all Indian trade to a store located on the agency yard and operated by T. E. Newlin, Mrs. Hoag's first cousin. While this brought more money into the Jones family ring, it also was a significant step in the ring's downfall. Merchants in nearby Seneca, Missouri, resented the loss of free trade. The merchants and citizens also began to suspect unfairness and fraud toward the Modoc.[52]

Lies, Deception, and Theft

[There is] fearful mortality prevailing among the Modoc Indians...[through] neglect and want of medical attention."[53]

H. H. Gregg, Seneca, Missouri, citizen, 1877

The Modoc dilemma was not solely a concern of the government. Gadflys among common citizens sprang up and had their say. One of the chief among them was H. H. Gregg, a prolific letter writer and critic of what he considered Jones's mismanagement of the Quapaw Agency. Deeply interested in the Modocs, he wrote a letter on Dec. 4, 1877, to Commissioner of Indian Affairs E. A. Hayt:

> There are instances when visitors to their camps—finding them sick without care or medicines—having come to this village [Seneca] and bought medicines and paid for medical attention upon them.

> These are an industrious and temperate people, and if anything can be done to stay the further ravages of disease among them, I respectfully submit that humanity demands that it be done.[54]

Two investigations were conducted in 1874 and 1875, but Enoch Hoag's influence was involved, so no problem showed. With Seneca merchants becoming more vocal, in 1878 Commissioner Hayt appointed Indian Office clerk Arden R. Smith to conduct an investigation into affairs on the Quapaw Agency. Smith's scrutiny uncovered nepotism and corruption. The Jones family ring exploits came to light. The investigation found that critical supplies, food, and services were diverted. The Modocs said it best through Bogus Charley, in his sworn statement during the 1878 investigation:[55]

> My people die eighty-six since we came here. (*The differences between his population and mortality figures and the official figures in government reports probably are accounted for by births and the high infant mortality rate.*) We were one hundred and fifty seven when we came. They died of chills and winter

fever. Agent Jones never came near us to see us when we were sick. When we first came here, Jones said, "I am going to take care of you the best I can." He has not done so. He has only been to our camps twice in the past year. We have found it hard work to get medicine from him. I have been to him and told him my people are sick, my people are going to die and he told me "I've got no medicine for you."

He said he was sorry he had got no money; the Government didn't allow any money for us. The flour which we get from the Agency is always bad. Never one time good....This year the beef is good because we kill our own. For three years we had bad meat. It was rotten and old bull...

I think Jones has our money; he didn't give my people any money. Last summer, I went to Jones and told him my people want money; white people have offered to buy the prairie hay at thirty cents an acre, but Jones told me "You can't sell it; hush; you will want the feed for your own stock"' But we had more than we could use for our stock. I showed him the bad flour and he told me "That is all the Government can allow you."[56]

Old wagons and horses were sold as practically new by Endsley Jones to his father. Modocs received substandard beef, and bad food of all kinds, in inadequate amounts, was consistently given to the Modocs. The prices in Newlin's agency store were inflated—a "valuable monopoly."[57]

The most shocking deception involved health services. No doctor, hospital, or medical supplies were available to the Modocs in a regular, ordered way. Most of the time these services were completely non-existent.

In October of 1875, Jones purchased ten coffins at $4.50 each from J. G. McGannon, who was part of the Jones ring. He had urged that the order be filled without delay. "They were necessary," Jones explained, "in order to induce the Modocs to abandon their barbarous habit of disposing of their dead (by cremation), and to induce them to adopt a civilized mode of sepulture." Contact with the Seneca coffin maker John N. Hall, showed that Hall received "$4.00 worth of goods for each coffin from McGannon, who was then paid the full price for the coffin."[58]

Hayt received Smith's report documenting practices ranging from dereliction of duty to defrauding the government. The Jones's system of nepotism was clearly and carefully laid out in a 120-page report. The government and Hayt did not respond. Nothing was done until another visitor to the agency, C. S. Buckingham of Poughkeepsie, New York, wrote his congressman in 1878. Buckingham said in his letter that Jones "ought to be forced to disgorge some of his ill gotten gains and to be indicted for *manslaughter* [italics are those of letter's author]. There is very strong testimony to convict him of this latter charge."

In April of 1879 Hiram Jones was relieved of his position as United States Indian agent.[59]

Carr's "China Wall"
*Started in 1877, the wall took seven years to build, with 300
laborers a day. Mountain in background is Mt Dome;
the seasonal dry lake is Souza Lake.*
(Photo by Jonne Goeller)

Modoc Color Plate 1

Captain Jack's Surrender Site
Located on Willow Creek, east of Tule and Clear lakes. The cave is
located in the center of the bluff—the large, black horizontal
opening at the top of the bushes.
(Photo by Bob Ernst)

Ivan Jackson (2/14/1948).
Modoc descendant who has studied and replicated items, including the
tule boat shown, from early Modoc culture.
(Photo courtesy of Klamath Tribes News Dept.)

Modoc Color Plate 2

Graves, 1945 – Modoc Leaders Hanged in 1873.
Ft. Klamath, Oregon. Discovery and re-marking in 1945 by Clyde L. and
Luella James. Left to right: Luella and daughter, Viola; daughter,
author Cheewa; Clyde L; and son, Clyde S. (Sonny) James.

Graves, May 28, 2006 – Soldiers in Period Dress.
Left to right: Kevin Fields (by Captain Jack's grave); author Cheewa
(Schonchin John's grave); Jerry Miller (Black Jim's grave);
and Steward Haley (Boston Charley's grave).

Modoc Color Plate 3

Ancestors of Cheewa Patricia James

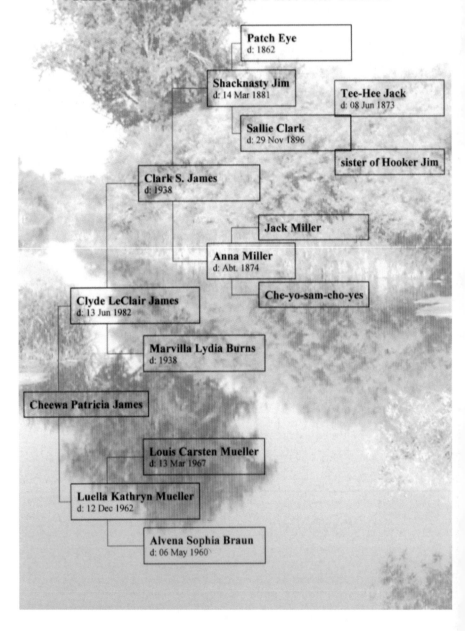

Patch Eye
d: 1862

Shacknasty Jim
d: 14 Mar 1881

Tee-Hee Jack
d: 08 Jun 1873

Sallie Clark
d: 29 Nov 1896

sister of Hooker Jim

Clark S. James
d: 1938

Jack Miller

Anna Miller
d: Abt. 1874

Che-yo-sam-cho-yes

Clyde LeClair James
d: 13 Jun 1982

Marvilla Lydia Burns
d: 1938

Cheewa Patricia James

Louis Carsten Mueller
d: 13 Mar 1967

Luella Kathryn Mueller
d: 12 Dec 1962

Alvena Sophia Braun
d: 06 May 1960

Modoc Color Plate 4

Shacknasty Jim (Shkeitko)
(abt. 1850 - 1881)

Clark S. James
(1873 - 1938)

Clyde L. James
(1900 - 1982)

Cheewa Patricia James
(1939 -   )

Modoc Color Plate 5

Cheewa James Family
Front Row: Son David James Easterla *(8/12/1961)*; granddaughter Tayla
Breanne *(2/11/1997)*, grandson Tanner Brian *(2/15/1993)*, and son Todd
Bryce Easterla *(8/12/1964)*. Back Row: Cheewa *(5/15/1939)*.
(Photo by Al Snyder)

Viola James Colombe *(8/23/1942)*.
*Sister of author, and her grandson
Shane Koepnick (8/19/1998).*

**David J. "Missouri"
Easterla**. *Pictured at age
6, this is a Modoc Indian
fighter in training!*

Modoc Color Plate 6

Clyde LeClair James *(3/9/1900).*
Photographed in 1980 in front of the Lava Beds National Monument
Visitor Center. The visitor center has since been razed and
replaced with an updated facility.
(Photo by Cheewa James)

Modoc Color Plate 7

Lost River

*Lost River country, winding through central southern Oregon and
northern California, was the ancestral home of the Modocs. Photo
taken near Merrill, Oregon, close to site of Captain Jack's village.
(Photo by Al Snyder)*

Modoc Color Plate 8

(After Map by Charles Banks Wilson)

QUAPAW AGENCY INDIANS TRIBAL RESERVATIONS

Quapaw Agency Indians Tribal Reservations
(Photo courtesy of Oklahoma Historical Society)

Redpath Lecture Company, 1874
Shacknasty Jim, Steamboat Frank, Frank Riddle, Toby Riddle,
Scarfaced Charley. Seated, Jeff Riddle. The dress is lecture performance
attire and is not traditionally Modoc.

Alfred B. Meacham
Organized the Redpath Lecture
Company. At each performance he would
talk about his role in the Modoc War and
the injustices done. He was very
sympathetic toward the Modocs.

Chapter 5
Enter an Old Friend

These Modocs have now found rest. They have no idea of ever again going upon the war-path.[60]

Alfred B. Meacham, 1874

A most suprising visitor appeared at the Quapaw Agency in 1874. It was Alfred Meacham, former Oregon superintendent of Indian Affairs, who had originally coaxed the Modocs onto the Klamath Reservation and who had met with eight Modocs at the 1873 Good Friday Peace Conference. Commissioners Gen. E. R. S. Canby and Rev. Eleasar Thomas had been killed, and Meacham had been badly wounded at the conference. The Modocs had attempted to scalp the unconscious Meacham. Hooker Jim had offered the comment to Boston Charley, who was doing the scalping, that if Meacham's bald head would produce a scalp, Boston was welcome to it.[61]

Meacham came upon an astounding scene:

> In front of the Agency building a game of croquet was in progress. The most dashing fellow among the players was Bogus Charley, who was dressed half-quaker and half Spanish. His head was covered by a broad-brimmed hat, his feet in high-heeled calf boots, with red lace at the top, and small tassels dangling on his instep, and he wore a red sash around his waist....Bogus Charley's keen eye caught sight of my face, and with hurried movements he...muttered in Modoc a few words to his companions, and ran into the agent's house.[62]

Bogus Charley's playing companions were Shacknasty Jim, Hooker Jim, and Steamboat Frank. As amused as Meacham was to see these once feared warriors playing croquet, he wasted no time in announcing the object of his visit. He came on a mission. Meacham was looking for Indians to join him in taking the story of the American Indian to the public. His intentions were to bring forward the plight of the Indian. Despite his Modoc-inflicted injuries at the peace conference, he still solidly believed that the Modocs had suffered injustice and that the war should not have happened:

> I submit that had Captain Jack and his band been protected
> while upon Klamath Reservation in 1869...or had patience
> been exercised in forcing the order for his removal to Klamath
> in Nov. 1872, no war would have occurred....Had no Modoc
> horses been captured by our army during the armistice or had
> they been returned when demanded and no further breech of
> the compact been made by the movement of our troops under
> the flag of truce, no assassination would have been committed,
> and peace would have been secured on amicable terms.[63]

He recruited Shacknasty Jim, Steamboat Frank, and Scarfaced
Charley to tour throughout the United States with him—along
with Toby Riddle, the Modoc woman interpreter during the war;
her husband Frank Riddle, also an interpreter but not Indian; and
their son Jeff, who was eleven years old at the time of the tour. The
Riddles had remained on the Klamath Reservation but were now
joining Meacham. In addition, Meacham brought several Indians
from other tribes, including Klamath Indians David Hill and
Tecumseh ("both now civilized and Christianized," according to
Meacham). Oliver Applegate, former Indian agent, also joined the
group,[64] which was sponsored by the Redpath Lyceum Bureau,
founded by James C. Redpath in 1868.

Meacham dropped the rather mundane name of the Modoc
woman Toby and substituted "Winema," which according to
Oliver Applegate came from a poem by writer Joaquin Miller.[65]
Meacham's group traveled in 1874 from city to city, beginning in
Sacramento, California, and ending in New York City. Meacham
started each appearance of the company with the story of the scar
around his forehead, a reminder of the Modoc's attempt to scalp
him. One of the featured acts of the company was the archery of
the Modocs.

* * * * * *

— Reluctant Archer —

*Shacknasty Jim sat in the gallery of a large
auditorium in a city whose name he'd already forgotten.
It was a lot like all the rest of the cities he'd been in—
bustling, paved, full of white-skinned people curious
about Indians.*

*The place was packed, and the audience was
buzzing as people settled into their seats. Jim watched
as men escorted elaborately dressed women down the
aisles. How they breathed in those clothes, Jim did not
know. He smiled to himself and thought about how
shocked they would have been if they had seen the
bare-breasted Modoc women of his village before the
coming of the non-Indian intruders.*

He became aware of the stares and silence around him. Indeed he'd never sat in the audience before, and everything from the brown of his skin to his casual dress was attracting attention. He looked disdainfully back at the curious stares. He was part of the Redpath Lecture Company and normally would have been backstage preparing for his part in the show.

Tonight he was rebelling. Having asked Alfred Meacham earlier in the evening as to what the box office receipts would be for the company's performance, he was vexed to learn that the returns were low even though there was a full house. Jim had gone to Meacham and let him know that he was a proud man and would not shoot his bow for the amusement of people who charged Meacham for everything and paid nothing. He remained in his room, and nothing anyone in the company said had any effect on him, even though he was told how disappointed the audience would be if he did not perform. Scarfaced Charley finally told Meacham, "It's no use. He won't come. Suppose you shoot him. It's all the same."

Shacknasty Jim was regarded as a top marksman during the Modoc War. He was also a legendary Modoc archer. Few even tried to match his skill with bow and arrow. His father was shot in a fight in 1858, from behind, through the right side of his face, the shot destroying the eyeball and a part of his nose. Legend has it that he turned to another warrior, snatched his handkerchief, then scraped the eye-socket with his finger, bound up the wound and rushed again into the fight. From that time he was known as Patch Eye. He was slain by the Shasta Indians in 1862.

Shacknasty Jim's mother, Madame Shacknasty, or Sallie Clark as she became known, inherited all the fighting blood of the royal house of Mo-a-do-cus. She had actually fought during the Modoc War. Her father was a celebrated warrior. He possessed the mysterious power of Ka-okes-a—witchcraft.

Jim had been forced into the war after attempting to reach the Klamath Reservation in Oregon to surrender. He joined Captain Jack in the Stronghold and became one of the most ferocious fighters, voting for war on most occasions.

Tonight, becoming bored sitting in his room, he had

decided to be a spectator at the evening's performance. As Meacham started the program he was startled to glance up and see Jim sitting in the audience. He walked to the front of the stage and began to apologize for his inability to present the archery performance with any prospects of success because one of his best archers was in the gallery. He pointed with relish to Shacknasty Jim, who was leaning over the railing above.

The audience began to clap their hands and stamp their feet. Jim was moved from being surprised to being flattered. Feeling that the applause was a compliment to his skill as an archer, he arose and came down to the stage to the accompaniment of great shouts.

He took up his bow and arrow as the target was being arranged. It had been the custom to hold the target at one side of the platform, and the archers to stand at the other side, thus making shots at very short range. To the surprise of everyone, Jim proposed that the target, a pine-board about six inches wide, should be placed on the stage and that the Modocs shoot from the middle aisle among the audience.

Intense applause met this proposal.

Each Modoc with his bow and arrows went halfway down the aisle. Shacknasty Jim, still standing on the stage, motioned to them and shouted "Back, back, I am no boy." Every eye was upon the target, when the first arrow by one of Jim's fellow Modocs was sent. It struck a little above the mark. The next man planted his arrow equally close. Then another still closer. At each shot, the audience shouted.

The most intense watcher, however, was Jim. Scarfaced Charley stuck his arrow within half an inch of the center, and a storm of applause greeted him as he strode back to the stage. Each Modoc had planted an arrow in the target, and their feathered ends stood bristling towards the audience.

Every eye was now on Jim, who seemed fully alive to the moment, going close to the target and scanning the arrows closely. He made a small white spot in the exact center, amid a silence so intense that every heart almost ceased beating. No man ever strode with prouder step or firmer nerve than did Shacknasty Jim walk down that aisle.

He did not stop midway where the others had, but continued back, back, until he was within a few feet of the remotest part of the long hall, then drawing his arrow and placing it on the string of his bow, he whirled, and almost before he had stopped, he sped the arrow forth with a wicked twang.

There in the little white spot in the very center of the target stood Shacknasty Jim's arrow, still quivering.

* * * * *

Meacham later commented on the performance by saying, "Shacknasty Jim, in this matter demonstrated that Indian nature does not differ much from human nature in general. But his archery differed so much from ordinary shooting, that he was an exception even to Indians."[66]

Despite the efforts of Alfred Meacham, the Redpath Lecture Company failed financially. The three Modoc "stars" returned to the Quapaw Agency. But once home, Shacknasty Jim found a way to pick up income using his unique skill. He would go to the railroad station and while travelers were stretching their legs between stops, he would notch a stick, place it in the ground and invite travelers to put coins in the notched end of the twig. Once the coin was in, Jim would draw his bow and send an arrow toward the coin. He rarely missed and, after scoring a hit, he pocketed the coin.[67]

Death Moves Among the Modocs

Hooker Jim died in 1879, only five years after arriving in Oklahoma Indian Territory. Bogus Charley died of tuberculosis (commonly called consumption at the time) in 1880, six years after arriving at the Quapaw Agency. Shacknasty Jim died of the same disease in March, 1881.[68]

Shacknasty Jim's obituary in The *Hallaquah*, published by the Wyandotte Mission near the Quapaw Agency, reads:

> In the time of the Modoc War...he had a reckless daring, a bravery which recognized not danger, and a skill in war which was a terror to his enemies....When removed to this territory in 1873...he was brought under the civilizing influences of Christianity and in time accepted its truths. Shoknosta [sic] was the first Modoc to declare against the custom [of cremation]. A few days before his death he said, 'When I die I not need these things, you must not bury them with me, you must let my wife and children have them, they will need them.' In this, leaving evidence of a fuller possession of the heart by Christians' hope, than has been given before by any other Modoc.[69]

Modocs adopted the custom of burial. But there was one very peculiar characteristic that the Quakers noticed—the Modocs accepted burial, but the deceased's head had to face east in the ancient tradition of the Modoc people when they were cremated.[70]

The Modocs also continued to practice another old tradition: the rite of keening and moaning at death. Quaker pastor Jerry Hubbard commented, "The Modocs are leaving off many of their old ways and customs. But to hear some of the old women wail at a funeral is wonderful."[71]

A piece of the old Modoc ways was still alive.

Sam Ball, *Ka Klo-litke. Fought in Modoc War.*
104 years old when photo taken (date unknown).
Photo by J. D. Shuck, Seneca

Pastor Frank Modoc (Steamboat Frank)
A minister of the Modoc Quaker Church in Oklahoma Territory, Frank
Modoc studied at the Oak Grove Seminary in Vassalboro, Maine.
He died in Maine in 1886.
(Photo courtesy of Oklahoma Historical Society)

Modoc Quaker Church, Oklahoma, 1880
This is Frank Modoc's home church at the Quapaw Agency,
where he often spoke.

Frank Modoc's Grave
Ann and Bob Miles of Portland, Maine, "adopted" Frank Modoc
and see that his grave in the Friends Meetinghouse Cemetery
is regularly visited. (Photo courtesy of Amy Woolls)

Chapter 6
More Modoc Death

Frank Modoc's good judgment and industry gave him influence with all classes of men. His word was taken as always reliable.[72]

Jerry Hubbard, Quaker minister, 1884

Steamboat Frank, a legendary name from the Modoc War, was a warrior turned missionary. His parents had died soon after his birth in the Modoc homelands, leaving him orphaned. He was adopted by a seventeen-year-old woman who was "gifted with a voice of extraordinary compass. From this fact she was called 'Steamboat' by her people."[73] When Steamboat Frank turned fifteen, his adopted mother made him her husband, and he was devoted to her. After her death, he married Alice Modoc, who came with him in exile to the Quapaw Agency.[74]

He was equally devoted to Alice and their son Elwood. He nursed her through her death from tuberculosis. One day, as her health failed, she said to Frank, "If only I could have some fresh fish, like in our old home in Oregon." He immediately went to the nearest railroad connection and telegraphed the express company to send out fresh fish.[75]

Steamboat Frank died of tuberculosis in 1886 in Maine, where he was studying in a Quaker seminary. His death carried with it great significance in terms of the in-roads of Christianity. He made the decision to enter the ministry of the Society of Friends and died as Pastor Frank Modoc, although his death precluded his being given an active pastorate. He was acknowledged in 1884 as being the first full-blood American Indian ever recorded as minister of the gospel in the Society of Friends.[76]

He had served as the minister of the Modoc Quaker Church, established in 1879, which was actively attended by the Quapaw Agency Modocs.

* * * * * *

— Dealth Stalks a Modoc Quaker —

As Frank Modoc looked out the window of the red brick Friends Meetinghouse in Portland, Maine, the view caused him to feel once again like he had lived many lives in the same old body that was now betraying him. He'd come so far, seen such wonders, and learned so much. He could not fathom why death was seeking him out at such an early age. The disease racking his lungs was consumption, the killer that had taken so many Modocs. The curse had not skipped him.

At forty-five years of age, he was just beginning to understand the intricacies of the Quaker teachings. He had a new mission in life—to go among the remnants of his tribe and carry the gospel to them. "Who," he thought to himself, "better than I?"

His analysis of himself was a true one. While still on the Quapaw Agency lands, he was recognized for his high level of intelligence and desire to learn. He had already succeeded in converting a good number of the tribe.

Frank was especially known among the Quakers for his eloquent preaching. He spoke English, but the Friends in Maine were particularly moved when this six-foot Indian would fervently speak and pray in Modoc. Understanding the words weren't important to those who listened. They felt the spirit.

He looked out the window again at the serene, pastoral image before him. Oaks, maples, and pines ringed the cemetery of the Friends Meetinghouse. The cemetery was as tidy as the meetinghouse itself, which was only some twenty-five years old. The painted white walls with blue wainscoting in the meetinghouse and the wide pine floorboards beneath Frank's feet all spoke to the simplicity and neatness of almost everything Quaker. Frank had come to love the Friends' ways. The serenity of the cemetery touched a chord in Frank. He knew quite well that the Quaker cemetery in Portland would most likely be his last home.

It was only a few years before that he had played as a boy near the wickiup that his father had constructed near Hot Creek in northern California. Frank knew nothing then of wooden houses or brick buildings, like the one in which he now stood, nor of the language he now spoke that still felt strange on his tongue.

His wife Alice had died only two years ago, taken by the cursed disease of the lungs that now gripped Frank. But their son Elwood, who was twelve, was staying with Frank's relatives at the Quapaw Indian Agency in Oklahoma. Thinking of Elwood brought a pang to Frank's heart.

The Quakers had always admired and appreciated Frank's ways with children. But what they didn't know was that when he was with children, he felt nearer to Elwood. Frank adored children, just as he loved his son. He fleetingly let his mind touch on the little daughter he and Alice had named Julie. She was with Alice now. Frank felt a slight tug of fear when he realized that he would most likely be joining them soon. He shut his eyes and let the fear dissolve into the image he had in his mind—the sun hitting the black, shiny hair of two women, one a child, one a grown woman. The woman was laughing and turned to wave at Frank. Slowly, slowly the panic subsided.

Frank had hoped to add to his knowledge of the Quaker religion by studying at Oak Grove Seminary in Vassalboro, Maine. He had wanted to return to Oklahoma with a greater understanding and even more powerful and meaningful messages for the Modoc people. Frank had been studying for just a short time at the seminary when his ailment had turned from annoying to serious. He had immediately decided to go back to Oklahoma and be with Elwood, or Lep-is, the affectionate Modoc name Frank often used for Elwood. Frank had only made it as far as Portland when he became too ill to travel.

A ragged cough seized Frank again, tearing through his body. He slumped into a nearby pew. He knew instinctively that his strength was failing and that he would not be able to come here again.

The great blessing in his life right now was the wonderful friends he had among the Portland Quakers. He knew they would stay by him and help him on his last hard journey.

* * * * * *

Frank Modoc's obituary in the Portland, Maine, *Daily Eastern*

Argus on June 15, 1886 read:

> At the house of J. J. Frye at Woodford's a very interesting
> person breathed his last on Saturday night. It was Frank
> Modoc, the converted Indian who had been attending school
> at Oak Grove seminary....[He] became desirous of thoroughly
> fitting himself at a white man's school for his chosen work of
> a missionary and teacher among the Indians...and won the
> respect and admiration of all...as a man of more than ordinary
> intelligence and capacity.

After Frank's death, the Quakers were amazed by the number
of scars Frank had, which were revealed when his body was
prepared for burial in Portland.[77]

Frank's son Elwood was to follow him in death four years
later in 1890 at sixteen years of age. His tombstone rests in the
Oklahoma Modoc Cemetery. Elwood was the end of Frank Modoc's
line.[78]

The Modoc Church and Cemetery

Religion, specifically Quakerism, took a huge step forward in
Modoc life in 1879. A church of the Modoc's own was built by
the government on Modoc land. The cost of labor, materials, and
furnishings totaled $462.00.[79]

The Quakers were impressed with the Modocs' zeal and
fervor. An early church worker described a huge Modoc Sabbath
turnout:

> A fierce blizzard was raging and the white man's church was
> empty. The snow beat into our faces as we drove along in
> the intense cold to the Friends' Meeting House in the Modoc
> camp....As we drew near we saw the Modoc coming from
> various directions through the storm. There were sixty of them
> present!...Scarfaced Charley, one of the old chiefs from the
> Lava Beds spoke. Faithful William, Robin Hood, Clinton...a
> marvelous testimony to the miraculous and conquering power
> of the Gospel of Christ.[80]

The Quakers made the decision to buy the Modoc Quaker
Church in 1891 and move it four miles north to its present location
adjoining the grounds of the Modoc Cemetery, eleven miles east of
Miami, Oklahoma, three miles from Seneca, Missouri. The building
was enlarged to include living quarters for the Quaker missionary
and family. Services were held on Sundays and Wednesdays.[81]

Modoc people who survived the bullets of the Modoc War only
to be struck by lethal lung diseases found a resting place in the
Modoc cemetery. The first marked grave was that of Rosie Jack,
the young daughter of Captain Jack and his wife Lizzie. Rosie died
in April of 1874, only seven short months after her father was
hung at Ft. Klamath, Oregon.[82]

A Life for a Pair of Boots

An unpaid bill for a pair of boots was the catalyst for what could have been a mini Modoc War in Oklahoma Indian Territory. In May 1879, five years after the Modocs were exiled to the Quaqaw Agency and only a month after the Jones family Indian ring had been exposed, a young Modoc by the name of Shepalina was murdered by a Seneca merchant. Eighteen-year-old Shepalina was the nephew of Bogus Charley, the son of Nancy Wild Gal Bogus, and the stepson of Hooker Jim.[83]

A foreboding telegram was sent on May 29 from Quapaw Agency Special Agent James M. Haworth, who had been sent to take over management of the Quapaw Agency after Jones's dismissal. The telegram went to Commissioner of Indian Affairs Ezra A. Hayt in Washington D.C. alerting the commissioner to the killing of the Modoc youth and promising him a follow-up letter. Two days later, Haworth detailed the grim, most unwelcome news. Having just waded through the mire of the Jones fiasco, the Indian Affairs Office was not looking forward to another battle.

The merchant, John Albert, had a delinquent bill for Shepalina on a $3.00 pair of boots. Seeing Shepalina enter A. J. Norris's store across the street from his store, Albert confronted Shepalina in the middle of the street as Shepalina came out. An argument ensued with Shepalina agreeing to settle the debt. But the disagreement accelerated, and the exchange became heated. Witnesses reported that Albert grabbed Shepalina's arm and slapped him in the face.

Shepalina turned and ran back into Norris's store. Albert went into his own establishment, obtained a gun and, with his brother, William, headed for Norris's store. A bystander and Norris tried to stop the Alberts, but they powered their way in. An unarmed Shepalina sought protection behind a large wood-burning stove. There, cowering behind the stove, Shepalina was shot three times by John Albert and died within three minutes.[84]

Several Modocs were in town and took the body back to the agency. There the lengthy Modoc ritual of wailing and moaning began as Modocs poured forth their grief, lead by Shepalina's mother. Emaline Tuttle, the Quaker teacher at Quapaw Agency, urged the Modocs not to seek revenge by attacking Seneca. With their eyes downcast as she spoke, a Modoc custom, the Modocs heard her praise them for the good example they had set over the six years they had been at the Quapaw Agency. She reminded them of what had happened the first time the tribe clashed with the U. S. Army and warned them that a second offense would bring even harsher punishment. Haworth met with the Modocs and urged them to remain calm because they would soon be permitted to return to their homes in Oregon.

When Haworth went into Seneca after the incident, he interviewed several witnesses and was able to piece the story together. He found many of the town's leading citizens, including religious leaders and professional people, believed the incident was unjustified and unprovoked.[85]

The *Joplin* [Missouri] *Globe*, in an October 2, 1949, article looking back on the incident, reported that later that evening Bogus Charley rode into Seneca and warned the citizens that the Modocs were incensed, and he feared an attack. He said the Modocs had pursued him almost to the outskirts of town. His horse was reported "flecked with foam and showed the severe strain of a mad gallop." The call for action went to townspeople and farmers in the countryside. Three hundred well-armed Seneca citizens readied themselves to protect the town and go to war if necessary.

It never happened. The next day townspeople met with the Modocs and a truce was finally reached. But the Modocs did not forget. The *Joplin Globe* reported that "several years after the episode, at regular intervals, a party of Modoc warriors would parade through the streets of Seneca to show that the killing of their comrade had not been forgotten. They never again caused trouble—only indicated a warning."[86]

John Albert was put on trial, but by the time the trial actually happened in August, 1881, over two years after Shepalina's murder, the charge had been lowered from murder to manslaughter in the fourth degree.

U. S. District Attorney for Western Missouri, Colonel Louis Waters, was sent by the government to assist in prosecuting the case against Albert. Waters presented his appeal to the court:

> If [you expect] to make peace with the Almighty and rest from [your] earthly labors in eternal glory at his right hand [you] must convict John Albert.[87]

His words did not move the jury. Albert was declared not guilty on the first ballot.

Several factors entered into the apparent miscarriage of justice. The nation was suffering a psychological humiliation at the defeat of Custer and the U. S. Army at Little Bighorn just three years before Shepalina's death. This was not a good time to be an Indian—an Indian was an Indian, no matter what tribe. The failure of U. S. Grant's "Quaker Policy" had resulted in bad publicity and lack of public trust, the local fallout being the Jones family ring scandal. Haworth was obligated to spend much time cleaning up the Jones mess, and that had forced him to leave agency representation in Shepalina's case to subordinates.

Looking back at history, historian Robert E. Smith, who researched the Shepalina killing, had this to say in 1991:

> Shepalina, the young man murdered for a pair of boots in 1879 in Seneca, Missouri, remains a symbol of the callous disregard for Native Americans in the late nineteenth century.[88]

As for John Albert, he was elected the first mayor of Seneca when it incorporated in 1882. He helped to organize the Methodist Church South and operated his store until his retirement. He died at the age of ninety.[89]

Annie Long Spicer
(d. -11/24/1923), daughter of Sallie Clark, half-sister of Shacknasty Jim, married at one time to Long Jim.

Kate *(1897-1921) and* **Ardella Stanley** *(1899-1911), daughters of Etta (Modoc) and Charles (Peoria) Stanley, whose land adjoined.*

Cora Pickering Hayman
(1870 - 1949), daughter of Anna Jim, half-sister of Clark James.

Winnie Lawver Crim, *Modoc and Ottawa mixed blood.*

Oklahoma Modoc Quaker Church, 2007
(Photo by Jimmy Sexton)

Oregon Sprague River Friends Community Church, 2007
(Photo by Cheewa James)

Chapter 7
Changing Cultures

The Indians of this tribe are the best of the lot...hard workers,
dress better, farm more intelligently, keep their houses cleaner...[90]

J. V. Summers, Quapaw Indian Agent, 1885

Eleven Modoc men in April of 1880 sent a letter to "Our Great Father in Washington" stating that a council had been held and the desire of Modocs was to replace their chief, Bogus Charley (who was by this time thirty-one years old), with Long George. The result: no chief at all. Commissioner of Indian Affairs R. E. Trowbridge ruled that, "a Modoc chief has no authority and is of no essential benefit to the tribe" and should therefore be abolished. In the future, any business with the government was to be conducted by individuals as they had a need. The Modocs would remain without a federally recognized leader for ninety-eight years.[91]

The Modocs were making an amazing adjustment to their surroundings. Without exception they were lauded as hardworking, thrifty, sober, and eager to learn. Their relationships with nearby townspeople and those living near them in more rural areas were agreeable and cordial. Quaker missionaries were their guides, and the Modoc traditions and religious ceremonies seemed to be fading.

Distinguished Linguist Takes Interest in Modocs

A remarkable anthropologist and linguist visited the Quapaw Agency in 1884. Harvard educated Jeremiah Curtin was acquainted with more than fifty languages, a large number of which he spoke fluently. He was a world traveler and had a special interest in mythology. The American Indian myths had a particular appeal. Curtin's memoirs claim that he always found "ancient crones, mammies and withered squaws" from whom he heard the myths of their culture.[92]

It was in Oklahoma Indian Territory that Curtin and his wife Alma met and worked extensively with Martha Lawver, whom he called Ko-a-lak'-aka, and her daughter Jennie (who in time would be known as Jennie Lawver Clinton). Martha Lawver was one of the older Modocs at the Quapaw Agency. As Modocs continued to die at an alarming rate, Martha remained steadfast and seemed impervious to death.[93]

Curtin said that Martha was "one of the most remarkable persons I have ever met. [She] possessed mental power of the first ability....Very little of the Modoc mythology would have been saved had I not met [her]." Martha spoke no English, so Jennie served as interpreter, often making comments on what her mother said. Curtin, in keeping with his genius at languages, spent his evenings learning the Modoc language. Eventually, Curtin ceased working with other Modocs and concentrated solely on Martha and Jennie. He "spent thirty days, from seven in the morning till six in the afternoon, taking down what Ko-a-lak'-aka told me."[94]

Curtin commented on the Quapaw Agency administration and the fact that the Modocs' transition to new ways of life was not complete:

> I discovered at once that harmony was lacking in the official circle. This situation was decidedly unpleasant. I found it was best to see as little as possible of the government officials....I had to endure many hardships which could have been easily avoided had the agency been under the control of proper officials. But I counted hardships as nothing compared with the treasure which I was obtaining. The Modocs were at that time quiet, and, for Indians, they were industrious. They tried, however, to keep up their customs and in that way caused the agent annoyance. The summer before I was there a woman died, and, following a Modoc custom, her family burned all of her clothing and several blankets....The Modocs still shave and tar their heads when a relative dies. They mourn for their "own country" [California/Oregon] where each mountain, valley and lake has a story and is connected with the religion and mythology of their tribe.[95]

Martha was a legendary storyteller, without equal among the Modocs. As Martha spun her tales for Curtin, his wife Alma wrote them down. As Alma said in a letter home to her family, "we have had Indians with us, an old lady and her daughter. The old one has more in her head of old times and traditions than I would dream it possible for one head to contain....She is very old, long ago a great-grandmother." The long summer hours spent by the Curtins and Lawvers were not easy. Alma recorded on July 7: "Very, very hot, almost impossible to work. Jennie & old woman so sleepy that it was very trying to work with them. Sweat stood in drops on one all day. We couldn't get a breath of cool air."

Alma also noted on a Sunday work day: "Very hot again. Worked with J & mother all day. Old woman worked on her cap [weaving basket hat]. Said she didn't belong to any of the churches [so] it wasn't wrong for her to work Sunday [;] every day was good for her."

The entire experience of working with her husband among Indians across the United States was a foreign one for Alma Curtin. In her own handwriting, she took thousands and thousands of words of dictation, both from her husband and from storytellers. She reflected in her journal on her involvement with her husband's work: "I am a regular copper color. How I'll get the sunburn off is a question, but it doesn't matter much. I wouldn't give up the knowledge of the U. S. and the Indians that I have gained for the past few months for a great deal."[96]

Although Curtin and his wife worked among many other Indian groups, they formed a special relationship with the mother and daughter. Alma writes on March 16:

> ...bought a wood-cock which we gave to Jennie's mother, whom we found quite sick. I spent all afternoon and took dinner in the Modoc hut. They killed a hen and baked biscuits and tried to get up a swell dinner, custard pudding with napkins. I was really surprised at what they could do in the shape of getting up a presentable table and I ate quite heartily.

Jennie, too, contributed to Curtin's work, and this comment was recorded by Alma:

> If a baby is sick and a doctor cures it, he gives it a medicine name. A child that has a medicine name is sure to live long. Jennie, whose Indian name is Bap-pee Binpatokit, told me that she had three or four medicine names, for she was sick several times before she was old enough to talk.[97]

Traveling a Rocky Road

Despite their struggles to succeed and attempts to integrate into the society around them, the Modocs were in trouble in the 1880s. Agency funds were so sparse that housing was severely limited, as was the Modocs' ability to build their horse and cattle herds. Perhaps most troubling was the agency's inability to provide adequate trade education. The Modocs were unable to acquire the skills necessary to enter the local labor market. Despite this, the Modocs continued to labor at what jobs they could get in town and work their land. School attendance of children was important to them, and even adults attended classes. Improving their lot in life was of paramount importance.

The Modocs' biggest problem was the one that had plagued them since their arrival. Their tribe was shrinking. One hundred fifty-three Modocs had arrived at the Quapaw Agency in 1873, but by 1885 their numbers had dwindled to ninety-seven. A full investigation by the Department of Indian Affairs on the condition of the Modocs concluded that they were suffering from disease, and despite their record achievements, the Modocs were not happy.[98]

Eight Modocs, most in poor health, were allowed to return to Oregon in the summer of 1886. This was the beginning of the return of many Modocs to Oregon. Upon their arrival at the Yainax

Peter and Lizzie Schonchin
The last surviving warrior of the Modoc War,
Peter returned to Oregon in the late 1880s and married Lizzie there.
(Courtesy of Klamath County Museum)

sub-agency on the eastern side of the Klamath Reservation, the eight Modocs requested a Quaker missionary teacher, although President U. S. Grant had placed the Klamath Reservation under the care of the Methodist Church. An article was placed in the Friends' paper, the *Christian Worker*. Modocs were reunited with their Quaker faith when Levi Gilbert responded to the ad and moved to Yainax.[99]

Gilbert was a little disconcerted after assuming his post to be approached by one of the leading men who was helping to plan a major feast. The Modoc said, "We want to know which loves the people the most, the Methodist or the Quaker, by giving [us] a steer for the feast." Gilbert reported that he could not become party to controversy on that scale.

Peter McCarty Schonchin, son of Schonchin John, was one of the returnees to Yainax and appears on the April 13, 1890, list of Modocs (some from Oklahoma, some who had remained in Oregon) joining the Yainax Quaker Church. He would live in Oregon many years and become a part of history as the last surviving warrior of the Modoc War.[100]

Modocs Become Landowners

The dream of many Modocs came true in February of 1887 when President Grover Cleveland signed the Dawes Act. This act provided authorization for the president to have all Indian reservation land in the United States surveyed and allotted to individual Indians.

In the eyes of the Modocs, "Uncle Sam" had finally heard their repeated request for a tiny piece of land for each tribal member. The Modoc Reserve was surveyed and platted between 1888 and 1891. The 4,000 acres were split into allotments, and in 1891, sixty-eight patents were transmitted to the Quapaw Indian agent "...in favor of the members of the Modoc Tribe...for lands in the Indian Territory." There was no rhyme or reason in the distribution of allotments. A person could have one part of their allotment on one side of the reserve and another piece on another. But it was home sweet home, and the Modocs were ready to nest.

Some, however, rather than stay as landowners, chose to return to Oregon, and so the exodus continued, with Modocs settling at Yainax. In the spring of 1893 only forty-seven Modocs were registered on the Quapaw Agency roles, although by 1899, the number had increased to fifty-five.[101]

One Modoc who did not return to Oregon was Curley Headed Doctor. He died in 1890 in Oklahoma Indian Territory. He was the shaman, the religious leader, during the Modoc War. Curley Headed Doctor was held in great awe by the Modocs for his mystical ways. The story of his death was the stuff of legends. It was recounted many, many times among Modocs. Jennie Clinton often related the story of his death.[102]

* * * * *

— The Coming of the Birds —

The day was a dreary one. It was one of those Oklahoma days when the black clouds move close to the earth and sounds cease, leaving an eerie quiet.

The attending nurse at the hospital glanced over at the old Indian known as Curley Headed Doctor. He had come to the hospital from the Quapaw Agency in very bad health, suffering from senile decay and arthritis. The nurse would have added "deep depression" based on what she had seen. He was a strange one, she thought—didn't say much, and you could only wonder what those old eyes of his had seen. As if he knew she was thinking about him, he signaled her to move closer to him as he was trying to talk.

"I'm going to die, you know," he whispered in his paper-thin voice. "You're going to be here when it happens, so I need to tell you what to expect. Do not be afraid, as you will not be hurt. Before I die, a great black thunderstorm with lots of rain, thunder, lightening, and hail will darken the sky. After the storm has ceased, a great flock of birds will come for my spirit."

The old Indian's words alarmed the nurse. If the truth were to be known, his message, as crazy as it was, gave her goose bumps. She offered him words of consolation, assuring him he was going to be okay, but his mind had obviously moved elsewhere. He did not seem to hear her words. She faltered in her speech, and then her words dwindled to nothing. She moved very quickly from his bedside.

The encounter had left her jittery and ill at ease. Thankfully her shift would end soon—not too soon for her. She wanted out of this ward and into her easy chair at home. She was a little concerned about the weather and hoped the coming rain would wait until she was home.

The clouds were moving even lower—as if they were reaching down to become part of the earth. The first thunderclap completely undid her, and she jumped with a scream. All the sky opened up. The heavens convulsed and roared, the rain drenching everything. The storm was a fierce one, one of the most violent she'd ever seen. But when it finally lifted, the sun came out immediately, causing the hailstones on the lawn to glisten.

A magical quiet prevailed on the land.

Then, in the distance, several pigeons came flying to the trees just outside the hospital. Then a few more pigeons came. Then many pigeons. Finally came the remaining multitude of pigeons. They lit in the branches of the trees, cooing, and waiting, and then all took off at once and flew away.

The nurse looked around at Curley Headed Doctor's bed. He was dead.

* * * * * *

Scarfaced Charley joined the shaman in death in 1896. He died of tuberculosis at the Quapaw Agency. He had no living biological children, although he was survived by step-children. Named for the scar that ran over the right side of his face from a childhood accident, Charley had gained respect during the Modoc War for his humane actions and military strategy. He was the Modoc who had fired the first shot of the Modoc War—as Lt. Frasier Boutelle had fired at Charley in the same instant.[103]

Another Modoc from the Modoc War made his final resting place in Oklahoma Indian Territory soil. Slolux, who was on the Quapaw rolls as George Denny, died in 1899 and was buried in the Modoc Cemetery. Slolux was spared from hanging when Captain Jack and three other Modocs were hanged in 1873 at Ft. Klamath, Oregon. He spent five years in Alcatraz Prison before coming to the Quapaw Agency.[104]

Jennie Lawver and Daniel Clinton were married in 1887 by Pastor Jerry Hubbard. Jennie Clinton was twenty-eight and Daniel twenty-three. They remained at the Quapaw Agency until 1903, when they decided to move back to the Klamath Reservation. They returned to the Quapaw Agency some time later but then went back again to Oregon, where they remained.[105]

Jennie was in her teen years during the Modoc War and was often assigned the task of taking ammunition and clothing from the bodies of the fallen U. S. soldiers. She, like all the Modocs transferred to Oklahoma Indian Territory, had the double trauma of war and displacement to a foreign environment. Jennie had taken refuge in the religion presented by the Quakers. She was one of three Modocs—the other two being Frank Modoc (Steamboat Frank during the war) and her brother-in-law Samuel Clinton—who became pastors.

* * * * * *

— Death Takes the Young —

There comes a time in a human being's life, Jennie thought to herself, when a person has to wonder what life is all about and why one is even born.

It was only the last week of January in 1896. But already it was one of the worst years of Jennie's life. It was late afternoon and the wind had kicked up, blowing the snow across the flat Oklahoma landscape. Jennie looked out the window at the dreary day and knew she had never really liked nor understood the extreme Midwest weather.

The ground looked so cold and hard. That brought the tears again, and Jennie's body shook with sorrow. Only five days ago she had been pulled away from the mound of fresh dirt covering her son's tiny body. Earl was frail from the beginning. He was on earth only two months when his cold turned into a hacking cough. Within a few days he was gone, disappearing beneath the earth of the Modoc Cemetery near the Modoc Quaker Church.

But that wasn't the worst. Ten days before that, on January 15, another day Jennie would never forget, she and Daniel had put their first-born child, Mary, in the frigid ground. For eight years she and Daniel had laughed and found joy in the little girl. She had been as cocky and lively as a child could be. Mary had adored Earl, and Jennie took great comfort in that. She hoped that Mary had gathered Earl up in her arms when he joined her in death, just like she'd done in life.

Where would it end? Four years ago it had been Mercy, and then Claudie last year. Five children the good Lord had given her, and four he had taken back. Only seven-year-old Augustus remained.

Jennie felt that her faith was being tested to the ultimate with the deaths of her children. She had to be strong. She had thrived under the care of the Quaker missionaries. The old Modoc traditions had always allowed women to speak and be heard, but being a religious leader, although not closed to women, was rare. The Quaker religion was different. Friends believed that men and women were equal and that either could hold any position in a church. Women were allowed to take a major role. Jennie had done so. One of the best days of her life was when she was ordained as a Quaker pastor. Daniel was strong in the faith, too, and was proud of her.

Jennie sank back into the chair where she had held and nursed her children over the years. She was glad of the quiet and the chance to rest, just rest. Augustus was spending the day with his grandmother, Martha Lawver. Jennie's mother had been an absolute rock in her life, during the war and now

in the years of adjustment in Oklahoma Indian Territory. She was a blessing.

* * * * * *

Jennie Clinton proved to be one of the hardest working and most revered of Modoc Quaker pastors. But as a mother, she experienced extreme despair. Jennie and Daniel Clinton had eight children, all of whom died at an early age. The Oklahoma Modoc Cemetery is filled with Clinton children.[106]

Scarfaced Charley
Highly revered fighter in the Modoc War of 1873. This picture shows the transition from fighting warrior to non-Indian lifestyle.

Jennie and Daniel Clinton with daughter Mary
*Taken around 1890, their first-born Mary died in 1896 at the age of eight.
(Courtesy of Francis Landrum Collection)*

Modoc Cemetery

A small, lonely sign on a little traveled country highway—a sentinel standing among the Midwestern grasslands—marks the way to the Modoc Cemetery, located between Miami, OK, and Seneca, MO.

Once there, only birds and the sighing of prairie winds whisper the story of sorrowful exiles brought to a new home. Tracing the letters on the moss-covered tombstones, the names of Modoc people, born in one land but dying in this one, are found.

Rosie Jack, the young child of Captain Jack, Modoc War leader, was the first to be buried in this cemetery —April 1874 — only five months after her arrival in Oklahoma Indian Territory.

A note from an Oklahoma Quaker record book reads: "Owing to the uncertainty of life among Indian children, no record of any tribes was kept of the births until 1884."

Chapter 8
The Last Historical Chief

In the void of official Modoc leadership, Ben Lawver, a Modoc who had fought in the war, assumed the mantle of leadership in the years around the turn of the century. Lawver, whose Indian name was Ha-kar-gar-ush, was one of the last Modocs captured in May 1873, as the war drew to a close.

Jeff Riddle, in his book *Indian History of the Modoc* War, describes a conversation he had with Scarfaced Charley in New York in 1874 when they had been on tour with the Redpath Lecture Company. Charley told Riddle that Lawver wasn't much of a warrior but was "a good Indian....He was such a coward [I] do not believe that he fired one shot at any white man during all their fighting in the lava beds."[107]

Charley had told him that a "manly effort had been made to capture Lawver. Ben Lawver was too fast." Pat McManus, who sold merchandise and goods to the soldiers during the war, witnessed the attempt to capture Lawver. "Begorra," he exclaimed, "I'll bet me auld hat against a dead rattlesnake that long-legged Injun will be in San Francisco by this time tomorrow."[108]

Lawver adopted the name Chief Yellowhammer. The Modocs in Oklahoma Indian Territory intermarried with white people to a greater degree than their counterparts in Oregon. Lawver was no exception. When he met a Quaker missionary by the name of Alice Perdin, Chief Yellowhammer lost his heart. His wife Sallie and daughter had died a few years before, as so many Modocs had. Lawver was ready to be part of a family again. Although not Modoc herself, this fair-skinned missionary would become a memorable part of Modoc history.

Alice Perdin was born in Memphis, Missouri, in 1876. She came from a prosperous ranching family. Headed by Mathew Perdin and his wife, Cynthia, the family had eight children. Alice, their third child, had shown great promise as a student. She eventually became a school teacher.[109]

Alice was a devout Quaker. As a young woman she "felt the

call" to serve on the Quapaw Agency as a missionary to the Modoc Indians. Her parents Cynthia and Mathew were shocked and dumbfounded when on January 22, 1897, Alice married an Indian—Ben Lawver—in the tiny Missouri town of Seneca.

Alice Perdin Lawver was promptly disowned by the Perdin family.[110]

* * * * *

— Starting A New Life —

Alice had conditioned herself not to think about her family, especially her mother. In the first few months after her marriage, she grieved for the family she had lost. "It is so senseless, with all the death around," she thought "that a family is torn apart because someone marries a man that doesn't meet with approval." But time took the edge off the hurt. Alice threw herself into her missionary work, teaching the children and working with the Modocs on everything from language to Bible study. Alice was fluent in Modoc.

Married life was agreeing with her. She liked cooking and experimenting with recipes. Ben never knew what delight (or sometimes mishap!) would be awaiting him at the table. Of course, these were times Alice really missed her mother. Her mother always spread a wonderful table of food, and so many times Alice wanted to write and ask her questions. But she couldn't do that, she knew.

Moving from missionary to the wife of a Modoc changed her relationship with the Modocs drastically. She was now one of them, rather than an outsider looking in. Alice's excellent command of Modoc was a huge factor in making her more and more a part of the Modoc community. Alice rarely spoke English now, unless working with Quakers in the church or townspeople with whom she had some dealings.

Ben's life suited her well. He had a short stint with one of the wild west shows, and his photos, in full headdress and regalia, gave them both a chuckle. Not exactly Modoc dress, but it was what the owner of the show liked, and the job helped bring in extra money for their growing family. Ben was also a U. S. Indian police officer, hired by the Quapaw Agency. The children loved his badge and once in a while, off duty, he would pin it on one of them.

Ben was known to most outsiders as Chief Yellowhammer. Alice and Ben had designed stationery that certainly caught the attention of those who received an official letter from Ben. Alice had a major hand in developing the stationery—tan and maroon with a picture of Ben in his regalia from the wild west show on the letterhead and on the corner of envelopes. She also became proficient at writing letters for him, or, for that matter, any Modoc who needed to communicate

Ben Lawver in Wild West Show regalia.
(Photo courtesy of Bert Lawvor)

in writing. Ben and Alice were advocates of a legislative endorsement allowing Modocs to return home to Oregon. Alice put her school teacher writing skills to work. Suddenly letters began to show up in legislators' offices talking about Modocs and their concerns. Alice was an incredibly efficient "power behind the throne."

Ben loved to run. In the morning, most days, he would rise early and run. He would come back into the house, his body dripping with sweat. It was a ritual. One day Ben delivered the surprising news that he had entered a 25-mile marathon with cash prizes. He'd never done that before. "You have dinner ready," he told Alice. "I'll be home at six with money."

He was home at 6:00 p.m. with money folded in his pocket. Alice was not at all surprised. Ben was a born entrepreneur, and this was obviously another way of bringing in extra money. The fact that he did it doing something he loved was special. Alice decided that not many women had a husband who was a wild west show performer, policeman, and runner—not to mention serving the Modocs as chief.

One of the true joys of Alice's life was a wonderful friend whom she had become close to in the early years of her marriage. Minnie Robbins, who was Scarfaced Charley's step-daughter, was her confidante and companion. The two women, one with rich copper skin, the other fair complected, formed a deep and

Ben and Alice Lawver with daughters
*Ben (1850 - 1915) and Alice (1876 -1968) with
Mary on Alice's lap and Lela on Ben's knee.
(Photo courtesy of Bert Lawvor)*

Minnie and Charles Robbins with son Hiram
Alice Lawver and Minnie, Scarfaced Charley's stepdaugter,
were close friends throughout their lives.
(Photo courtesy of Coke Crume)

permanent bond.

Alice and Minnie had one significant thing in common: they had married men outside their own cultures. Minnie had married a white man by the name of Charlie Robbins.

On this particular hot, humid Oklahoma summer day in 1905, they were talking and laughing together in the cool shade of the grove of trees near the Lawver house. Their children, about the same ages, played nearby. They were engaged in the popular frog-leaping contest: the child jumping the greatest distance from a crouching position was the winner. Lela, Alice's seven-year-old, loved the game. Once Lela started, it was sometimes hard to stop her. She did it over and over, long after the other children had ended the game. Lela Lawver was developmentally disabled.

Alice could honestly say that she loved her three children equally and fiercely. Whatever happened in life, she would always be there for her little ones. Alice realized she carried the scar of rejection herself: she would never for any reason, disown or turn away from her flesh and blood.

* * * * * *

Sometime during the first decade of 1900, long-time Miami, Oklahoma, resident Arnold Richardson remembers going to watch Ben Lawver dance.

> The Indians on the Quapaw used to have 'stomp dances,' where each tribe would put on a different dance. There was a lot of cheering as people supported their tribe. My dad and I picked up Ben and his kids Shelby and Lela one time, and we headed out for a stomp. Ben performed his well-known turkey dance. He would dance with two turkey wings—crouch down real low and drag those wings through the dirt. Then he would suddenly leap up, turning in the air, and gobbling for all he was worth. He was a huge favorite with the kids.[111]

An event in Lawver's life in 1905 forced him to make a major decision. He chose to forsake Modoc tradition. When his brother Billy was killed by lightning, Billy's widow Eliza presented herself to Ben with the expectation of being taken in. Modoc custom held that a man married the widow of his brother. Ben explained that Modocs no longer practiced polygyny (a man taking more than one wife). He had a wife and children of his own and could not have her living with him as a second wife.

Eliza was not to be dissuaded and went after Ben with a knife. In desperation, Ben turned to the law. United States Commissioner

F. C. Adams intervened and sentenced the angry woman to a short cooling-off period in jail. The June 10, 1956, *Miami* [Oklahoma] *Daily News-Record*, has this quote from Commissioner Adams, who, fifty years after putting the Modoc woman in jail, still remembered the event:

> He [Lawver] was afraid she might kill him and he was probably right, for numerous writers have mentioned the unpredictable temper and fierce disposition of Modoc women.

In appreciation, Ben Lawver presented to Judge Adams a bow, predominantly painted in black. It is made of bois-d' arc, an orange-hued wood noted for its hardness, flexibility, and durability. It is strung with rawhide that Yellowhammer had processed and softened by long hours of patient chewing. The bow is now housed at the Dobson Museum in Miami, Oklahoma.[112]

The year 1905 was not only noteworthy for the Lawver family feud, but it also presented some accurate Modoc population statistics. There were fifty-six Modocs enrolled in the Oklahoma Indian Territory and 223 on the Klamath Reservation. Yainax, the Modoc area of the Klamath Reservation, was increasing in population.[113]

Arnold Richardson
(6/29/1906 - 4/14/2008) Born in Oklahoma Indian Territory. Honorary member of the Modoc Tribe of Oklahoma. (Photo by Jimmy Sexton)

Orville "Ram" Lawver, Jr. with Bow
Ben Lawver's grandson Orville (6/6/1936 - 5/29/2000) holds a bow made by his grandfather for Commissioner F. C. Adams. (Photo courtesy of Yvonne Lawver Kays)

Billy and Eliza Lawver
Billy, brother of Ben, was struck and killed by lightning in 1905.

Chapter 9
The Return to Oregon

Federal legislative action would drastically change the lives of Oklahoma Modocs. The May 26, 1908, *Klamath Falls* [Oregon] *Evening Herald* headline blared, "Coming to Old Home. Remnant of Captain Jack's Band will Start for Klamath." The article maintained:

> The Modocs are thrifty and have not spent the time in idleness. They are extraordinarily good workers and for years have maintained themselves solely on their own manual labor....It is thought by the more progressive mixed bloods on the Klamath Reservation in Oregon that the coming of the remnant of Captain Jack's once warlike band will have a splendid effect on the entire tribe....

> Senator Curtin of Kansas, himself part Kaw Indian, prepared the report on this bill and he dipped his pen in sympathetic ink. 'The rapid decrease in population,' he says, 'seems to be the result of mental anxiety caused by their forced separation from their families and friends....The agent at Klamath Agency reported...that they [the Modocs] would be kindly received and that there was ample opportunity for them to secure a good livelihood...where their friends and relatives would be glad to greet them....There is no question but what their removal can be accomplished through the plan proposed.

Thirty-six years after the exiled Modocs arrived in Oklahoma Indian Territory, the Congress of the United States officially restored the Modoc Indians to the Oregon Klamath Reservation rolls. On March 3, 1909, the Oklahoma Modocs were granted permission to return home.

The question was, what was "home?" Many Modocs had been born in Oklahoma Indian Territory, and the land of exile had become home. There was no memory of a California Lost River...or lava bed...or a Yainax. Some Modocs had already migrated back to Oregon, selling their allotments in Oklahoma to non-Indians. According to the May 26, 1908, *Klamath Falls Evening Herald* article, only seventeen of the original Modocs placed in exile in Oklahoma Indian Territory were still living.

The superintendent of the Seneca Indian School now managed

all Modoc affairs as the Quapaw Agency had been closed in 1901. Although selling or leasing the Modocs' land in Oklahoma was approved, officials now administering the Modocs were concerned that the Indian land was not governed by more stringent regulations. There was no way to prevent non-Indians from gaining control for small sale prices or lease fees. There were Modocs who sold their land for little more than the price of a ticket to Oregon.[114]

The Modocs who went back to Oregon faced opposition. A March 25, 1909, *Klamath Falls Evening Herald* headline proclaimed, "Klamaths Object to Modocs Coming." The newspaper went on to say, "The Modocs are to be allowed to share in the tribal funds of the Klamaths. This latter provision is what has caused the greatest objection to the return of the Modocs. The Indians [Klamath] are not any too anxious to having the Modocs brought back to live with them, but they certainly object to sharing with them their funds."

The paper stated, "It is not believed that anything except an act of Congress repealing their former act will prevent the Modoc from being brought to the Klamath Reservation." The Klamath Falls paper was exactly right. The Modocs were coming.

Nearly forty years earlier, in 1870, the Modocs had come to the Klamath Reservation. That had been ordered by a treaty. Living in close proximity to the Klamaths on this large reservation didn't work. The difference this time was that the Modocs were situated at Yainax, the sub-agency on the eastern side of the reservation, some forty miles from Klamath Agency on the western side. Yainax was founded in 1869 partly to quell dissention among the Indian tribes on the reservation and provide separate areas to live. The approximately one hundred Modocs who had not defected under Captain Jack had inhabited this area since the end of the Modoc War.[115]

Yainax

Education was a high priority for Modocs in Oregon, just as it was for those in Oklahoma. The 1876 Annual Report to the Secretary of the Interior from Klamath Reservation Indian Agent L. S. Dyar stressed the need for a school:

> In my last annual report I explained the necessity of a boarding-school at Yainax Station....Those Indians who have grown up in the habits and superstitions of the savages, although they may be improved, can never be raised to an advanced state of civilization or respectability, and it is to the rising generation that our efforts must be directed if much good is to be accomplished in this direction.[116]

A school, predominantly of Modoc children, opened in 1882 with thirty-one students. Attendance was mandatory, and for students not brought in by their parents, Indian policemen, appointed by the Klamath Agency, did the chore. As with other reservation schools of this era, children boarded at the school for ten months out of the year and were trained in ranching, farming, housekeeping, cooking, and other practical areas. They also received a basic education much like non-Indian children of their time. They were fed, clothed, and schooled without charge to their parents. By 1897, 110 students were enrolled at Yainax School. Holidays brought special celebrations, picnics, and parties to the school. Christmas was a big event with a tree, gifts, and community involvement.[117]

Ivan Applegate, the commissary in charge of the Yainax sub-agency, had high expectations for the school. He laid out some of his plans in a June 8, 1871, letter to Alfred Meacham, who was then superintendent of Indian Affairs in Oregon:

> First establish some order and discipline among the young Indians....I would hope not only to educate the rising generation but, by a very gradual process, greatly to improve the present pitiable condition of the parents. In this connection I would say that one year ago I selected four Indian boys and kept them about the Agency in order to teach them our language...[and] the use and value of domestic animals, tools, etc.; this project has been crowned with the most flattering results. All the boys understand and speak our language very well, milk the cows, drive teams, cut wood...[118]

There was definitely a community that had sprung up at Yainax. Residences, doctor's and matron's houses, dormitories for boys and girls, jail, store, and post office were all there. The Yainax Post Office, with Ivan Applegate as postmaster, was established in 1891. But the big draw in Yainax was the store. Operated by Robert Spink, the store was on the bottom half of the building, and the Spink family lived on the second floor. Spink's daughter, Claudia Spink Lorenz, writing about her childhood during the years of 1903-1910, remembered Yainax as she first saw it:

> A passage of bottomless mud in winter and a repletion of dust in summer...the settlement had a stark look as it faced barren Yainax Butte, overlooking gray sagebrush flats....The only time that there was a general semblance of softness and beauty was when the grain and hay fields were growing.[119]

Spink's store was far more than a store. Indeed bacon, beans, lard, crackers, bright calicos, and neckerchiefs flew out the door, but the primary function of the store, in the eyes of the Modocs around Yainax, was as a meeting place. Coming to the store was a social event for Modoc families, especially the women. They came early in the morning and, depending on the time of year, would either perch near the stove or sit on the store porch in the sunshine. It was a chance to meet and visit with friends. To prolong the day, the women would purchase their goods one item at a time between enjoyable conversations. It made for a good day of socializing. Looking back on the event, Claudia Lorenz distinctly remembered that "on a chilly day the store would get pretty crowded at times and the air pretty pungent as well."

Toby Riddle
Died of pneumonia in 1920 at Yainax. (Photo courtesy of Klamath County Museum)

Toby and Frank Riddle, prominent interpreters during the Modoc War, and their son Jeff and his wife, Amanda Schonchin Riddle, were often seen at Yainax, especially at the store. Lorenz recalled the awe with which the children held Toby, re-named Winema. "Winema... quite over-shadowed her husband Frank. However he seemed content to remain in the background, proud of the respect and recognition that she received from her own people as well as the whites."[120]

When the store moved to a bigger building, a new service was offered. Spink also performed some of the duties of an undertaker. Funeral caskets were standard merchandise, and he displayed them on the second floor. He became quite proficient at embellishing the exterior of the coffins with metal plates and ornaments. His wife made the head pillows and shrouds from heavy white china silk.

The old ways of Modoc cremation had faded, and the Modocs were good customers for caskets. A funeral was a significant happening for Indian families. Vast amounts of food were served, large crowds were present, and the event lasted all day.[121]

It was inevitable that a town would spring up near Yainax. It did. In 1915 Sprague River blossomed some six miles north of Yainax. It eventually completely replaced Yainax. Many buildings at Yainax were actually physically transported, with the store building one of the first to be moved. Modocs who had chosen to leave the Quapaw and move to Yaninax, moved again. The Modocs who had remained behind in 1873 also moved.

Things were changing on the reservation and in Yainax. Business with people off the reservation was flourishing as Indian land was leased and cattle sold. As the Modocs' standard of living improved, they looked for more services and merchandise.

The Indian boarding school, a major hub in Yainax, changed to a day school in 1907. Dormitories closed and many residences were no longer needed. With the establishment of Sprague River, the school eventually closed. Modoc children integrated into public schools.[122]

The Journey West

A letter addressed to Benjamin J. Lawver on May 11, 1910, from the U. S. Department of the Interior, Office of Indian Affairs, answered the question many Oklahoma Modocs were asking:

> The Office has received your letter of May 2, 1910, written at the request of "your people", regarding allotments to the Modoc Indians in Oklahoma on Klamath Reservation, Oregon. You ask if the Indians of your tribe can be allotted on the Klamath Reservation without the necessity of going to that reservation....

> ...Before allotments on the Klamath Reservation, Oregon, can be made to any of the Modoc Indians formerly enrolled at the Quapaw Agency, it will be necessary for such Indians to remove and take up their residence on the Klamath Reservation....It was not contemplated...that allotments would be made...to those members of the Modoc Tribe of Oklahoma who failed or refused to leave their present locality.[123]

Ben was twenty-one at the time of the Modoc War. At fifty-eight years of age, he had forgotten much of the California-Oregon area where he had spent his childhood and early years. But he remembered enough to make him feel that it was time to go home. Besides, in order to claim land on the Klamath Reservation, he had to return. If his children were to have any legacy or land claim in the homeland, he had to act right away. He was ready.

* * * * * *

— Going Home —

The train trip back to Oregon in 1910 was far different than the one Ben had experienced going to Oklahoma Indian Territory as a prisoner of war. He would never forget the cold, crowded conditions of the railway cars headed for Indian Territory in 1873 and the humiliation of wearing irons on his wrists and on his legs at night. The last part of the trip from McPherson, Nebraska, to Baxter Springs, Kansas, had been tortuous. There had been some bad times at Quapaw Agency but nothing to rival the hunger and extreme cold the Modocs had experienced on the cattle cars.

After the long train ride from the Midwest, the Lawver family made the final journey to the Yainax area in a buckboard. They spent the night on the banks of the Sprague River. The next day, in the dark of early morning, they started on the last leg of their trip. Just before dawn broke, Ben suddenly reined in the horses at the foot of a large butte in front of him.

After a few whispered words to Alice, he began to run. He was nearing sixty years of age, but he felt like the twenty-one-year-old who had left Oregon. With the cool air whipping his face, Ben started his ascent, running until he could feel his heart thudding violently in his chest. He made it to the top of the hill just as the sun arose. Falling on his knees and praying aloud in the Modoc language, Ben Lawver celebrated his return to the homeland.

Ben felt incredibly strange to be back after nearly forty years. The majestic, white-shouldered Mt. Shasta, sacred to the Modocs, had been replaced in Ben's life with the wind-swept prairies of Oklahoma. He had left his homeland speaking little English and adhering to the cultural traits of his Modoc ancestors. He belonged to a group of people that newspapers of the 1870s branded "savages." He now wore the clothing of a turn-of-the-century non-Indian, shiny shoes for dress, and even a stove-pipe hat for special occasions. He had traded the Modoc deity Kumookumts for the Quaker God. He would be buried, not cremated in the old way. He now looked to a pastor, not a shaman, for guidance. He ate beef he raised instead of venison from deer he stalked and killed. He now not only spoke English but was a fluent and articulate spokesman for the Modocs.

His first visit back to the lava bed and Captain Jack's Stronghold left him shaken and emotional. He had taken Lucky with him that day. The active, babbling six-year-old had been the perfect companion, helping to focus Ben in the present and not bury himself too deeply in the past. Soon after arriving in the desolate lava flow, Ben went to a spot he remembered. It was here during the war, while in flight from the soldiers, that he had hastily dug a hole and thrown guns and ammunition in.

While Lucky happily played on the lava rocks, Ben found a big stick nearby and began to dig. The stick hit something solid, and Ben yelled. Lucky came at a gallop, just as his father hauled a bayonet from the ground. Ben turned and ceremoniously placed the dirt-encrusted weapon in his son's hands.

In time the Lawver family settled permanently at Yainax. The day school at Yainax provided great schooling for the Lawver children. Alice worked with the three developmentally disabled children that were part of the Lawver family. Ben and Alice's other two children, Ham and Mabel, made an easy adjustment in school. Ham, from the very beginning, took to ranching and the rough-riding Modoc horsemen he saw around him. Alice reminded him that his father had been a wild west performer back in the Midwest.

The family settled in one of the resident houses in Yainax. For Alice, the best part of the arrival in Oregon was that Minnie and Charlie Robbins had migrated from the Quapaw Agency, too. Minnie and Alice enjoyed the Spink general store like the rest of the Modocs did. Many years later, Alice's grandson Bert, who lived with her in her later years, said, "You couldn't tell grandma she wasn't Modoc! She was always an Indian in spirit."

* * * * * *

Ben Lawver died in 1915 at sixty-three years of age and was buried in Schonchin Cemetery, the Modoc cemetery near Yainax. That left Alice to raise the eight children that they now had. Five years after Ben's death, in the spring of 1920, the unbelievable happened. Lela, Lucky, Lucille, and Mary were placed in the Oregon State Institution for the Feeble-Minded in Salem, Oregon. Lela was pregnant. The child was born in the institution, and Lela named her Alice after her mother.

Over the next five years Alice wrote hundreds of letters to the superintendent of the institution in an attempt to follow her children's progress in school. She waged a relentless campaign to have her children returned to her. Her granddaughter Alice died in the institution of pneumonia at two years of age.[124]

An Institution Challenged and a Church Built

In July of 1922, seven years after Ben Lawver's death, Alice Lawver married Daniel Clinton, who was at one time husband to Jennie Lawver Clinton. Alice and Daniel were married in Yreka, California, as mixed marriages were illegal in the state of Oregon. Daniel and Alice were firmly committed to two things: to the Quaker faith and to bringing Lela, Lucky, Lucille, and Mary home. Alice knew that the Oregon State Institution for the Feeble-Minded did not consider her able to care for her children because she was not married. Her marriage was a significant step in getting her children returned.[125]

Meetings among the Modocs were held regularly to keep the Quaker beliefs alive and active in the Oregon Modoc country. Gatherings were held in Alice and Daniel's home. Many of the

Quapaw Agency Modocs who had returned to Oregon attended. Charles and Carrie Hood, who had been Mol-ak-ak and Wi-ka-in on their 1873 arrival in Oklahoma Indian Territory, appeared on Sundays. Peter McCarty Schonchin and his wife, Lizzie, whom he married after returning to Yainax, attended regularly. Jennie Clinton and her former brother-in-law Samuel Clinton often delivered the Sunday message.

Samuel Clinton, Daniel's older brother, began actively preaching once he arrived in Oregon. At one point Samuel was ready to quit. "I did preach, but there was never such a failure. I went home sick at heart, getting on my knees and saying, 'Didn't I tell you, Lord?'" But those Quakers listening didn't feel the same. One Quaker parishioner said, "He was as good a preacher as one could wish to hear." Whether it was that kind of praise or his need to serve, Samuel continued on his path.[126]

Jennie Clinton lived on the western side of the reservation near Klamath Lake. She traveled with a team and buggy throughout the reservation ministering to the people. Jennie is reported to have told someone that she and Alice Clinton had the same last name because they were married to the same man at different times. The exact circumstances of these marriages and how one woman replaced the other is lost. But Jennie Lawver Clinton and Alice Lawver Clinton, as well as Daniel Clinton, appeared on the same November 1924, Sprague River Quaker membership list. They obviously worked closely together.[127]

Alice Clinton's constant letter writing insisting that her children be returned, including a letter in August 1924 to Oregon Governor Walter Pierce, brought results. After nearly five years at the Oregon State Institution for the Feeble-Minded, Lela, Lucky, Lucille, and Mary Lawver were released on January 14, 1925, to the care of Alice and Daniel Clinton. This was done only after the Clintons agreed to have all four children sterilized in keeping with a ruling from Oregon's Board of Eugenics.[128]

A Church is Built

An effort to build a Quaker church went into full swing in 1925. Lucky Lawver, twenty years old at the time and always known as a hard worker, put in hours and hours of work on the Sprague River Friends Community Church. Daniel Clinton, Samuel Clinton, Pastor Ivey Clark, and other Quaker members hauled logs to the government mill in the nearby community of Beatty. The sawn lumber was brought back to Sprague River for the church. The thirty by forty-eight foot building was constructed for $3,000 with donated labor and some materials contributed. Although not completely finished, the church was dedicated on Easter Sunday, 1925.

It was a common sight on Sunday mornings in Sprague

River to see Alice with her four children, returned from the State Institution for the Feeble-Minded, marching in line to church, oldest to youngest. Lela was now twenty-seven years old and led the line.[129]

Ben Lawver Family
(Front, left to right) Lucille, Luscum (Lucky), Shelby (Ham) and Lela. (Back row) Mary in Alice's arms and Ben. (Photo courtesy of Bert Lawvor)

Yainax
*Sub-agency of the Klamath Reservation, established
in the 1870s to separate the Modocs from the Klamaths.
(Photo courtesy of Klamath County Museum)*

Yainax Indian Boarding School
*School operated for Modocs by the U. S. government.
(Photo courtesy of Klamath County Museum)*

Chapter 10
Two Tribes

The dividing of one tribe into two started with the forced split in 1873 when Modoc War prisoners of war were sent to Oklahoma Indian Territory. Half a continent apart, the two groups of Modocs, who shared the same blood and ancestral heritage, took separate paths and developed different lifestyles. Travel back and forth between Oklahoma and Oregon became less common. Most Modocs by the turn of the century, wherever they were, called their land home. They ceased to know each other.

Modocs associated with the Modoc War were becoming fewer and fewer. Toby Riddle (Winema) died in Yainax of pneumonia in 1920. She was seventy-nine years old. She was not sent to Oklahoma Indian Territory, so spent her later life in Klamath country. She is buried in Schonchin Cemetery. Peter McCarty Schonchin, son of Schonchin John, was the last surviving warrior of the Modoc War. Sent to Oklahoma as a prisoner of war, he returned to Yainax in 1886. He died in 1939 at age ninety-five and is also buried in Schonchin Cemetery.[130]

Memories of the Quapaw Agency faded for those who returned to Oregon. Some Modocs simply kept their silence. Bert Lawvor, grandson of Alice and Ben Lawver, who changed his last name from Lawver to Lawvor, remembers that Alice never discussed her past life in Oklahoma. Neither did Minnie Robbins. Minnie raised her granddaughter Coleen Crume (better known as "Coke" because, yes, she liked Coca-Cola!). Coke remembers conversations back in the 1940s when Minnie, too, would clam up when the subject of the past came up. She passed little of the Modoc culture down, including the language. Minnie, born at the Quapaw Agency in 1878, five years after the Modocs arrived in exile, must still have felt some of the old fear. At times she would caution Coke not to talk about being Modoc. The grandchildren of Alice and Minnie remember the great amount of time the women spent together. But they always spoke in Modoc, so the thoughts they shared with each other stayed with them.

Alice was remembered by most in Sprague River as a kind, honest

Jo Anne Tuning Magee
Born (8/11/1934),
daughter of Pastor Evert
Tuning. Basket was gift
from Dora Walker,
daughter of U. S. Grant.

woman, devoted to her church, and a wonderful cook. "People were always welcome at her table," Coke remembers. Grandson Bert relates, "She never said anything bad about anyone. She was quiet, understanding, and never raised her voice. Only one time did she use corporal punishment on us kids. She tried to paddle my brother Ben with an old wood shingle. It broke before she could do a good job, so she quit. That was the end of my grandmother's spankings."[131]

Jo Anne Tuning Magee was the daughter of Evert Tuning, who was the pastor for the Sprague River Friends Community Church beginning in 1942. Jo Anne recounted many memories of Modocs on the Klamath Reservation. Her first meeting with Alice Lawver was when her dad accepted the pastorate at Sprague River:

> We had driven all the way from Idaho with our milk cow in the trailer. We finally arrived in Sprague River, and my mother had a terrible migraine. Alice came over and cooked dinner for us all. Her kindness was immediately obvious to us.

She had vivid memories of Minnie, too:

> Minnie was quite a person. She was definitely her own boss. One day Minnie showed up for church with her shoes on the wrong feet. My mother mentioned the fact to Minnie, but the conversation ended abruptly when Minnie told her, "They feel better this way."[132]

Come mid-June, it was a tradition for Alice to take her children, grandchildren, and their friends hunting down by the river for epos, a staple in the Modoc diet for eons. The carrot-like leaves and little white flowers of the plant signaled good eating below the earth. The epos were dug out with an *umbda*, a long pole with a cross-bar on it. The pole was used to pop the bulbs, which came in clusters of two or three, out of the ground. The bulbs were thumb-size and had brown skin. When the skin was scratched off with a fingernail, white meat was revealed. Eaten either raw or cooked, epos were crunchy and had a nutty flavor.[133]

Ham Lawver, one of Alice's children, continued to build his childhood interest in horses and riding. By 1915, when he was fourteen years old, he was riding for ranchers in the area, bringing money home to his mother Alice, who was now a widow. Buttons Bodner, an area Modoc rancher, describes Ham at a later age as

Kla-Mo-Ya Casino
*Located twenty-two miles north of Klamath Falls, Oregon. The casino
name is an acronym of the three tribes that form the Klamath Tribes:
Klamath, Modoc, and Yahooskin band of Paiute.*
(Photo by Karen Weatherby)

Modoc Color Plate 9

Alvin Lawver (3/15/1966).
With daughters Alison (6/24/1999),
lower left, and Darenzie (8/19/1993).
Descendants of
Alice and Ben Lawver.
(Photo by Karen Weatherby)

Bert Lawvor Jr. (7/2/1964).
Son of Bert Lawvor. Descendant of
Ben and Alice Lawver.
(Photo by Jim Hackbarth)

Richard Tupper (10/22/1950).
Son of Bill Duffy.
(Photo by Jim Hackbarth)

Bert Lawvor (12/27/1942).
With granddaughters Mikaela
(2/27/1998) on left and Aiyanna
Lawver (6/11/2000). Descendants
of Alice and Ben Lawver.
(Photo by Jim Hackbarth)

Modoc Color Plate 10

Bill Duffy and wife Rachel Tupper
(1924 - 2001), descendant of Minnie Robbins. Photo taken to exhibit in Klamath Falls photographer's window.

Bill Duffy, AKA Phil Tupper
(2/9/1929). 1957 Nat'l. Intercollegiate Rodeo Assn. Bronc Riding Champion. Descendant of Watson Duffy.
(Photo by Jim Hackbarth)

Rayson Tupper *(1/14/1947). Son of Bill Duffy and daughters Taylor David (4/8/1969) on left and Torina Case (2/25/1968). Daughters descendants of Old Sheepy on mother's side. (Photo by Jim Hackbarth)*

Taylor David *(4/8/1969). Descendant of Old Sheepy and Watson Duffy, nephew of Bogus Charley. (Photo by B. Taylor)*

Modoc Color Plate 11

Colleen "Coke" Crume
(6/14/1940). Descendant of Minnie Robbins.
(Photo by Jim Hackbarth)

Helen Crume Smith *(9/9/1934 - 3/26/2008). Cousin of Coke. Descendant of Minnie Robbins. Served on Klamath Tribes council.*
(Photo by Karen Weatherby)

Alfred Meacham's great-grandchildren
(Left to right) Margaret Berlin (3/13/1943), Judith Masters (8/17/1939), and William Byrne (12/18/1944)..

Richard Rambo
(11/23/1948). Klamath County Circuit Court Judge. Descendant of Matilda and Robert Whittle. Lives today on Whittle property (originally Whittle's Ferry). (Photo by Laddie Tofell)

Modoc Color Plate 12

Debra Herrera *(4/9/1951).*
With mother Christine Allen
(3/13/1927). Descendant of Toby/
Jeff Riddle and Schonchin John.
(Photo by Karen Weatherby)

Phil Follis *(8/9/1936).*
Descendant of Long Jim. Serves on
Modoc Tribe of Oklahoma council.
Author's second cousin.
(Photo by Jack Shadwick)

Bert Lawvor and author Cheewa.
(Photo by Jim Hackbarth)

Arnold Richardson *(6/29/1906 -*
4/14/2008). With daughter
Oklahoma "Oma" Potts (12/1/1928).
Early OK. Indian Territory resi-
dents. (Photo by Jimmy Sexton)

Modoc Color Plate 13

Ivan Crain (5/29/1971).
With daughter Salalie
(1/20/2000) in Spirit of
Captain Jack
Pow-wow regalia
(not traditional Modoc).
(Photo by Jim Hackbarth)

Harold Wright (6/25/1933).
Modoc and Klamath descent.
(Photo by Jim Hackbarth)

Eloise Ohles (2/10/1934).
Modoc and Klamath descent.
(Photo by Jim Hackbarth)

Modoc Color Plate 14

Cassie Mitchell *(8/8/1987).*
Daughter of Jeff Mitchell, who
serves on Klamath Tribes council.
Descendant of Old Sheepy.
(Photo by Jim Hackbarth)

Ramona Rosiere *(1/30/1946)*
Descendant of Long Jim. Serves on
Modoc Tribe of Oklahoma
council. Author's second cousin.
(Photo by Jack Shadwick)

Author Cheewa James
(5/15/1939). With sons (left to right)
David J. (8/12/1961)
and Todd (10/4/1964).
(Photo by Karen Weatherby)

Katerra Hicks *(1/14/1992).*
Modoc/Klamath descent.
Klamath Restoration Celebration
Queen in 2004 and 2005.
(Photo by Taylor David)

Modoc Color Plate 15

Sonlatsa "Sunshine" Jim-Martin *(6/14/1972). With daughters (left to right) Zunneh-bah Martin (4/1/1997), Nizhoni-bah Martin (7/25/2005), and Shundeen-bah Martin (8/16/2001). Modoc and Navajo. Daughter of Sonny Jim James. Author's niece.*

Codi Colombe *(11/29/1972). Modoc and Rosebud Sioux. Daughter of Viola James Colombe. Author's niece. (Photo by Al Snyder)*

Tayla Easterla *(2/11/1997) and* ***Clyde Captain Colombe*** *(7/12/1996). Second cousins—great-great-great grandchildren of Shacknasty Jim. Modoc, Rosebud Sioux, and various European blood. (Photo by Cheewa James)*

Modoc Color Plate 16

"a good old cowboy, tough and hard to hurt." Ham was known for his ability to roll a cigarette while riding full speed on his horse. Bill Duffy, another Modoc rancher, "liked buckarooing with him." Ham was a tribal stockman with the Klamath Reservation re-issue program.

This program was a unique plan designed to help Indian ranchers. Once a rancher showed that he had hay and a good place to keep livestock, he was issued a permit in the program. The idea was that a given number of heifers would be distributed by the reservation agency. A rancher's brand could be placed anywhere on the cow but the tribal ID brand was on the right rib.[134]

When the cows distributed by the tribe calved, Klamath tribal agency stockmen would check the herds and sort out heifers to repay the livestock debt. They picked out top heifers, as these animals would go back to the tribal herd for distribution to other ranchers. The rancher would keep the remainder of the spring calves. When a rancher wanted to sell a cow, he had to get a permit from tribal authority. Usually twenty-five heifers were allotted to the rancher, and he was given five years to return that number of animals to the re-issue program. Bill Duffy remembers the rigs that the tribal stockmen drove. "They were little coupes but instead of a trunk, they had a small bed that carried branding irons." A breeding service for cattle was also offered to Klamath Reservation Indians.

Back in Oklahoma

There were more than 150 Modocs sent as prisoners of war in 1873 to the Quapaw Agency in Oklahoma Indian Territory. One hundred Modocs remained in Oregon on the Klamath Reservation. Within a few years, because of the excessive number of deaths at the Quapaw Agency, Modocs in Oregon outnumbered those in Oklahoma. More Modocs returned to Oregon in the early 1900s than stayed at the Quapaw Agency, bringing an even higher number of Modocs to the West. Population statistics in 1905 show fifty-six Modocs in Oklahoma and 223 in Oregon. Those families that remained in Oklahoma represented seven families originally sent back as exiles. One significant Modoc death occurred in 1913. Martha Lawver, the incredible storyteller with whom Jeremiah Curtin worked in 1884, died at around ninety-five years of age and was buried in the Oklahoma Modoc Cemetery.[135]

At the turn of the century, the Seneca Indian School, some seven miles from Seneca, Missouri, was open to any American Indian in the United States. But most of the students came from the local Quapaw Agency. The Indian boarding school was much like the Yainax Indian School in Oregon, which Modoc children attended.

Arnold Richardson, born in 1906, spent his entire life in the

Seneca-Miami area, and although not of American Indian descent, he knew the Modocs well. He was made an honorary member of the Modoc Tribe of Oklahoma on his 100th birthday in 2006. He believes that the Indian school students "had a better education than the rest of us. The school was self-supporting. I remember they used to butcher their own hogs. Out of every tribe there came some highly skilled musicians and artists from that school."

Richardson's daughter Oma (after Oklahoma) Potts was born in 1928. She says the students coming out of the Seneca Indian School were "so far ahead of us when they went into high school. They were sharp with fractions and anything involving math."[136]

Clyde L. James (1900 - 1982)
His daughter, author Cheewa, possesses a button from the uniform he is wearing.

Clyde James, born in 1900, grandson of Shacknasty Jim, entered the Seneca Indian School at six years of age. There were over one hundred students at that time. Boys, for dressy occasions, wore military uniforms with brass buttons that had a U. S. eagle and "U. S. Indian Service" in raised letters. James talked about the school attire in a television interview in 1981.[137] "We dressed in uniforms during certain occasions. The flag was raised. We would march to school, to dinner," he remembered. "All the boys looked alike. The girls did, too."

James baked bread, scrubbed floors, and made beds in dormitories that had some fifty beds in a room. "As a kid, I mean a little chap, I had to get up at 4:00 in the morning to help milk the cows." He always felt that his years in the Indian school gave him discipline and a work ethic.

One of the punishments for misbehavior was to darn socks on Saturday afternoon instead of going into town. James admitted that he got pretty good at darning socks, "and could do it yet today." Another punishment at the Wyandotte Indian School was picking plantain, a green weedy plant. "We had to dig those up, the number depending on the severity of the misconduct. We got smart towards the end and instead of dumping them like we were supposed to, we hid them, kept them watered down, then the next time someone was punished they would dig out of the gunny sack what they needed.

It was kind of cheating, but it worked."

One common occurrence in the Indian boarding school was children running away. "No one liked to be away from home. We were taken in the first years of our life." He remembered one time when he and two of his cousins, older than he was, took off for the cousins' farm, some ten miles away. "It got dark and I played out. I was just a little boy. They had to carry me most of the way." James remembered how frightened he was of "wild animals we could hear yowling. I think my hair stood straight up." They made it home, but the next morning when they got up, "there was the buckboard, with two horses, sitting out front. They came from school to pick us up and take us right back. This happened day after day. Different kids, but all headed home."[138]

Wilma Bellm, the grandaughter of U. S. Grant, was born in 1916. At five years of age, she entered the Indian school and rarely went home. Her three brothers were also enrolled. Wilma made it clear in later years to her son Jack Shadwick that she would never send her children there. She felt this way, he thought, because of the rigid routine and schedule that had to be followed. Not only was her uniform regulation, but her haircut, too.

Wilma especially remembered getting her tonsils out. It was done without anesthesia. Having tonsils removed was standard procedure for everyone in the school. It was believed tonsil removal prevented infection and colds. Wilma was placed in a dental chair. They opened her mouth and snipped out her tonsils.[139]

Oklahoma Modoc Life

From the first days in Oklahoma Indian Territory, the small group of Modocs had been accepted and held in high esteem by agency personnel, other Indians, and citizens of the near-by communities. Thus, a pattern of successful adjustment to a condition of forced or directed change was established.

Intermarriage with non-Modocs was common for Oklahoma Modocs. That was because there was a great degree of contact between Modocs, non-Indians, and other Indian groups. The Modocs in Oregon, by contrast, were more isolated from the non-Indian community. There also seemed to be less prejudice against Indians by non-Indians in the Oklahoma area as contrasted to Oregon.[140]

Jack Shadwick (9/13/37)
Great-grandson of U. S. Grant,
grandson of Ruth Grant Bellm.

Ben Lawver, Minnie Robbins, Wilma Bellm (and her son Jack), and Clark James (and his children, Clyde and Viola), married non-Indians. Etta and Charles Stanley had adjoining land allotments. Etta was Modoc and Charles was Peoria. Once married, in the late 1900s, the two joined their land, built on Stanley's land, and raised five children.

A letter from the Department of the Interior (United States Indian Service, Seneca School and Quapaw Agency), dated Dec. 8, 1916, to Daniel Clinton read:

> In the name of O. M. McPherson, Chairman of the Competency Board, I present to you a purse and a citizen button, also copy of ritual which declares you to be a full citizen of the United States in as much as you have received a patent in fee for your allotment of Indian land on the Modoc Reserve.[141]

These letters went out to every adult Oklahoma Modoc. Clyde L. James remembered his father's button, which read "Citizen of the United States." James spoke with obvious pride that Oklahoma Modocs became citizens. He talked of his father who could then "go in any bar or store without any trouble and buy alcohol." When he returned to the Klamath Reservation in 1939, he found that neither he, nor any other Indian on the Klamath Reservation, could buy liquor.[142]

Last Voice of the Modoc War

Jennie Clinton was the last survivor of the Modoc War. A dedicated Modoc pastor, Jennie for many years traveled throughout the reservation sharing the word of the Quakers and extending care where needed. She was a Modoc icon on the Klamath Reservation. In her later years, when she was not able to travel as easily, many people came to her.

Viola Hayworth, great-granddaughter of Old Sheepy, as a small girl in the late 1920s, would often stay for several days at a time with Jennie. She and Jennie would take wocus seeds, from the water plant that was a staple for the ancestral Modocs, and make a meal. Rather than grind it as the old Modocs did, they just cooked the wocus seeds like rice or cereal and then topped it with milk and sugar. Jennie liked foods from her childhood. "When Jennie could get someone to take her," Hayworth remembers, "she would go back to northern California, the Lost River country, and pick wild plums and epos."[143]

In her later years, Jennie was blind. Even after losing her sight, she was known for her leather craft and beading work. Hayworth still owns a purse made by Jennie. Helen Crume Smith, a descendent of Schonchin John, remembers "the moccasins Jennie made for me. Even though she was blind, the patterns of her beadwork were always neat, and the moccasins always fit. We would talk to her for ages and she told stories. She was fabulous."

When Jennie could no longer go to the Quakers and their meetings, they came to her. Pastor Tuning and his wife, Virena, visited Jennie regularly, often bringing their daughter Jo Anne. Jo Anne recollects the time they went to Jennie's to get buckskin pouches with beading around the edges that Jennie had made for the Tuning children. "As it turned out, Jennie thought there were only three of us, instead of four, and since I was the oldest, my mother decided I should give mine up. I could have kicked my mother!"[144]

Minnie Robbins and her granddaughter Coke used to visit Jennie often, as so many of the Modocs who had once lived in Oklahoma Indian Territory did. Coke reminisces over their trips from Sprague River to Jennie's house near the Williamson River on the western side of the Klamath Reservation. "It wasn't an easy trip. Grandma didn't have a car but she always got around—the mail truck or school bus. Once we got to Aunt Pearl's, she would take us on to Jennie's." Robbins continued to visit faithfully. Minnie died in 1955 at the age of seventy-seven.[145]

Modoc rancher and rodeo rider Harold Wright would often go over to Jennie's house and cut her wood. Using her handle pump, he would fill her buckets with water and bring them into the house. "She would always give me a piece of cake or whatever she had. We didn't have old folks' homes. We were a real community and took care of each other."

Throughout the early and mid-1940s, Clyde L. James, wife Luella, and three children, including the author, visited Jennie on Sunday afternoons. Jennie sat on the porch of her weather-beaten, one-room house with the three children at her feet. She pulled out her Bible, turned to the appropriate page and following the text with her finger, she would "read" to the James children. Knowing her eyesight was going, she had in the years before memorized vast portions of the Bible.

The children would listen patiently but always were anxious for her to end because they knew what she had for them. Finished, she would snap the Bible shut, open the door and shuffle over to her bed. From underneath the bed she pulled out an ancient leather trunk with a strap around it. She always had a struggle undoing the strap, with all three children wishing she could move a bit faster, and finally pulled from its depths a bag of candy from the Williamson Store. To three small children, it was the highlight of Sunday trips to see Aunt Jennie.

Jennie always claimed that during the war, a large amount of gold, saddles, and other valuables had been hidden in a cave in what had become the Lava Beds National Monument, California, some seventy miles south of the Klamath Reservation. Although totally blind, she assured Clyde that if he would drive her down, she could give him directions to the cave. She remembered the landmarks and felt that her blindness would not hinder her.

The selected day for the cave search came—some seventy years after the Modoc War had ended. Jennie and Clyde began the drive by car to the Lava Beds National Monument with anticipation and excitement. Jennie told him once again of how in great panic and haste, she and other Modocs had carried everything into the cave and sealed the cache when they were done.

Then the day began to change. The wind kicked up and black clouds moved over a sky that a short time before was clear and blue. As they approached the Lava Beds, raindrops pelted the windshield. The sky opened up. With limited visibility and whipping wind, the decision was made to return to the reservation and try for a better day.

The location of the cave went with Jennie to her grave in 1950. She was ninety-one. She is buried in the Schonchin Cemetery. With Jennie Clinton's death, the last voice of the Modoc War was gone.

Sharing and Caring

During the 1940s, Sprague River had a community pigpen. People shared responsibilities in taking care of the pigs. When they needed pork, they took their share. Helen Crume Smith remembers the pigpen. It was a community playpen for her. "My brother Melbern Walker would get in the pen, grab a baby pig, and throw it over the fence so I could play with it. We were careful to always put the pig back."[146]

Harold Wright recalls when WWII brought rationing and hardship to the reservation:

> Things were needed overseas. Servicemen needed things first. Beef was hard to come by then, so those of us who were hunters would go out after deer. Clyde James had returned by then, and he and I would ride together. We'd shoot the deer, throw them over a horse, bring them in, cut them up, and distribute venison to anyone on the reservation who had a need.
>
> I remember one particular day when we had hunted long and hard. It was late and darkness settled in. We were zig-zagging up a hill with the horses loaded with deer. On an especially steep part, one of the pack horses carrying two deer lost his footing and slid all the way to the bottom, rolling over a couple times. That was a tense time. But that horse stood right back up at the bottom of the hill. We dragged the deer out to the nearest road with ropes. The horse had done his work.
>
> We'd make jerky by placing strips of venison on a screen made out of chicken wire, build up hot coals, and then throw willow or mahogany bark on the smudge fire. The jerky would slowly cook. We'd pass the jerky out, too, to reservation folk who needed it.[147]

The Puzzle of Curley Headed Jack's Remains

At the close of the 1873 Modoc War, a weary band of Modoc prisoners of war were moved from Boyle's Camp (sometimes known as Peninsula Camp), located near the Modoc War battlefield, to Ft. Klamath, Oregon. They left on Friday, June 13. On the following Sunday, June 15, Curley Headed Jack, one of the Modoc warriors involved in the killing of Lt. William Sherwood in April 1873 shot himself in the head. Fearing a death sentence for killing the lieutenant, Curley Headed Jack opted to die in his Lost River homeland. He was buried near the Natural Bridge that same day.[148]

As a result of the 1989 National Museum of the American Indian Act, the Smithsonian Institution began repatriating the remains of Indians. Risa Diemond Arbolino, an anthropologist at the Museum of Natural History, assigned to connect skeletal remains and funerary objects to present-day tribes, found a letter with human remains No. 42109:

> These are the bones of Curly Head Jack, who died June 8, while encamped at Lost River, a prisoner with the Modoc Indians en route from the peninsula on the Tule Lake to Fort Klamath.

The letter was written by Army Surgeon Edwin Bentley.[149]

Erwin Thompson in *Modoc War: Its Military History and Topography* has this listing: "Bentley, Edwin, Asst. Surgeon, USA. Took charge of general field hospital, May 25, 1873".[150]

According to newspaper reports and military records, Curley Headed Jack was very much alive on June 8. However, it was on this date that four Modoc prisoners of war, Tee-Hee Jack, Mooch, Pony, and Little John, traveling with several other Modocs, including women and children, from the west side of the battlefield en route to the hospital for treatment, were shot to death in the back of a wagon. There was speculation that Oregon vigilantes had committed the murder. There is no record as to what happened to the four bodies.[151]

The Oregonian article concludes:

> All agree the Modocs wept, thinking Curly Headed Jack had been buried. But in fact, the Army surgeon shipped his body to the Army Medical Museum in Washington, D.C., where his head was cut off and lost.

But the date and name do not match. Did the Army surgeon put the wrong name on the remains? Or did he have the wrong date? History has buried the truth.

Ulysses S. Grant and Grandchildren
*(Left to right) Ruth Grant Bellm (1892 - 1920), Ana Greenback, Ulysses S.
Grant "Akekis" (fought in the Modoc War), Charlie "Jock" Robbins
(Photo courtesy of Jack Shadwick)*

James Family - 1906
*Viola James Fryatt (1898 - 1975), Irish immigrant mother
Lydia Marvella Burns James (1875 - 1938), Clyde L. James,
(1900 - 1982), father of author Cheewa.*

**Klamath Reservation
Dignitaries**
*(Back, left to right)
Oliver C. Applegate,
prominent in Modoc
War; Jeff Riddle, son of
Toby Riddle; Chaplain
C. C. Hulet.
(Front, left to right)
Klamath Reservation
Indian policemen David
Chock-toot and Watson
Duffy, nephew of
Bogus Charley.
(Photo courtesy of
Klamath County
Museum)*

Jennie Clinton
*(1859 - 1950)
Last survivor of the
Modoc War, with
(standing) Clyde S.
(Sonny Jim) James
(12/28/1940), Viola
James Colombe
(8/23/1942), and
(seated) author
Cheewa Patricia James
(5/15/1939).*

Chapter 11
The Closing Chapters

The Lava Beds National Monument was established in 1925, permanently preserving the rugged terrain and landmarks of the 1873 Modoc War. Approximately 46,500 acres in northern California, with the California/Oregon border as a northern boundary, were set aside. The purpose for establishment was to protect and interpret the rich geologic, cultural, historical, and natural resources of the area. Major historical Modoc War sites are marked today.[148]

A dramatic event in the history of the Klamath Reservation came in 1954 with the passage of Public Law 587, terminating the Klamath Reservation. Some 1l8 million acres were taken by condemnation. This ended the Klamath Tribe as a federally recognized entity. The official language of the law read, "to provide for the termination of Federal supervision over the trust and restricted property of the Klamath Tribe of Indians consisting of the Klamath and Modoc Tribes and the Yahooskin Band of Snake Indians, and of the individual members thereof."[149]

Cheewa (Patricia Easterla) James, U. S. National Park Service Ranger-Interpreter, Lava Beds National Monument, CA., summers - 1979 and 1980.

The Modocs in Oklahoma, who were enrolled on the Klamath Reservation, and the Modocs in Oregon, who both lived on and were enrolled on the Klamath Reservation, were no longer legally classified as American Indians. The two groups of Modocs now had one major thing in common. Federal supervision over both groups was terminated.

The Klamath roll officially closed on August 14, 1954, and "no child born thereafter shall be eligible for enrollment." Just prior to

Oklahoma Flood, July 3, 2007
*A devastating flood in Miami, Oklahoma, put the Modoc Tribe of Oklahoma
tribal headquarters under water. The building was subsequently razed.
Being the tribe that wouldn't die, tribal offices were rebuilt in 2008.
(Photo courtesy of Ben Barnes)*

The Stables
*A joint venture of the Modoc Tribe of Oklahoma and the
Miami Tribe of Oklahoma, this off-track betting facility has national
simulcasts of top thoroughbred horse races, high stakes bingo, and
electronic games. It opened in September, 1998. (Photo by Cheewa James)*

the closing of the rolls, a census showed a total of 2,086 enrolled members. The census was not broken down as to how many were enrolled in each of the three tribal groups. But the Modocs were certainly a smaller percentage.

The government purchased approximately 15,000 acres of the Klamath Marsh, the heart of the former reservation, to establish a migratory bird refuge. The government also purchased large forested portions of the former Klamath Reservation. This forest land became part of the Winema National Forest. By these two purchases, the government became the owner of approximately 70 percent of the former reservation lands. The balance of the reservation went into both private Indian and non-Indian, ownership either through allotment or sale of reservation lands at the time of termination.

As a result of this legislation all members of the Klamath Tribes had the choice of being removed from the rolls and terminated with a cash settlement or remaining and having the United States National Bank of Oregon manage their undivided share in the tribal lands. The latter group, which numbered only about 470, would receive per capita payments. Most chose the cash settlement. Approximately four years after the passage of Public Law 587, those members received between $43,000 and $45,000 each.[150]

From that point on, the two Modoc groups took different directions.

The Modoc Tribe of Oklahoma

The Modoc Tribe of Oklahoma is based in Miami, Oklahoma, and has an enrollment of around 200 Modocs. There is no blood quantum required for tribal enrollment, only a proof of ancestry as determined by the tribe. Seventy-one members of the tribe live in Oklahoma, thirty-eight in Missouri, twenty-six in Kansas, and the balance of sixty-six live in twelve other U. S. states.[151]

The Modoc Tribe of Oklahoma, established an unofficial tribal government in 1967. The Oklahoma Modocs joined the Intertribal Council, Inc. of Northeastern Oklahoma, a 301 (c) 3 nonprofit corporation, in 1968. The Inter-tribal Council consists of eight

Bill Follis – Chief, Modoc Tribe of Oklahoma, 1978 - present.

of the old Quapaw Agency tribes: Eastern Shawnee, Miami, Ottawa, Peoria, Quapaw, Seneca-Cayuga, and Wyandotte.

The purpose of the council is both external—"to enlighten the public towards a better understanding of the Native American race"—and internal—"to enhance...economic opportunities...health, education and welfare of Native Americans residing within the service area of ITC."[152]

Modoc Tribe of Oklahoma logo

The Modocs in Oklahoma were restored to federal recognition in May, 1978, eligible for all benefits established for qualified American Indians by the U. S. government. In that year Bill Follis, great-grandson of Modoc warrior Long Jim, became the first federally recognized chief of the Modoc Tribe of Oklahoma in ninety-eight years. Bogus Charley in 1880 had been the last official chief. Follis remains the chief as of 2008. The tribal council is made up of five tribal members, elected every four years.

In a joint casino venture with the Miami Tribe of Oklahoma, the Modoc Tribe of Oklahoma operates The Stables. This casino offers off-track horse race betting, electronic bingo, slot machines, and other games. It is said that on Kentucky Derby day, Miami is packed to the brim with people—motels filled, highways clogged, and the town bustling. Red Cedar Recycling is a tribally operated non-profit business collecting paper and plastic products. Other enterprises include a flooring company, technology services, personnel and bookkeeping management, and a smoke shop.[153]

Although the tribe has no cultural ties to the buffalo, they now own a herd of over 100 buffalo. The herd supports a meat processing business that was started in 1994 with eight buffalo. A major emphasis in building the buffalo herd, in the words of Tribal Land Manager Phil Follis, Chief Follis's son, is "to work towards the restoration of cultural and spiritual integrity of the bison."[154]

Education is of high priority with the Modoc Tribe of Oklahoma, and fellowships are offered to tribal members for higher education and other academic pursuits. Some two and a half million dollars has been given since October 1995 to community families and providers, including over a half million dollars in grants to local daycares, schools, and libraries. Tribal members also benefit from programs such as home energy.[155]

The Klamath Tribes

The Klamath Tribes is based in Chiloquin, Oregon, and has an enrollment of around 3500. It consists of the same original three Indian groups. Modocs still only make up a small percentage of the tribe. All persons whose names appear on the final roll as of midnight, August 13, 1954, before termination, are automatically enrolled members, although an individual can be enrolled in only one federally recognized tribe. Those born after that date must have one-quarter blood of at least one of the three Indian groups.

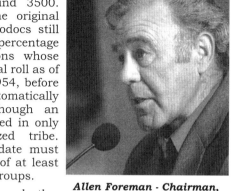

Allen Foreman - Chairman, Klamath Tribes, 1998 – 2007.
(Photo by Taylor David)

Minor provisions paved the way for restoration of the Klamath Tribes. The U. S. Supreme Court ruled in 1974 that Klamath fishing and hunting rights granted by treaty survived the termination process. Another legal victory in 1979 guaranteed minimum stream flows in the Klamath River to protect fish and wildlife.

Klamath Tribes logo

Federal recognition and restoration came to the Klamath Tribes in 1986, eight years after the Modoc Tribe of Oklahoma had been restored. Provisions read: "The tribe and its members shall be eligible, on and after August 27, 1986, for all Federal services and benefits furnished to federally recognized Indian tribes or their members without regard to the existence of a reservation for the tribe."[156]

Directed to compose a plan to regain economic self-sufficiency, the plan reflected the Klamath Tribes' commitment to play a pivotal role in the local economy. The Klamath Tribes opened the doors to Kla-Mo-Ya Casino in 1997, the first enterprise in the forty-five years since termination.

The casino name is an acronym of the three tribes that form the Klamath Tribes. Built over forty acres along the Williamson River, the casino is four miles from Chiloquin and twenty-two miles from Klamath Falls. The casino provides jobs for approximately 150 individuals, 60% of whom are members of the

Joe Kirk - Chairman,
Klamath Tribes, 2007 - present.
(Photo by Karen Weatherby)

Klamath Tribes or other tribes. The goal of the Klamath Tribes is to make Kla-Mo-Ya a premiere resort destination with the addition of a hotel and other lodging. Thousands of dollars have been contributed by the casino to community, youth, education, and Native American charities and activities. Beginning in 2007, benefit checks went to tribal members.

The tribe provides health and family services and drug and alcohol abuse support. College, adult training, and employment assistance is available. The Natural Resources Management Department of the tribe works to protect the fish, wildlife, and natural habitat of the reservation. The Culture and Heritage Department programs are designed to preserve the traditional cultures and values of the three tribes.[157]

Two major celebrations bring the tribe together each year in fun, social interaction, and a rememberance of days past. The Spirit of Captain Jack Pow-wow and Rodeo is held in Klamath Falls over the Memorial Day weekend. The annual Restoration Celebration, commemorating the restoration of the tribes in 1986, is held in Chiloquin the fourth weekend in August.

Allen Foreman, a Modoc descended from Old Sheepy of the Hot Creek band of Modocs, served as tribal chairman from 1998 to 2007. Joe Kirk, who also has Modoc blood, took the tribal reins in May 2007. Ten members make up the tribal council and are elected every three years.[158]

Quaker Churches

The last service in the Modoc Friends Church in Oklahoma was held in 1978. The church adjoins the Modoc Cemetery. After tribal recognition in 1978, the Modoc Tribe of Oklahoma applied to the U. S. Department of Housing and Urban Development to purchase the church and the four acres on which it stands from the Society of Friends. The tribe sought to restore the church to its original structure. Funding fell short, but an additional $24,000 grant from the Oklahoma Historical Society allowed purchase and restoration of the church.

The Modoc Friends Church and Cemetery were placed on the National Register of Historic Sites in 1980, the first site so designated in Ottawa County, Oklahoma. The official dedication was celebrated on June 10, 1984.[159]

The Sprague River Friends Community Church, built by a joint effort of Modocs and Quakers, was dedicated in 1926 in Sprague River, Oregon. The church occupies the same building today. It is operational under the leadership of Pastor Robert Adams and has a membership of approximately twenty-five. Church membership no longer includes any Modocs.[160]

Alice Lawver, the Quaker missionary instrumental in the building of the church and in keeping Quakerism alive among the Modocs, died in Klamath Falls, Oregon, in 1968, at the age of ninety-two. Many of her children, grandchildren, and great-grandchildren, all with Modoc blood, live in the Klamath area.[161]

Last Four Modocs to Return Home

After the hanging of Captain Jack and three other Modocs on October 3, 1873, the four heads were surgically removed and shipped in barrels to Washington, D. C.'s Army Medical Museum. They were moved in 1904 to the Smithsonian Institution, the United States' national museum. Stamped across the forehead of each skull was a number: 1018, Captain Jack; 1019, Schonchin John; 1020, Boston Charley; 1021, Black Jim.[162]

J. Lawrence Angel, the curator of physical anthropology, Smithsonian Department of Anthropology, in a letter dated February 25, 1974, to the *Klamath Falls Herald and News* explained that:

> ...in accord with ethics and practices of that time, many Indian and other remains in the Army Medical Museum before 1900 were collected after executions....Today, in an extremely different ethical atmosphere, we show our respect for the first people of our land by trying to recreate their lives and times.

Angel's studies show the skulls having the front of the faces flattened to achieve the "flat face" look, desirable among Modocs. He found evidence of sharp childhood sickness or starvation in the late 1830s or early 1840s. He also found verification of past poor nutrition "possibly from the stressful winters of hide-and-seek with General Canby's forces."[163]

The *Herald and News* article made mention of Smithsonian Acting Secretary Robert A. Brooks' comment that "requests from a relative of any of the victims might result in release of the skulls."

That's exactly what happened. In 1974 Don "Duck" Schonchin, a descendant of Schonchin John, received permission to take possession of the skulls. His mission ended tragically. While in Washington, D. C. to retrieve the skulls, he died of a heart attack.

On July 13, 1983, Klamath Tribe Chairman Charles E. Kimbol, Sr. addressed a letter "To Whom It May Concern." In the letter he expressed the thought that the tribe should not become involved in the return of the skulls but that it should be handled by descendants of the four Modocs. He gave his support for efforts to return the remains but with this stipulation: "...for proper religious burial."

Deborah L. Riddle Herrera, a descendant of Schonchin John, began the quest in 1983 to have the skulls released to her. She had the support of several other Schonchin descendants who gave "moral and physical support to Debbie Riddle Herrera to retrieve the four Modoc men...and give them traditional, cultural, and hereditary burial in a designated area."

Herrera also had the support of the Klamath County Museum, the Klamath County Historical Society, and other organizations and officials. The Klamath County Board of Commissioners, in a July 15, 1983 letter to the Smithsonian Institution, said it had "identified the religious reasons, and supports personal family comfort that will result when you assist Debbie in bringing her ancestral remains to their proper burial place."[164]

Smithsonian Institution shipping invoice, registrar file No. ACC 321090, showed "two packages containing 4 Modoc skulls packed 2 per box, No. 1018 - 1021." The skulls were released to Debbie Herrera on June 26, 1984.[165]

A *Klamath Falls Herald and News* article shortly after that date reported the return of the skulls. J. Lawrence Angel of the Smithsonian stated, "I think it's proper at this time that people should know. We kept it strictly confidential—no information at all. The Herreras wanted it that way." He also said that Herrera "indicated the skulls would be re-buried, but does not know what has happened since June."

Several requests by the Klamath Tribe were made in the years following, requesting information from Herrera on the skulls. A January 3, 1994, letter from Chairman Thomas J. Ball, Klamath Tribes, reads:

> It has been brought to the attention of the General Council of the Klamath Tribes that those remains either have not been properly administered to in terms of burial or these remains have been neglected and left unattended. Concerned direct-line descendants want to know how their ancestral remains have been administered to. Also, some of these direct-line descendants do not feel that they have authorized giving any one individual the responsibility to take on this sacred responsibility.

> Rather than concentrate on rumor and innuendo, I would like to invite you to come forward to inform the Executive Committee and the General Council of the Klamath Tribes of what you know about the situation.

There was a follow-up letter to Herrera on February 7, 1994, from the new Klamath Tribes Chairman Marvin Garcia reminding her that the skulls "are a concern of the General Council and will continue to be pursued until it is resolved."[166]

Herrera refused to meet with tribal officials to provide any information. A letter from Herrera, along with the letters from Ball and Garcia, appeared in the February/March 1994 issue of the Klamath tribal newspaper, *The Klamath News.*

> I will remind you that the disposition of my ancestors' remains has never been of interest to the Klamath Tribe as you now suggest it is. In fact, the Tribe was requested on more than one occasion by the Smithsonian Institute to repatriate the remains.[167]

The battle between tribe and the keeper of the skulls was never resolved. The last chapter of the Modoc War is not yet written.

Epilogue

With no knowledge of where the last remains of the Modoc war chief, Captain Jack, and the other three leaders from 1873 rest, Modocs, and others who care, will have to honor them in an inward way. The significance of these men has grown. They represent many lives. They symbolize the massive struggle of a people who wouldn't give up, despite the odds. Their story parallels the chronicles of many Native people of America, who are united in spirit and memories of days gone by.

The waves of rebellion stirred in history by the Modocs have long ago been quelled. The intricate culture these people created is indistinct and faint in the swirl of time. The once mighty voices of the Modocs are silent.

Yet even as parts of the Modoc world died, Modocs themselves refused to die. They were possessed of a spirit that was bold yet flexible, proud but accepting. They kept their strength of mind open to life even as death constantly dogged their trail.

The Modocs were a solid, enduring people of great history. They had tenacious staying power over thousands of years. That tenacity carried them through years of unrest, war, and then disease.

The bloods of many cultures and nations mingle in the veins of Modocs today. That mixing of bloods speaks to an appreciation of uniqueness and a spirit of tolerance for all people.

As long as the heart and soul of a people have tolerance, tenacity, and boldness, they will never die.

Clyde S. "Sonny Jim" James.
(1940 -)
*All-Around Indian Cowboy 1969 and 1970. World Champion Indian
Bareback Rider, 1970. World Champion Indian Steer Wrestler, 1982.
Great-grandson of Shacknasty Jim and brother of author.*

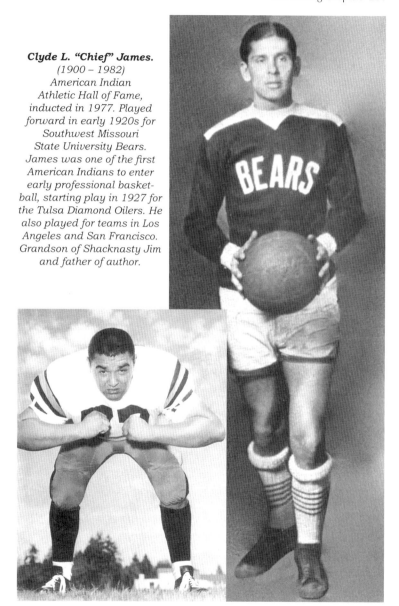

Clyde L. "Chief" James.
(1900 – 1982)
American Indian
Athletic Hall of Fame,
inducted in 1977. Played
forward in early 1920s for
Southwest Missouri
State University Bears.
James was one of the first
American Indians to enter
early professional basket-
ball, starting play in 1927 for
the Tulsa Diamond Oilers. He
also played for teams in Los
Angeles and San Francisco.
Grandson of Shacknasty Jim
and father of author.

Orville "Ram" Lawver, Jr. *(1936 – 2000)*
Green Bay Packers, 1959 - 1960. Coached and taught at the Chemawa
Indian School, Salem, Oregon, 1963 - 1995. Lawver Stadium at that school
was dedicated to him in 2000. Grandson of Ben and Alice Lawver.

Appendix
Ancestral Modocs
by Cheewa James

Primitive Pragmatists by Verne F. Ray (1963, University of Washington Press) was used as a reference for "The Ancestral Modocs." Ray's ethnographic account is based on original field research done in 1934 by Ray and five students.

Informants on the Klamath Reservation included Sally George, Usee George, Peter Schonchin, Lizzie Schonchin, Evaline Schonchin, Celia Lynch, Elmer Lynch, Cora Lynch, Jennie Clinton, Anderson Faithful, Mary Chiloquin, Stonewall Jackson, and Arthur Chester.

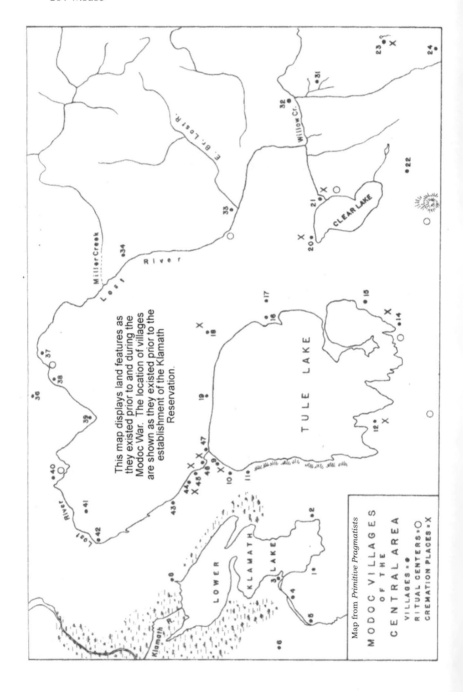

This map displays land features as they existed prior to and during the Modoc War. The location of villages are shown as they existed prior to the establishment of the Klamath Reservation.

Map from *Primitive Pragmatists*

MODOC VILLAGES
OF THE
CENTRAL AREA

VILLAGES = ●
RITUAL CENTERS = ○
CREMATION PLACES = X

Chapter One
In the Beginning

How good I have felt when the sun has shone on me and warmed me on a cold day. You are our great sun. Thank you for your care.

Modoc prayer

— A Child's Life —

Ku-cin's tule doll was her pride and joy. It seldom left the soft-spoken Modoc girl's side. She had made it herself when she was just seven years old. She was now nine, and the year was 1670.

The Modoc land was one of lakes and rivers, and it was in those waters that the tall water plant known as the tule could be found in abundance. Tule Lake was named for the plant. The tule reeds were softened in water so they were easy to weave. Even so, making her doll had been a difficult thing to do as the reeds slipped so easily from the girl's tiny fingers.

There had been times when she had wanted to throw the whole thing away. But praise was a powerful motivator for Modoc children. So she had worked hard to make every strand tight and straight. Her care had brought great rewards. Her mother had been proud, so very proud.

Ku-cin hoped that her fingers would become more and more skilled at basket weaving as she grew older. She knew that her ability to learn the art of basketry was important as she moved toward taking an active role in her Modoc band. Already she was starting to weave solid, well-rounded beginnings to her baskets— a sign that the basket sides would rise as they should. Often her friends would have basket races to see who could weave the fastest. The loser was always considered a poor achiever.

She was content to play with her doll, bending the doll over the river now and then for a sip of water. Ku-cin was like a happy little brown beaver, occasionally slipping into the water to cool herself and enjoy the feel of the clear water on her skin. She wore a discarded skin of a water snake around her arm. This was known to be a magical aid to swimming, and Ku-cin was eager to get all the help she could. She was a strong swimmer and loved to beat any of the children who challenged her to a swimming match.

The last time she had come down to the river, a swarm of butterflies engulfed her, spinning in a myriad of colors, up and down. The sky seemed to fill with them. She sucked in her breath, afraid to breathe at the wonder of it and feeling absolutely magical as the color swirled around her. The wings of the butterflies occasionally brushed her cheek, and when that happened, Ku-cin felt sure it was Kumookumts blessing her. When one butterfly actually landed on her, she knew something special was happening. She wasn't exactly sure how this god worked, but she knew her father put great faith in Kumookumts. The prayers during the hunting season seemed to work. She could hardly wait to ask her father if she had been blessed that day. It felt like it.

When Ku-cin was born, one of her parents, as was the Modoc custom, remained awake throughout the night to be with the newborn infant—who as custom dictated had been powdered with finely pulverized white clay. When Ku-cin was only a few weeks old, she had been placed in a cradleboard. A pad of folded buckskin had been tied high across her forehead. The binding had resulted in a flattening of her head. The care taken to flatten her head made it obvious that she had parents who cared very deeply that she would grow into an acceptable and beautiful woman.

A girl living near Ku-cin had never had her head bound. She often wore a tule basket hat to hide the deficiency. But everyone knew why she wore the hat.

Ku-cin's thoughts drifted to the girl with the round head. She felt sorry for her. Ku-cin was grateful for the family she had. Earlier in the day she had played with her father, who had rolled her around in the grass, tickling her and making her laugh. Like most Modoc children, she received nearly all of her hugs and holding from her father, more than from her mother. Fathers had more time than mothers, Ku-cin understood. There was much work for a woman to do to keep her family fed and provided for. Her father often cared for Ku-cin and her brothers.

Her father had been especially pleased when she brought back, in her small burden basket, mud hen and duck eggs from the swampy places in the lake. He had given her a small bead necklace for her successful foray. He had also promised Ku-cin that he would go with her next time. They hoped to bring back Ku-cin's favorite food, the wonderful delicacy known as bol'ooqs, duck embryos.

Ku-cin especially loved the times in the evenings when her dad and other adults told myths and anecdotes relating to Modoc tradition and culture. She was a smart little girl and knew that when adults were telling stories, they weren't just amusing the young ones. It wasn't just coincidence that there was always a lesson about behavior and ethics. Ku-cin was most willing to get whatever message she was supposed to because the stories were so good—great stories that stirred her imagination and spirit.

Respect and obedience to all adults, relatives or strangers, were strongly emphasized, and the act of lying was condemned. Advice was frequently given regarding relationships with others and not fighting with other children.

With a little shudder, Ku-cin remembered a time she had been belligerent and outspoken to her mother. Sometimes a child was punished by being given very little to eat. But in this case, the punishment was more severe, and Ku-cin was placed in the sweathouse with the entrance blocked. The hot stones covered with water made the environment very uncomfortable, and Ku-cin truly wasn't sure she would come out alive. Now, she gave a little chuckle at the memory, and she watched her tongue a little more carefully.

It was a happy life, in a culture that went back for centuries. Ku-cin was glad she was who she was, and with that thought, she placed the doll carefully on the bank and slipped once again into the water.

* * * * * *

The early territory of the Modoc people, stretching back to ancient times, was on both sides of what is now the California-Oregon border, immediately east of the Cascade Range. The Modocs were spread over considerable territory, with about 5,000 square miles of hunting range. The semi-nomadic Modocs ranged in the summers from the foothills of Mount Shasta in California to Goose Lake on the Oregon-Idaho border.

The Modocs were located to the south of the Klamath Indians, a much larger tribe. The name "Modoc" is believed to be of Klamath tribal origin and means "people to the south." The sharing of a language and frequent intermarriage resulted in a fairly amicable relationship between the two tribes, although animosities occasionally surfaced.

The Modocs were a small group. Before 1800, reliable estimates are that they numbered only 400 to 800 people. Modoc tribal territory was divided into three geographic areas. Modocs identified themselves by these designations. The Gumbatwas were "people of the west," meaning west of Tule Lake. All bands living to the east, except for the lower valley of Lost River, were Kokiwas, "people of the far out country." The Modocs of Lost River Valley were Paskanwas, "river people."

Every man and woman had a basic affiliation to one of these groups. This was determined by primary or earliest long-term place of residence and usually reflected family and kinship ties. These group names were used by Modocs when greeting one another.

The formal greeting was, "What is your people?" The answer: "I am Gumbatwas. And you?"

Governing by Consensus

There was never a tribal government in the ancestral life of the Modocs. Only in times of war might they unite under a war leader. Modocs lived in autonomous bands or villages consisting of ten to forty or more people. In the latter half of the nineteenth century, approximately fifty bands were identified. These individual bands lived along the shores of Tule Lake and the rivers and other tributaries flowing into the lake. Families averaged five people. Each band governed itself, headed by the *la`qi*, which in the native tongue means, most appropriately, "leader." The *la`qi* was a domestic advisor, not authoritarian in any sense of the word. Bands also had religious leaders or shamans.

Although men held the position of *la`qi*, women had a say in the affairs of the band. Consensus of the people was the final ruling in Modoc society, so the ability to persuade others was considered a great asset in a person. Modocs did not consider silence golden. Rather, the silver tongue was a desired trait, and the top talker of a Modoc band was often the *la`qi*.

The *la`qi* was more like the chair of a committee than a ruler or despot. He could be deposed at any time by simple voice consensus. He was in every sense an instrument of the people, there to do their bidding and fulfill their desires. Modocs were one of America's first democracies, although voting was rare. More commonly the *la`qi* kept his ear to the ground and was aware of where public opinion rested.

Because a *la`qi* was selected by consensus, positive psychological traits and strong ethics were important individual characteristics for a man selected to lead. Patience, diplomacy, altruism, control of temper and jealousy—these all were important character traits for a *la`qi*.

An important legal mechanism of the Modocs was the assembly. The assembly recognized democratic principles and the strength of the majority. Any matter that concerned the community came before the assembly. Assemblies could be called for a specific reason but more often were held regularly as a peacekeeping, unification function. Although the meetings were informal in nature, everyone, regardless of gender and age, was encouraged to participate.

* * * * * *

— Coming Together of the People —

Loldam had spent a relatively lazy morning. Upon awakening earlier, he had smeared his face with dry ashes, soaking up some of the facial oil so that his fingernails could get a solid grip on the sprouting whiskers. It was only when plucking facial hair that Loldam secretly (very secretly!) envied women.

Today being the special day that it was, the day of the assembly, he had parted his hair and arranged it into two clubs, or bundles, at either side of his head. His best hair ties, made of otter fur, swung in front, below his shoulders. Deer fat and bone marrow from the leg bones gave his hair the tidiness and sheen he liked.

He felt that being la`qi in his band meant more than just living up to the qualifications of his office. He had the responsibility to look like a leader, and on this day he looked the part. He swelled his chest at the thought of the community assembly later in the day.

As la`qi, Loldam advised in domestic affairs. Three things were considered when a leader was selected by consensus: wealth, the size of a man's household, and his oratory skills. The latter quality was considered of greatest importance.

Loldam's name translated in Modoc to "North." His father had given the name to him. His father saw the North with its white snow as a match to the silver hair of the elders. Elders represented the collective wisdom of the tribe, and Loldam's father honored and respected knowledge. He was determined that his son be strong of mind, and he had schooled Loldam well—he had drilled Loldam in oratory skills especially. Loldam knew he was highly revered as one who talks well, a man of the silver tongue.

La`qis were expected to have sound judgment and act with promptness in an emergency. Affability and diplomacy were highly desired traits of the selected leader. Modoc society was, after all, based on compromise and consensus. The people followed the advice of the leader if it didn't run counter to firmly held views. Even if it did, argument and oratory sometimes prevailed.

The la`qi terminated disputes, mediated, and negotiated. Loldam received no specific compensation for his services, only what an individual he helped chose to give him as a gift. But Loldam was aware that indirectly he did profit. For example, when hunters returned with an especially large bag, he would often get a more than fair distribution. That made for a nice bonus, but Loldam held the position because he had a sincere desire to serve his band. He had become good at what he did. Quite frankly, Loldam loved his job.

Loldam had been a la`qi for many years. He had made a blunder or two along the way and in early years had tried to place his opinion above those of others. He had come to realize that, in most cases, if people were helped to work things out themselves, they would do a good job.

* * * * * *

Chapter Two
The Land is Our Brother

The banks of the Lost River and the nearby streams were favored grounds for villages and camps. It was here that lush green meadows spread down to the water, providing a pleasant environment for living. The Modocs had at least twenty small, semi-permanent villages used in the winter.

The annual cycle that the Modocs lived was a rigid one simply because survival was dependent on when and where food was available. They were a hard-working, hard-hunting, get-it-done kind of people. Their life related directly to the land, and they understood their environment: how best to use animals and plants for the needs and health of tribal members and yet stay attuned to the surrounding ecosystem.

The Modocs were semi-nomadic: in the winter they inhabited sturdy, well-built houses called *wickiups*, and through the summer they moved around, living in temporary shelters made of brush and willow boughs. As the season changed and snow began to melt, usually in March, winter homes were dismantled. Small, mat-covered houses were built for the elderly or disabled, and throughout the summer, various members of the band would return with food for them. This meant more travel for younger members of the band as they made return trips to care for the band's needy.

The greater part of the band moved in search of food. Fishing villages were established early, usually at locations where fishing efforts were most rewarding. Suckers were the most common species to grace the belly of Modocs. They tasted good and had few bones. When the spawning season came and the suckers ran up from Clear Lake, located to the southeast, the suckers could be scooped up by the basketful. The men fished, and the women cleaned, cooked, and dried the fish. The women, who were wise in the ways of nature's abundance, searched for vegetables. Vegetable gathering occupied major parts of the Modoc woman's days, spring through autumn. Women did the bulk of the manual work in the tribe.

The waterways were good to the Modocs, and continually yielded a wealth of food. Ducks, geese, swans, pelicans, and gulls sought the wetlands. The wocus, or water lily, was a staple in Modoc diet, and its seeds were ground into a fine meal and made into bread. The epos, a wild, nutritious root somewhere between a potato and a carrot, and a mainstay in the Modoc diet, was ready for harvest soon after the spring fishing.

The epos had a very short season—only three or four weeks. The challenge was set by nature. The women worked at top speed, dawn to dusk, to dig from the ground this lifeblood plant of the Modoc. The tubers were collected in conical, open burden baskets. The plant had to be cleaned within three days to avoid spoilage, and then the race was on again. A woman who picked epos quickly and efficiently was prized as a wife.

Late June or early July brought the fields of nutritious, bittersweet camas, a rare and highly valued bulb. In late August huckleberries ripened in the higher elevations for the women to pick.

For the men, the time had come to hunt, which would continue from springtime until the snow fell. Hunters used numerous calls for the game they pursued. A rabbit call was made with the lips, and deer were called using a leaf in the lips and inhaling. Using obsidian, a black volcanic glass, to tip their arrows, Modoc men hunted deer, antelope, big horn sheep, and other animals. There were no great honors for the successful hunter. It was merely a duty that every man was expected to master.

* * * * * *

— A Proud Day to be Modoc —

En-te-as shivered slightly in the fresh summer dawn air. The light was still dim through the heavy tree cover. He felt a thrill run through him. It was going to be a glorious day. This was what life was all about.

En-te-as knew he was a good father and husband. He pulled fish dutifully from the streams and brought home the meat that would sustain his family through the winter. But what he was about to do made him truly Modoc. A feeling of invincibility surged through him. He stopped to savor the moment.

His friend to the left of him gently nudged him in the ribs. "Hey, dreamer, wake up," K'-amps-so taunted him. "You're the one who's convinced we'll get the grizzly. So you'd better be alert."

Searching out, confronting, and finally killing this

*powerful animal was as much a matter of sport as it
was a fulfillment of economic duty among the Modoc.
The six men with En-te-as had tracked the grizzly
through the pre-dawn hours, but now they separated
and scattered into the low brush as they silently
resumed tracking the giant bear. They knew they were
getting closer to him.*

*Much as his blood thrilled to the hunt, En-te-as hoped
that when night came, the day's search for the grizzly
would not move into his sleeping mind. He knew that
dreaming of a grizzly would bring an enemy of some
kind into his life. That he did not want. En-te-as swung
a few yards to the south. He wore, as most hunters did,
only a breechcloth covering him from the waist to his
upper thighs. He glided effortlessly through the lightly
forested terrain, at home among the trees. The trees
were just turning golden at their uppermost tips as the
sun rose above the skyline.*

*"Yi-yi," the call came, and En-te-as knew the bear
had been sighted. Now his time had come—it had been
acknowledged that he was the fastest runner of the
seven. He would now move forward to confront the
bear. He ripped off his breechcloth as he moved. As
Modoc tradition prescribed, he must be naked to meet
the mighty creature. He moved into the clearing ahead
where he had heard the call.*

*The bear was already alerted to danger and was
turning as En-te-as broke into the clearing. The bear
bellowed out a roar that mixed the young Modoc's
feelings of thrill and jubilation with fear. As the bear
charged, En-te-as pulled the string of his bow as far
back as he could, sent forth the arrow and then,
without a second of wasted time, turned and bolted for
the shelter of the trees behind him.*

*He heard the bear's cry of pain and the pounding of
the bear's feet as the grizzly began chasing him. But
even through his fear, En-te-as knew that at least six
other arrows, one from each of his companions, would
be aimed at the bear.*

*"Make my feet like the wind," he silently prayed to
Kumookumts, who had all power.*

*The scream of the bear behind him let him know an
arrow had found its mark. Another scream. Then the
woods shook as the great body of the bear fell to the*

earth.

"Brother!" he heard in his ear as K'-amps-so grabbed him, stopping him in flight and embracing him with abandon. "It is a proud day to be Modoc."

* * * * * *

In aboriginal times, clothing for the early Modocs was scant in the summer for both men and women. Children wore nothing, but decorum dictated that those having reached puberty wear a loincloth at all times, although both men and women could be bare-chested. Above those naked chests were usually perched hats, partly as protection from the sun but also as a decorative statement on the part of the individual.

Women habitually wore a basket hat of twined tule. A basket hat was occasionally worn by men, particularly as protection against chafing the forehead when carrying a pack supported by a head strap. A cylindrical bark hat was in vogue for men in summer and a peaked fur hat in winter.

Winter brought out the fashion parade of fur. Women preferred the fur of the coyote, but men tended toward groundhog skins. Women wore skirts and everyone wore buckskin leggings. For extreme winter wear, robes took the bite out of low temperatures. These robes also doubled as blankets. Robes were made of elk, deer, or bear fur or from tule or swamp grass. The deerskin robe was the most desired, equally serviceable in wet or dry weather since it had no seams producing weak spots. As contact was made with the Plains tribes, buckskin was used in clothing.

Tule, sagebrush bark, and swamp grass were common materials for clothing and even footwear in the summer. Adults wore moccasins only when necessary to protect the feet against extreme elements. Barefoot was most common in camp, in the *wickiup*, and always in canoes, even in winter. Moccasins of animal skin, with a string tied around the ankle, were worn in the summer.

In the winter, crudely woven fiber shoes lined with fur, swamp grass, or shredded sagebrush bark made for warm, comfortable wear. But fiber shoes were short lived. Tule shoes were good for ten or twelve days of continuous wear, whereas the sagebrush shoes lasted several times as long. However, sagebrush shoes took much longer to weave. So tule shoes were most often used. A man walking over crusted snow would take several pairs along if he knew he would be gone for a length of time.

The faces of the Modocs were often painted black with charcoal for protection against the sun. Charcoal from the burned pits of the wild plum was considered the finest. The areas around the eyes, including the lids, were thickly painted in winter to avert snow blindness.

The watery marshes of the Modoc homeland produced the marvelous tule, used by the Modocs in every facet of their lives. This water plant, in the skillful hands of Modoc women, was woven into baskets, which were used for carrying and storage. Basketry was also one of their art forms. The Modoc were especially known for intricately made willow baby carriers. Mats, sandals, roofs for their *wickiups*, and even boats were made from the pliant but sturdy tule.

Home, Sweet Home

The earth-covered *wickiup* was a structure of some architectural note. The inverted, bowl-shaped structures, dug partially into the ground, were entered through a hole in the top. Logs, preferably of pine, were used for the framework. Construction was substantial and a major project for Modoc families. Digging for the circular pit was done from the center outward to a depth of about four feet. The excavated earth was used to cover the top when the framework was up and topped by tule matting. Generally women dug the pit while men collected the timbers.

Building a *wickiup* with the opening to the east was very important, although a northern or southern entrance was acceptable. The land of the dead was to the west, and fearful things could come from that direction. The favored position in the *wickiup* for sleeping was near the ladder or the east. Those who found themselves in the western part of the *wickiup* slept in their sleeping mats of twined tule or robes of fur with their feet pointing to the west, reversing the normal sleeping direction.

Housing for the Modocs proved to be very comfortable with temperature regulated. The fire in the center of the room was allowed to die at night and was re-built in the morning by a woman specially delegated to take care of the fire.

Those who lived in the *wickiup* entered on ladders placed on the east side. One faced the ladder when going up or down, with children clinging to the backs of adults. Common *wickiup* etiquette asked that household members avert their eyes when a person of the other sex used the ladder.

Wickiups were placed at some distance from each other and were owned jointly by the adults living there. A smaller *wickiup* might house one or two families, but the larger ones, up to forty feet in diameter, could house six to eight families.

Two meals a day, one early in the morning and one late in the afternoon, were prepared. One unusual aspect of life in a *wickiup* was the fact that each family stored their food in a special cache outside the *wickiup*. The respective family carefully guarded the location of the cache, located a quarter mile or more from the *wickiup*. Furtive care was taken to keep one's fellow villagers from knowing when stores of food were brought from the family cache to the *wickiup*. Food was often brought from the cache at night or camouflaged so others did not know food was being transported. Surface indications of the cache were hidden so that even the family used a secret sign to allow them to find the cache again.

* * * * * *

— The Killer Snow —

It was unlike anything that anyone, even the oldest of the elders, had ever seen. The winter of 1830 was a season of desperation for the Modocs.

It started with a snowstorm that increased in fury and strength. The young men had returned late in the season from a successful hunt, and there was no apprehension about what lay ahead. But the snow continued to fall in a blinding blizzard for seemingly endless days. Deeper and deeper it piled up until nothing in the landscape was familiar. Ridges, stunted trees, rocks, and bushes had vanished. Everything was flat. Even the wickiup was buried. The world had become strangely silent.

Desperation set in and frantic efforts to reach the caches resulted in failure. Strong men struggled, combating the snow, only to return to their families exhausted and hopeless—and the stores of food remained hidden under the snow. The tiny brown faces of the children, pinched in hunger, drew the men out into the unrelenting whiteness again and again until, in a weakened state, they could try no more.

Kak had been named for the raven, and he would have loved to hear his namesake's call, or the call of any bird, for that matter. The quiet was frightening.

Inside the wickiup the hush was extended. Kak was only thirteen years old, but in those thirteen years he had always remembered winter as a time for games and laughter around the fire. Indeed, the days were long and dark, but he had always felt that having his family near was good.

His grandmother had been the first to go. It had been so heartbreaking to see her body carried up the ladder and placed in the cold outdoors. Kak thought of her often, up there lying in the snow. The baby was much too quiet now, and Kak hated the hush that replaced her gurgling. Even his sister Che-um-nas laid aside her basketry and she, too, simply sat—hungry, like Kak was.

The family had eaten everything that could possibly be eaten, including deer and antelope skins, the skins of wild fowl used as bedding—and even, to Kak's horror, the family dog. He would push that horrible memory from his mind during the day, only to have the image of the dog haunt his dreams at night, whimpering and licking his hand.

Kak's puberty crisis quest had happened only a few months earlier, before the terrible snows had hit. A puberty crisis quest, a ritual in which young people coming of age roamed the wilderness, was a major part of Modoc life.

Curled in a ball to fight the cold, Kak thought back to his five-day puberty vigil, his quest for talents and power, reaching for the dreams that would guide his future life. He had fasted for five days and thought the growling hole in his belly then was as bad as it could get, but it was nothing compared to the hunger that now consumed both him and his family.

Tears formed in the corners of his eyes as he remembered the joy he had felt during his quest. He had done the ritual bathing, swimming under water to touch the five stones, or "rabbits" as they were known. He had done the ritualistic breaking of shrubs, stripping bark from small trees and tying knots in limbs as he moved half-clothed through the rough country surrounding his home.

He especially remembered his rock piles. A significant part of the quest had been taking materials at hand as he traveled and building a stack of rocks, big ones on the bottom. His grandest joy had been the height he had attained with some of his piles—a private accomplishment that only he ever saw.

He closed his eyes and began to recite his rock prayer to himself: "My good helper, stone pile, you give me good luck. I am going out to hunt now. I give you this. Help me to have good luck hunting deer. That is what I want you to do." Maybe, maybe, the power of the stones would slice through the cold and snow that gripped the land and somehow bring food.

He opened one eye, then the other, but his heart told him before his eyes that absolutely nothing had changed in the wickiup. His sister hadn't moved at all, the fire still sent a stream of smoke to the hole in the ceiling, and no venison had miraculously appeared. He obviously had not learned much about prayer on his quest.

Kak wondered bitterly if this was the future that his puberty quest had brought on—cold, hunger, and death. As he huddled miserably on the floor of the wickiup, the tears began to flow freely, and Kak didn't care that at thirteen he wasn't supposed to cry.

Now, just as Kak's rock piles were out there somewhere, the family's food cache was also buried. Snow rarely fell in this region deep enough to even consider the possibility of preventing access to the caches. But this year was different. When his father had dug out of the wickiup after the fury of the storm abated, he had confronted mountainous snowdrifts over his head. Like other Modoc men, he had tried to search for the cache, but the snow itself made movement practically impossible.

Kak knew that until the day of his death he would remember his father dropping down into the wickiup exhausted and shivering. He had never felt more strongly that his father was a man devoted to his family. This winter had proved to Kak how much his father loved him. This knowledge helped sooth the horrible hunger pangs a bit.

Curled in a fetal ball, listening to the wicked howl of the wind, Kak wondered if this was happening to all his friends and their families. Would they all die in this Winter of the Big Snow?

* * * * * *

When spring came and the snow mass receded, it was found that death had crept into every *wickiup*. The Big Snow of 1830, it was said, had taken half of the Modoc people.

Chapter Three
The Modoc as a Social Creature

The Modocs, with their great emphasis on talking and expressing views, were naturals when it came to socializing, game playing, and singing. *Ca'gla* was the Modoc word for games of the non-athletic variety and for gambling. It must have been a happy word for most Modocs because the word embodied camaraderie and bonding, all a part of the game. Women were permitted to gamble, but the teams were predominantly of men.

Ca'gla had great importance to the Modocs. A man's status as a gambler affected both his social and economic standing. Considerable quantities of goods changed hands. Because gambling usually had an extensive playing time, there was little sense of urgency. If there wasn't a win today, then it would come tomorrow.

No man who won heavily in one game could take his winnings and quit. The only man ever allowed to quit had to be consistently unlucky. Anyone who decided to gamble was in for the long haul. His wife back in the *wickiup* knew those were the rules of the game, so it was not a wife's option to ask him to come home early or stay home for the evening.

Modocs gambled both within the tribe and against other tribes. The major game within the tribe was the hand game. Between tribes, the basket game was played. Both games were between two key players, although often competition was between teams with one player selected as leader.

In the hand game, marked gaming pieces called bones were used. They were cylindrical sections of certain trees, deer bone, or deer horn. Bones were used in two pairs, one pair plain, the other marked with a center wrapping of buckskin or a painted band of black. Their size was such that they could be hidden in a closed hand.

The bones were held by two active players from the opposing team. The active players were rotated so that all might take part in the course of the game. Determining which bone was in which hand of each active player was done by the key player, or guesser.

Each of the active players shifted his pair of bones from one hand to the other, with much swinging of arms from side to side. Periodically, a player would display the arrangement—sometimes one piece in each hand, sometimes both in one, hoping to confuse opponents by showing that they could not follow his rapid shuffling of bones.

Gambling Materials. *Gambling bones and mats are seen here. The pointed wooden counter sticks in the foreground were used to keep score.*

Play ended when each player holding bones crossed his arms and held his fists tightly closed near the shoulders. The guesser on the opposing side now had to guess how the bones were held. Score was kept with a counter, a wood stake pointed at one end that was thrust into the ground in front of the winning team.

Intertribal gatherings were occasions for intense gaming, and in these games the opposing teams were always from different tribes. Competition was fiercest and the stakes highest in the intertribal contest. The basket game, never played among Modocs, even subdivisions of the tribe, required gaming pieces, a covering plaque, and counters.

The gaming pieces, or bones, and counters were similar to those used in the hand game. A covering plaque, which covered the gaming pieces, was spirally woven and had deer dew hoofs fastened to the top center to serve as rattles. The plaque was kept flexible by periodic dampening, and raised sides were formed by bending it over a stick. The resulting semi-basket shape gave the basket game its name.

The idea was for the opponent, or guesser, to determine the order of the pieces, which the opening player had hidden beneath the plaque. Luck certainly was a part of the gambling. But the guesser could make unlimited guesses, without being locked into a final decision until he gave a formal hand signal to end the round. That gave him time to study the situation and, even more importantly, his opponent.

The opening player, however, could move the pieces wherever he wanted until the formal signal was given. He, too, was in a flexible position. The flicker of an eye and subtle body and face movements were closely watched. What developed were two Modocs working to project poker faces.

Men who could interpret an opponent's actions accurately and move swiftly with the signal were the more successful players, with the comfortable economic position that came with it. The left hand clapped suddenly against the chest on the right hand side signaled the decision time—no more switching pieces, as there was now a winner and a loser.

Team playing took on a frenzy, with lesser players trying to buddy up with known winners. Players were required to squat on the right leg with the left knee raised. As a wager, a weapon, tool, robe, article of clothing, or anything of value would be thrown onto the blanket, mat, or buckskin robe resting between the two teams. A horse or canoe would be offered by name. Women could watch from a distance but not participate in the basket game.

Singing with an accompaniment of beating on a raised pole or log placed before the players was very common. Some songs were specific for a certain game, and the repertoire was quite large. Sometimes a particular song was used for a particular opponent. Gambling night was anything but quiet.

The Thrill of Victory, the Agony of Defeat

Modoc men were active athletes, with "Modoc soccer" a great favorite. Played on an open, flat field with teams of five or six on each side, the game would start with two men grasping each other's shoulders in the center of the field. They would try to throw the other off balance and then kick the grass or deer hair-filled buckskin ball to a teammate. The goal was to put the ball through a willow arch or paired posts—an opening six or eight feet wide. There were few formal rules. Kicking, hair pulling, and other aggressive moves were not unusual. All this was accompanied, as all good sports competitions are, by loud and continual shouting.

Women had their sport, too. In a contest known as the shinny game, each woman had a straight willow pole some four or five feet in length. Played on the same sort of game field as the men used, again with five or six players, two women would pair off like the men. But they played with a six- to eight-inch long piece of thong connected to the middle of two sticks. The idea was for a woman to grab the thong with her playing stick and try to throw it toward the goal.

Children played sporting games as well. Water splashing contests, boys against girls, trying to get the other team to retreat, were popular as were contests to see who could hold their breath under water the longest. Ball kicking, slingshots, bow and arrow, and spinning tops were all used in childhood games. Perhaps the most joyous game of all was the one with each team trying to laugh the longest and hardest.

The Ritual of Marriage

Major events in Modoc life involved a formal ritual or ceremony. A puberty quest, marriage, disposal of the placenta following birth, and mourning rituals, are examples.

Polygyny, the practice of having two or more wives at the same time, was an accepted custom, but the majority of Modoc marriages were monogamous. Only four or five marriages in a hundred might include more than one wife.

A woman who was widowed was taken in by her brother-in-law as a wife. The older brother-in-law was usually first in line, but an unmarried brother-in-law had priority. In the absence of brothers, nephews or cousins might step in. A widower was allowed to choose any of his former wife's unmarried sisters.

Love at first sight had virtually no meaning among Modocs. Marriages were arranged, with the choice of a mate made by parents. Young people were married as soon as possible after their puberty quests, which were performed by boys and girls alike. Not much time or opportunity existed between puberty and marriage to establish any ties of affection. The activities of girls during this period were carefully guarded to avoid any clandestine meetings that could result in an illegitimate birth.

Mates were not always matched in age, as sometimes the mate was a widow or widower. Personal qualities were emphasized above age in a match. The parents' primary consideration in selecting a woman was that she be industrious. The ability and willingness of a woman to spend long days digging roots was a strong qualifier. It was said that a proficient root digger was always beautiful. A quiet, retiring, and serious woman was held in high regard. Strength of character, bravery, and wit made a man desirable. He should also be a reasonably able participant in the economic pursuits of men.

The actual marriage arrangement involved a sashaying back and forth between the homes of the two families. When a boy's family felt they had found a suitable mate for him, they paid a visit, bearing a plentiful supply of food, to the girl's family. Neither the boy nor girl were present. The only difference between this and a casual visit was that there was more food brought and none was taken back, as was the custom in more informal visits. Not a word was spoken of a possible match, the discussion considered improper and unnecessary. Days of anticipation passed. A return visit from the girl's family would bring the matching process into play, with both sides fully engaged.

The time of gift giving had arrived, and the possibility of a match was increasing. Furs, skins, beads, bows, arrows, canoes, and baskets all served as gifts. In later years as horses became available, they became the ultimate gift.

A close male relative was chosen for the role of gift giver. At dusk on a given day, he arrived at the girl's home and hastily deposited his treasures. Then the boy's family began a period of waiting.

The arrival of the gifts created much excitement and discussion in the girl's family. Accept him. Accept him not. The game played throughout the night. The girl's family mulled over the gifts and the marriage offer. The following morning the answer was given, almost always yes.

* * * * * *

—Here comes the Bride—

Lo-ki knew she had never looked so fine. She was wearing a beautiful new buckskin dress, and she had never had so many beads on a garment. The whole household was giddy and anxious—and all because of her. Her little sister fussed at her feet, rearranging Lo-ki's leggings so that they fell in perfect alignment against her legs. Lo-ki suddenly felt a wave of sadness sweep over her. It would be strange to wake up every morning without her sister beside her.

The time had approached when she would walk with her family, bearing gifts, to her new home. The giggling and laugher stopped and all looked at Lo-ki, waiting for her to begin the walk that signaled a journey to a new life—a life with a man.

Although she'd known him throughout her childhood, she hadn't seen much of her husband-to-be in the last year. Even stranger to her was the fact that she would soon be sleeping and eating with this man who, only a few weeks ago, had been selected as her husband. For a period of time, she would now go to live with his family in their wickiup.

Lo-ki knew that she and her new husband would return to live permanently with her family, but even the short period of separation from her family would be hard.

Lo-ki suddenly realized that everyone around her had become very still. They were waiting for the wedding party's walk to the groom's home to begin.

"Psst," her mother whispered to her. "Put your back straight. All eyes are on you." With those words, Lo-ki felt the anxiety drain out of her a bit. Her mother was still talking just like her mother. Perhaps the change would not be too bad. Her family would still be very close.

The walk was short, and the boy's mother met the wedding party at the door. Lo-ki had so many times in her life waved to this woman as she ran along the path that connected their homes. But today Lo-ki's breath came in short gasps, which she hoped others could not hear, as she realized she would now actually be living with this woman. But as her new husband's mother took her hand, Lo-ki felt a tiny squeeze. Lo-ki was warmed by that little gesture and knew she would remember it until she was an old woman.

This woman, who would be grandmother to Lo-ki's children, guided Lo-ki to her place in a corner of the wickiup, at the groom's sleeping place. Lo-ki's mother had coached her well, and Lo-ki folded her knees beneath her as she moved to the ground, sitting with her back to the room. Here she would remain for the next four days, leaving the corner only momentarily, as the wedding was celebrated around her. When she spoke to her new mother-in-law, she was allowed only to whisper.

Lo-ki heard, but could not see, her own family and friends enter the wickiup and join in the wedding celebration. At one point a small amount of food was placed in front of Lo-ki. She knew this procedure would be repeated for the next few days.

The day was long, but for Lo-ki it was filled with anticipation. She knew that when the day ended and the wedding celebration died down, in the dark of the night, her new husband would join her in their corner of the wickiup.

* * * * * *

Chapter Four
Sun, I Pray to You to Guide Me

The heart and the soul of the Modocs cannot be adequately interpreted without understanding the roots of their spirituality. The harshness of life for the ancestral Modoc was reflected in their never-ending endeavors to be at peace with their surroundings. For the Modocs, holy places were everywhere they looked in their own land. Mountains, trees, animals, and other things of nature had stories associated with them that brought wisdom and guidance.

There are varying versions as to how Modocs came to be, but they all involved Kumookumts, who had the leading role in the religious views of the pre-history Modoc people. Kumookumts had the attributes of a human form, characteristics, and behavior. This spiritual being was part male and part female and traveled about as an old woman, a basket maker who never finished her baskets. One can only wonder about the metaphysical or philosophical meaning of that to Modoc women whose primary craft was basket making. But history has buried any clue about a profound message for basket weavers.

The world in these early days was envisioned as a flat disc, the center of which was located on the east side of Tule Lake. On this spot was a small hill that was the original earth matter. From this point, the work of creating people took place. One common interpretation of creation involved Kumookumts scattering seeds throughout the world to create tribes. Races other than Indians were eventually created but at a later time. Another version has the creator plucking hair from her armpit to create human beings.

In the mystical world of the Modoc, there were animal-like beings that possessed extraordinary supernatural skills. Weasel's power came from his ability to travel under water, over land, and from treetop to treetop. Spider could rise straight up in the air and move as fast as a bird.

Medford Eagle was the greatest of Kumookumts' lieutenants. From mountaintops he could look down on everything, and his sight allowed him to see as far as the ocean. When he flew overhead, the beings below gained much—they lived better, fought more courageously, and gambled with improved luck. With gambling having such significance to the Modocs, there must have been fervent hopes when the gaming started that Medford Eagle would fly over.

Councils held by these spiritual beings determined much that affected human beings. The comparative lengths of summer and winter were discussed and a decision reached. Should humans be mortal or immortal? It was determined that humans should die. But when Kumookumts' human daughter died, he went westward, where the land of the living was separated from the dead by a mountain, and he attempted to return with his daughter. Five times he tried. Five times he failed, so he gave his daughter to Death.

Kumookumts gave much to human beings—knowledge of edible and poisonous plants, instructions to the shamans, and the introduction of the sweathouse.

Praying, Sweating, and Dying

The sweathouse, spu'klas, was of primary importance to the Modoc and served as the altar where prayers were offered. The powers addressed included the sun, moon, earth, and stars. In addition, such parts of the earth as mountains and bodies of water were the receivers of prayer.

Prayers did not ask for specific things like killing a certain number of deer, winning a particular prize at gambling, or gaining the affection of a named woman or man. Rather, prayers were for certain skills or good luck in areas like health, relationships, and wealth.

The sweathouse was a unique place of worship that offered a cleansing of the spirit at the same time as a cleaning of the body. A humble but efficient structure, it was small and airtight. Rocks heated to the maximum were brought in and sprinkled with water from time to time. The result was steam rising into the air producing a sauna.

As a place of prayer and communication with the supernatural, mourning rituals took place in a sweathouse, and a shaman would sometimes treat a patient there. Men would spend whole days in the sweathouse and were free to nap there, although it was not used at night to sleep.

Modocs did not believe in an immortal soul but rather in a life force in the heart that escaped through the top of the head. Modocs believed in cremation, not burial, and even when hunting, traveling, or in battle, an attempt was made to bring the body home, partially cremated if necessary for preserving the body. A complete fast by primary mourners began immediately upon death and continued for three or four days. A primary mourner was one who had lost a spouse or a child.

The body was prepared for cremation by a female relative who was not a primary mourner. The body and hair were washed and the hair braided in the normal way. Old clothing was laid aside to be burned with the body. New clothing and many ornaments and decorations were added, particularly necklaces and other beadwork. The arms were crossed across the chest.

Cremation normally took place at a communal cremation place on the paternal side of the family. A pyre was constructed and white buckskin, if available, was used as a body wrapping. The head faced west, the direction of the supernatural world. The deceased person's possessions were placed around him or her and taken by those present. In return, those taking the possessions were expected to leave beads or offer a service to the family of the deceased. What was left was burned with the body.

The reason for giving away or destroying the deceased's property, on occasion even burning the home, was the desire to eliminate any reminder of the dead person, and thus to ease mourning. A name taboo, a deliberate attempt to forget the dead, was put in place. For a period of two years, and even as much as a generation, the name of a deceased person was not spoken. That person was only referred to when necessary by terms like, "he of such-and-such-a-place" or "the one I lost."

In a way not typical for Modocs, most were silent at funeral ceremonies. No prayers, speeches, or songs were uttered. Even conversation was hushed. Weeping, moaning, and wailing of the primary mourners dominated the silence. In the days following the cremation, the weeping and wailing continued, usually practiced in the mornings and evenings.

An intense mourning period of ten days followed the cremation. All ordinary activities were suspended for primary mourners and formalized grieving substituted. The vision or crisis quest, a time of isolation and re-building, happened immediately following cremation. A new sweathouse for primary mourners was constructed. Usually the mourner remained in the sweathouse during the day and returned home to sleep.

Both men and women cut their hair if the deceased was a spouse. Women, but rarely men, smeared their hair and face with pine pitch. It was customary to rub charcoal over the pitch to render the resin less sticky. When men used pitch, it was removed after ten days, as was the facial pitch of women. But after the death of a husband, a woman kept pitch on her hair for about a year. She carried a supply in a buckskin bag.

Crisis Quest: Seeking Enlightenment

Dreams were the unwritten holy books of Modoc belief. Dreams were critical to any crisis quest (*spu'do*), the attempt to seek a path of action.

Certain crises in life were occasions for observance of a quest involving fasting, strenuous artificial activities, isolation, and ritual bathing. The acceptable bathing places were spots where some unusual event had occurred in mythical times. The occasions for such ritualization were puberty, the birth or death of one's spouse or child, consistent and serious gambling losses, and chronic illness. Adolescents understood that the quest was part of their approach to adulthood. The *spu'do* was viewed as a quest for talents and power. Bereaved persons recognized that the quest helped them to forget their sorrow.

The framework of the *spu'do* was a quest in which the individual wandered in areas isolated from human settlements. Most quest sites were within Modoc territory, but sometimes distant trips were made. Crater Lake, located in what is today Oregon, was frequently visited. That which was sought in the quest was a prophetic and satisfying dream. This was achieved by energy-consuming activities and exertion, followed by a short period of sleep. Exhaustion and hunger were not uncommon for those on a crisis quest.

The interpretation of dream symbols was fairly straightforward. Dreams were all favorably interpreted. For example, if a boy dreamed of furs, buckskin, or meat, he would have good luck at hunting. If a man dreamed of his puberty quest or a woman her puberty dance, this was an indication that the dreamer would remain young for a long while. Most individuals interpreted their own dreams, although adolescents sometimes consulted their parents.

The Shaman Cometh

Shamans were usually men, but a woman could become a shaman in the span of her life following the ability to bear children.

A shaman's call to serve as a spiritual leader came in a dream usually in mid-life. Several days were spent on a vision quest in which personal contact with the spirits was sought. Often the ruins of a former shaman's home would be the location of the vision quest.

Becoming a shaman was high risk because when a shaman's powers failed and a patient died, the shaman could be killed by the deceased's relatives. A person preparing to become a spiritual leader knew the risks. A peaceful death in bed at an old age was not a common passing for a shaman.

* * * * * *

— The Healer —

Jackalunus was jerked from sleep by his invoker, La-da-da. Jackalunus had been working with La-da-da ever since he'd become a shaman. No one needing his medical help ever came to him directly. When Jackalunus was needed, the invoker came to his wickiup with a summons. A shaman worked only at night, never in the daytime. So La-da-da was on night call, too.

It was the invoker's job to call Jackalunus's assisting spirits out in preparation for the night's work. La-da-da was chanting in a monotone voice outside the wickiup, calling up the right spirits to work with Jackalunus. The shaman knew that if he looked out he would see the invoker with his right hand raised palm downward, touching his forehead. La-da-da would turn in all four directions, look up, then down, as he chanted to entice spirits from all directions to venture out.

But there was no need for Jackalunus to look. What he needed to do was put on his clothes, grab his hat, and go wherever illness in the night had called. Jackalunus had worn the red buckskin skullcap adorned with woodpecker feathers for many years now. It settled down around his ears just where it belonged. As the shaman followed his invoker into the night, he felt the chill that had settled in. The moon was covered with clouds and a sudden flash of sheet lightning let Jackalunus know that rain might not be far behind.

Ko-mut's wickiup was crowded with spectators as the duo walked in. Ko-mut's wife, sweating and obviously in pain, was stretched out on a wooden plank in the middle of the wickiup, naked except for a robe covering her. Casually, using only his peripheral vision, Jackalunus let his eyes pick up the objects dangling from beams above. He immediately saw the rawhide thong. Ah-ha! A good night this would be. The dangling objects represented what the shaman's payment would be, and the thong was the symbol of a horse. Pay that good would keep him there two nights, all night, if necessary. The bag of the camus plant, a tiny gift, was just an added token.

He was pleased to see the chorus of a few women standing by to assist in his songs. They were good, he knew. Everyone present would sing, but having the women to lead the chorus made the evening go much more smoothly.

The room became still as Jackalunus lit his pipe, drew deeply, and blew smoke upon his hands. He then blew smoke three times on the woman extended before him. He laid his pipe to the side and reached forward, placing both hands on her body.

As he touched her, a flash of lightning lit up the room, and a clap of thunder reverberated. Even Jackalunus felt the drama of the moment. The shaman began to sing the special song that he knew would summon the first spirit he needed that night. The women behind him picked up the melody, leading family and friends of the stricken woman in the singing.

Jackalunus invoked spirit after spirit, with the singers accompanying him in the appropriate song. Then his powerful voice rolled across the room, talking to the spirits, trying to find the cause for the woman's illness. Thunder and lightning punctuated his words and the songs. Finally both the elements and the shaman became still. A recess was called.

It was at this point in a curing that a shaman could declare that there was nothing more he could do for the patient, and his services were terminated. Sometimes it had to do with too small a fee, but often the shaman was unwilling to attempt a cure because of probable failure. Failure for a shaman could mean possible death for himself at the hands of the patient's relatives.

Jackalunus's mind churned. He felt certain he knew what the illness was. He had seen it before. It was controllable—he could help her. The spirits guiding him were numerous and strong. He signaled his readiness, and a murmur of appreciation ran through the wickiup. The moment had come for his most important work.

Jackalunus resumed his place beside the woman. A basket filled with water was placed near the woman. He dipped his index and middle fingers alternately into the water and then into his mouth, preparing for the sucking. He placed his lips on the woman's temple and began to suck, accompanied by loud, explosive sounds. He then moved to her neck. The singing from the people crowded into the wickiup continued and *grew in volume. Jackalunus felt the spirits responding to their individual songs.*

Jackalunus's breathing became labored. He choked and then gasped. A violent jerk threw his head back, and he fell back as if pushed by a great force. The shaman held the back of his right hand over his mouth and emitted a gargling sound.

He reached into his mouth with his forefinger and thumb and pulled something out. The crowd surged forward to see. Nestled in Jackalunus's hand was a sliver of yellowish quartz-like stone, a symbol of a chest disease.

Jackalunus had earned his horse.

* * * * * *

Baskets from Pacific Northwest Tribes.
The Modocs made use of the tule water plant to make baskets.
In the foreground is the tule plant in various stages of preparation.

Chapter Five
Warfare Modoc Style

Modoc conflicts, in aboriginal times, were infrequent and brief, but bloody. War parties were small, the fighting unit consisting of ten to one hundred men. The bigger parties usually comprised more than one Modoc band or a combined effort with another tribe. When an attack was made combining other bands or tribes, there was a single war chief.

Because battle was relatively rare, maybe once a year, the men who actually fought were usually different in each battle. The war leader for each encounter was one of the regularly recognized war leaders. Once accorded the title of war leader, that designation was held for life until the selected leader gave it up, commonly done by older men.

Because battles usually were short, men took small supplies of preserved food, such as dried roots and meat. Although women, who accompanied men on longer trips, were useful in setting up overnight shelter and other camp tasks, most women did not go for one single reason—fear of seeing their husbands killed. The only women who went were those whose husbands wore armor, relieving their wives's fears.

Modoc armor was a most unusual sight. Made of elk rawhide, full armor was a kind of overcoat that reached from neck to the ground. A major disadvantage overshadowed the impenetrable value of the armor. The man wearing it was unable to run. Thus only a few men wore the gear. Most men opted to have the ability to fight and to run when necessary. They wore only breechcloths and moccasins. No headgear was worn.

A civil leader, or la`qi, could never be part of a warring party. It was acknowledged that their competence was in handling civil affairs. Losing a civil leader in war could jeopardize non-combatants and the stability on the home front. The majority of a Modoc community always stayed at home during a battle.

Having a shaman accompany the war party was common. On overnight forays the shaman was especially needed. Not only did he have rituals important to guarantee a successful outcome, but he also curbed the impatience of waiting men, keeping them alert and busy.

The People Decide

Decisions regarding battle rested in the hands of the people. The *la`qi* would lead a discussion on the pros and cons of a proposed raid. Had there been a good amount of time since the last battle? Would economic ventures or ceremonials be interrupted? Was the location of the enemy known? Did it look like the spoils of war would be good? Many other concerns and thoughts were brought forward. The people were invited and urged to speak. The war leader was a participant with substantial information, but the decision rested with a consensus of the people.

Once war had been decided upon, the undertaking was carried out with little delay. The organization and planning of the venture was under the direction of the war chief. If the party was small, the planning was carried out informally en route. A larger encounter required that all participants gather prior to departure. Tactics and the route of travel were discussed. Lieutenants were chosen. At times a dance was held to incite and prepare those fighting. The dance involved imitation of fighting, women's songs which were scornful of the enemy, and ritual performances by shamans.

The fighting men usually left early in the morning with the women following behind, singing a song that called for success. The men marched in mass formation. At an appropriate point, scouts were sent out.

Speed was critical when the attack was made, so it was the responsibility of those without armor to rush ahead first. Those wearing armor could not move fast enough. When they fought, the Modocs spread over a wide front, irregularly spaced, so they did not present a concentrated group for the enemy to fire upon. They fought with bow and arrow in groups of two or three, with one man keeping watch while the other aimed and released the arrow. The roles were reversed for the next round. If one partner ran out of arrows, the other shared.

Modocs were fair-weather fighters. Fighting in the winter or even during inclement weather was rare. There were unplanned battles, such as those caused by an enemy party trespassing on Modoc territory or retaliation for stolen property. A planned raid's purpose was to gain property and captives. The Pit River and Shasta Indians were traditional enemies, as were the Paiutes after the introduction of the horse. The Modoc and the Klamath, in more recent times, often fought together as allies. They were acknowledged to be superior fighters.

Most of the captives who were taken in battle were sold to the

Klamath Indians. The few who were kept by the Modoc were those to whom the owners became attached. A captured woman was sometimes made a concubine. When a male taken as a young boy reached marriageable age, he became essentially free to marry a Modoc girl, although some stigma remained throughout his life. Although assigned hard work, retained captives were well treated. They were free to participate in ceremonies and enjoyed complete freedom of movement within the village and beyond. Although there is no question that a captive could escape, his or her own people would not take the captive back.

The Modocs became environmental tacticians as a result of these raids. They singled out advantageous ground for their conflicts. They used skillful techniques for throwing their enemy off balance. They were masters at using the land to their advantage against the enemy—rather than allowing the environment to stop them. It was this Modoc strategy that U. S. military troops faced in the extraordinary Modoc War of 1872-73.

Clyde L. James at Crater Lake
Commercial photograph sold throughout Oregon and California as post-cards and pictures in the 1930s. Crater Lake was spiritually significant to the early Modocs. Dress in this photo is not traditional Modoc.

End Notes
Part 1

Chapter 1

1. Meacham, *Wigwam and Warpath*, p. 409; (can be found at http://soda.sou.edu).
2. Howard, p. 39; maxpages.com/modocwar/Fairytales.
3. Murray, p. 20; Howard, p. 9.
4. Meacham, *Wigwam and Warpath*, p. 300; Palmberg, pp. 17-19; Dillon, *Burnt-Out Fires*, p. 53; Quinn, p. 12; Murray, pp. 26-27.
5. Bancroft, p. 556; Odeneal, p. 5; Dillon, *Burnt-Out Fires*, p. 58; Murray, p. 36.
6. Murray, p. 38; Dillon, *Burnt-Out Fires*, pp. 59-62; Bancroft, p. 557.
7. Palmberg, 47; Murray, p. 35.
8. Bland, p. 10; Palmberg, p. 48, 51; Bancroft, p. 631; Faulk, p. 26.
9. Bancroft, pp. 559-560; Murray, p. 56; Quinn, p. 37.
10. Dillon, *Burnt-Out Fires*, p. 97, Murray, p. 15, 39.
11. Dillon, *Burnt-Out Fires*, p. 100.
12. Murray, p. 57.
13. Riddle, pp. 34-35.
14. Ibid., p. 37.
15. Bancroft, pp. 560-561; Murray, p. 58; Palmberg, p. 57.
16. Cornwall, p. 21.

Chapter 2

17. Odeneal, p. 26.
18. Putnam, pp. 5-6.
19. Murray, p. 34.
20. Ibid., p. 42.
21. Palmberg, p, 21; Murray, p. 44.

22. Quinn, p. 6.
23. Bland, p. 6; Thompson, p. 52.
24. Landrum, p. 24.
25. Faulk, p. 35; Murray, p. 45.
26. Odeneal, p. 14; House Documents, pp. 6-7.
27. Bancroft, p. 562.
28. Murray, p. 36.
29. Bancroft, p 562; Faulk, p. 42.
30. Palmberg, pp. 37-38.
31. House Documents, p. 74.
32. Quinn, p. 40; Murray, pp. 61-62.
33. Murray, p. 62.

Chapter 3
34. Johnson, p. 3.
35. Ibid.
36. Ibid., pp. 5-11.
37. Ibid., p. 2.
38. Ibid., p. 28; House Documents, pp. 13-14.
39. Murray, 60; Palmberg, 60.
40. Johnson, p. 29.
41. House Documents, pp. 6-7.
42. http://maxpages.com/modocwar/Petitions; Odeneal, p. 10;
    House Documents, p. 8.
43. House Documents, p. 13; Odeneal, p. 10. There has been
    much confusion about whether Ivan or Oliver Applegate
    was the Yainax commissary. Murray (p. 82), Riddle (p. 254),
    and Cornwall (p. 21) claim Oliver. Thompson (p. 7) claims
    Ivan as does the maxpages.com/modocwar. In House
    Documents, No. 122, the Yainax commissary name on the
    petition reads "commissary A. D. Applegate"—a non-existent
    person. In Odeneal's printed work, the same petition has
    been corrected to "I. D. Applegate." Also found in several
    other letters in his work is the reference to " I. D. Applegate,
    commissary in charge of Yainax."
44. House Documents, pp. 12-13.
45. Ibid., p. 6; Dillon, *Burnt-Out Fires*, p. 114.
46. House Documents, p. 13. In comparing the petition signed
    by 40 settlers and Applegate's letter, there is a great
    similarity in the writing style. Applegate most probably was
    involved in writing the document.
47. House Documents, pp. 13-14; Dillon, *Burnt-Out Fires*, p.

117.
48. Thompson, p. 52.

Chapter 4

49. House Documents, p. 38; Brady, p. 273.
50. Murray, p. 71; Dillon, *Burnt-Out Fires*, p. 118.
51. Thompson, p. 13; Murray, p. 77.
52. Bancroft, p. 573.
53. Ibid., p. 573.
54. Brown, p. 6; Quinn, p. 7.
55. Trolinger, "List of Modoc Prisoners of War".
56. Odeneal, p. 45.
57. Murray, p. 78.
58. Bancroft, pp. 573, 573 (footnote); Murray, p. 79.
59. House Documents, p. 42; Murray, p. 85; Faulk, p. 55.
60. Odeneal, p. 39.
61. House Documents, p. 173; Landrum, p. 125.
62. Brown, p. 51; Murray, pp. 87-88.
63. Brady, p. 267.
64. House Documents, p. 8.
65. Meacham, *Wi-ne-ma*, p. 81; Thompson, p. 17; Bland, p. 14.
66. House Documents, pp. 42-43.
67. Ibid., p. 106.
68. Bland, p. 13.
69. Riddle, p. 45.
70. Brady, p. 269.
71. Bland, p. 14.
72. House Documents, p. 26.
73. Ibid., p. 47.
74. Brady, pp. 265-270.
75. Palmberg, p. 173.
76. Bancroft, p. 574; Murray, p. 79; Thompson, p. 22.
77. Murray, p. 93; Meacham, *Wi-ne-ma*, p. 82.

Chapter 5

78. House Documents, pp. 174, 253; Landrum, p. 126.
79. House Documents, p. 187; Murray, p. 91; Dillon, *Burnt-Out Fires*, p. 134; http://maxpages.com/modocwar/Lost_River_Murderers.

80. Murray, pp. 83, 92.
81. Bancroft, p. 576; Dillon, *Burnt-Out Fires*, pp. 143-145; Thompson, p. 20; Murray, p. 92.
82. Dillon, *Burnt-Out Fires*, pp. 146-147.
83. Moore letters.
84. Thompson, p. 27; Murray, p. 97.
85. Riddle, p. 38; Quinn, p. 62; Murray, p. 97.
86. http://maxpages.com/modocwar/Hot_Creeks_Incident.
87. Dillon, *Burnt-Out Fires*, p. 147; Brown, pp. 57-58.
88. Bancroft, p. 579; Stone, p. 74; Dillon, *Burnt-Out Fires*, p. 92; Author's note: Historian Francis "Van" Landrum told me Muntz once worked for Fairchild.
89. http://maxpages.com/modocwar/Hot_Creeks_Incident; Bancroft, p. 579; House Documents, pp. 30-31; Muntz, in the summer of 1886, killed an Indian picking wild plums on his farm. A preliminary trial found him guilty of second-degree murder, and bail was set for $6,000. He jumped bail and the bail money was used to build the first courthouse in newly established Klamath County (Stone, p. 74).

Chapter 6

90. House Documents, p. 55; Dillon, *Boyle's Personal Observations on the Conduct of the Modoc War*, p. 9.
91. www.nps.gov/labe.
92. Brady, p. 292.
93. Brown, p. 64.
94. Ray, p. 144.
95. Brady, p. 284; Thompson, p. 29.
96. Brown, p. 64.
97. Dillon, *Burnt-Out Fires*, p. 266.
98. Murray, pp. 63-65; Palmberg, pp. 5-6.

Chapter 7

99. House Documents, p. 48.
100. Interview with Harold Porterfield, current owner of the John Fairchild Ranch (2007).
101. House Documents, p. 58; Thompson, p. 43.
102. Thompson, pp. 33-34.
103. Murray, p. 103.
104. House Documents, p. 50; Dillon, *Boyle's Personal Observations on the Conduct of the Modoc War*, p. 8; Brown, p. 60.
105. House Documents, p. 50.

106. Ibid.

107. Dillon, *Boyle's Personal Observations on the Conduct of the Modoc War*, pp. 23-24; Thompson, p. 35.

108. House Documents, p. 55; Bancroft, p. 589.

109. Brady, p. 294.

110. House Documents, p. 54; Bancroft, p. 591.

111. House Documents, p. 55.

112. Ibid., p. 51; Brown, pp. 62, 64; Thompson, 44.

113. Brady, p. 296.

114. Brown, p.61.

115. Brady, p. 296; Murray, p. 124.

116. Brown, p. 61; Dillon, *Burnt-Out Fires,* p. 194.

117. Thompson, p. 39; Dillon, *Boyle's Personal Observations on the Conduct of the Modoc War*, p. 24; Murray, p. 120.

118. House Documents, p. 59.

119. www.homeofheroes.com/gravesites/states/idaho; Brady, p. 293; Dillon, *Boyle's Personal Observations on the Conduct of the Modoc War*, p. 71; Murray, p. 124.

120. Thompson, p. 43; Bancroft, p. 562.

121. House Documents, p. 61.

122. Dillon, *Boyle's Personal Observations on the Conduct of the Modoc War*, p. 28; Bancroft, p. 596.

123. Brown, p. 63.

124. Dillon, *Boyle's Personal Observations on the Conduct of the Modoc War*, p. 28; Thompson, p. 41; Murray, p. 127.

125. Moore letters.

126. Brown, p. 69; Murray, p. 154.

127. Meacham, *Wi-ne-ma*, p. 88.

128. Ibid., p. 91.

129. Author's note: As a child in the early 1940s, I spent many Sundays with my parents visiting Aunt Jennie on the Klamath Reservation. She talked of taking clothing and weapons from the bodies of soldiers.

130. Meacham, *Wigwam and War-path*, p. 407.

131. Putnam, pp. 8-9.

132. Dillon, *Boyle's Personal Observations on the Conduct of the Modoc War*, pp. 27, 30.

133. Moore letters.

134. http://maxpages.com/modocwar/1st_Battle_for_the_Stronghold.

135. House Documents, p. 50; Thompson, p. 44.
136. Murray, p. 131.
137. Thompson, p. 44.
138. Meacham, *Wigwam and War-path*, p. 411.

Chapter 8
139. Bancroft, p. 601.
140. Quinn, p. 103.
141. Meacham, *Wigwam and War-path* , p. 420.
142. Knight, p. 128; Bancroft, p. 601; Brown, p. 71.
143. Brown, p. 72.
144. Bancroft, p. 595; Meacham, *Wigwam and War-path*, p. 416.
145. *San Francisco Chronicle*, 2/23/73; Meacham, *Wigwam and War-path*, p. 423.
146. Dillon, *Burnt-Out Fires*, p. 191; Murray, p. 144.
147. Thompson, p. 51.
148. Knight, p. xiii.
149. Ibid., xii-xiii.
150. Dillon, *Burnt-Out Fires*, p. 196.
151. Knight, p. 126; Dillon, *Burnt-Out Fires*, p. 197.
152. Meacham, *Wigwam and War-path*, p. 423; *Wi-ne-ma*, p. 44.
153. Thompson, pp. 54-55; Dillon, *Burnt-Out Fires*, p. 208.
154. House Documents, p. 67.
155. Dillon, *Burnt-Out Fires*, p. 208.
156. Bland, p. 23.
157. Landrum, pp. 2-3, 6; Brady, p. 231.
158. Murray, pp. 158-159.
159. Thompson, p. 57, pp. 130-132; Brady, p. 298.

Chapter 9
160. Riddle, p. 72.
161. Murray, p. 51.
162. Bland, p. 25; Meacham, *Wigwam and War-path*, p. 441.
163. Murray, pp. 166-168.
164. Brady, p. 298.
165. Bancroft, p. 608; Murray, p. 171.
166. Bancroft, p. 608; Quinn, p. 107.
167. Landrum, p. 5.
168. Murray, p. 153; Brown, p. 71; Meacham, *Wi-ne-ma*, pp. 57-

62.

169. Dillon, *Boyle's Personal Observations on the Conduct of the Modoc War*, pp. 36-37.

170. Bancroft, p. 613; Bancroft reported exactly what Moore did, even referring to "the officer at the signal station overlooking Mason's camp," which was Moore.

171. Moore letters

172. Meacham, *Wigwam and War-path*, p. 415.

173. Author's note: I was a keynote speaker at the 1988 "Symposium on the Modoc War," sponsored by the Lava Beds National Monument. Having arrived in Klamath Falls, I was unpacking my car in the parking lot of the motel. A woman next to me was doing the same thing, and in the conversation, which we struck up, it developed we were going to the same conference. I told her I was a great granddaughter of Shacknasty Jim. She exclaimed, "Your grandfather shot my grandfather's finger off!" Melissa Stewart was Alfred Meacham's great-great granddaughter. I apologized profusely, we both laughed and enjoyed getting to know each other over the next few days.

174. Bancroft, p. 614; Riddle pp. 227-229; Murray, p. 202. *Yreka Journal* 5/21/1873: "President Lincoln and General Canby, who was one of the president's warmest friends and confidential advisers during the war, were both assassinated on Good Friday."

175. Palmberg, p. 144; Dillon, *Burnt-Out Fires*, p. 248.

176. House Documents, p. 77.

177. George Custer, killed in the battle of the Little Bighorn in 1876, was a lieutenant colonel in the regular army. His promotion to brevet major general lasted only until the end of the Civil War.

178. Author's note; Of course, people like myself, who are descendants of those who fought in the war, might not be in existence at all today if history had taken a different bend in the road at any given time.

179. Quinn, p. 154; Murray, p. 204.

180. Murray, p. 174.

181. Murray, p. 209.

182. Dillon, *Boyle's Personal Observations on the Conduct of the Modoc War*, p. 32.

Chapter 10

183. House Documents, pp. 85-86; Murray, p. 202.

184. Thompson, pp. 70, 68; Brown, p. 85.

185. Jones, p. 376.

186. Dillon, *Boyle's Personal Observations on the Conduct of the Modoc War*, p. 29; Thompson, p. 68.

187. Dillon, *Boyle's Personal Observations on the Conduct of the Modoc War*, p. 43.

188. Murray, p. 206.

189. Ibid., p. 209; Dillon, *Burnt-Out Fires*, p. 254.

190. Moore's life was cut short at twenty-nine years of age when on May 9, 1878, five years after the Modoc War, he was reported missing at Ft. Klamath. The next day his body was found floating in Ft. Creek. It was determined the drowning was accidental as he had fallen from a footbridge and was strangled by his own scarf as he passed through the flume.

191. Thompson, p. 72; Murray, p. 212.

192. Bancroft, p. 617; Dillon, *Boyle's Personal Observations on the Conduct of the Modoc War*, p. 43; Murray, pp. 212-213, 215.

193. Dillon, *Burnt-Out Fires*, p. 270.

194. Brady, p. 300.

195. Murray, p. 214.

196. Ibid., pp. 215-216; Quinn, p. 142; Dillon, *Boyle's Personal Observations on the Conduct of the Modoc War*, p. 44.

197. Dillon, *Boyle's Personal Observations on the Conduct of the Modoc War*, p. 44.

198. Jones, p. 378.

199. Putnam, p. 10.

200. Thompson, p. 75.

201. Murray, p. 217.

202. Thompson, p. 76; Palmberg, p. 88.

203. Thompson, pp. 76-77; Brown, p. 86; Murray, p. 215.

204. Murray, p. 218. Forts can still be seen in the Stronghold.

205. Thompson, p. 75; Jones, p. 379.

206. Pentz letters.

207. Landrum, p. 7; Murray p. 216; Thompson, p. 80; Riddle, p. 103.

Chapter 11

208. Dillon, *Boyle's Personal Observations on the Conduct of the Modoc War*, p. 54.

209. House Documents, p. 109; Dillon, *Burnt-Out Fires*, p. 269.

210. Dillon, *Boyle's Personal Observations on the Conduct of the Modoc War*, p. 47.

211. House Documents, p. 108; Thompson, p. 83.
212. Meacham, *Wi-ne-ma*, p. 66; Murray p. 225; Dillon, *Burnt-Out Fires*, p. 267.
213. Riddle, p. 112; Thompson, p. 85; Dillon, *Burnt-Out Fires*, p. 268; Murray, p. 223.
214. Brown, p. 88.
215. Dillon, *Burnt-Out Fires*, p. 275.
216. Thompson, p. 86; Brown, p. 90; Dillon, *Burnt-Out Fires*, p. 270.
217. Brady, p. 310.
218. Thompson, p. 88.
219. Brady, pp. 307, 309.
220. Ibid., p. 314; Thompson, p. 89.
221. Dillon, *Boyle's Personal Observations on the Conduct of the Modoc War*, p. 54.
222. Brown, p. 93, Thompson, p. 91.
223. Pentz letters.
224. Bancroft, p. 623.
225. Thompson, p. 136. The man's name is seen as "Gode" in many books. However, in Pentz's writings, which came to light fairly recently, he refers to him as "Gude." The two men were very close friends, and Pentz's penmanship was very clear and distinct.
226. Brady, p. 308.
227. Dillon, *Boyle's Personal Observations on the Conduct of the Modoc War*, p. 52; *Burnt-Out Fires*, p. 271.
228. House Documents, p. 84.
229. Ibid.; Murray, p. 244.

Chapter 12
230. Quinn, p. 157.
231. Riddle, p. 125; Palmberg, p. 138.
232. Bancroft, pp. 624-625; Brown, p. 95; Murray, p. 246.
233. Bancroft, p. 625; Dillon, *Burnt-Out Fires*, pp. 283-284; Thompson, p. 98; Quinn, p. 158.
234. Brady, pp. 321-322; Murray, p. 247.
235. Shacknasty Jim's mother ("Madam Shacknasty" or Sallie Clark) and Ellen's Man George's father (Slolux or George Denny) were sister and brother.
236. Murray, p. 250; J. Howard manuscript.
237. Brown, p. 98.

238. www.arlingtoncemetery.net/johnosca.htm.

239. House Documents, p. 110.

240. Bancroft, p. 626.

241. Palmberg, p. 137; Dillon, *Burnt-Out Fires*, p. 289.

242. Thompson, p. 102.

243. Bancroft, p. 626.

244. http://maxpages.com/modocwar/Surrender; House Documents, p. 110; Bancroft, p. 627; Murray, p. 260; Dillon, *Burnt-Out Fires*, p. 290.

245. Bancroft, p. 627; Murray, p. 261.

246. Dillon, *Burnt-Out Fires*, p. 301.

Chapter 13

247. Murray, pp. 254-255.

248. Ibid., p. 264; Dillon, *Burnt-Out Fires*, p. 294.

249. Bancroft, p. 629; Murray, p. 266.

250. Landrum, p. 64; Dillon, *Burnt-Out Fires*, p. 296; Jones, p. 369.

251. Jones, pp. 382-383; Murray, p. 268; Dillon, *Burnt-Out Fires*, p. 297.

252. Brady, pp. 303-304.

253. Brady, p. 304; Bancroft, p. 630; Brown, pp. 103-104; Dillon, *Burnt-Out Fires*, p. 300. It is likely that Humpy Joe is the Modoc that became known as Jerry Hubbard, a POW in Oklahoma Indian Territory (Riddle, p. 107).

254. http://maxpages.com/modocwar/Surrender

255. Putnam, p. 12.

256. Dillon, *Boyle's Personal Observations on the Conduct of the Modoc War*, p. 58; Murray, pp. 308-309; www.austintxgensoc.org/calculatecpi.php.

257. Bancroft, p. 633; Landrum, pp. 20-21; Murray, pp. 272-273.

258. Murray, pp. 221-222; Putnam, p. 6 (photos).

259. Brown, pp. 101-102; Murray, pp. 277-278. Author's note: Big Jack Dawals, who is thought to be Tee-hee Jack, was the father of Sallie Clark, my great-great grandmother, mother of Shacknasty Jim.

260. Palmberg, p. 147; Murray, p. 278.

261. *San Francisco Call*, June 25, 1873.

262. Murray, p. 280; Landrum, pp. 25-26.

263. Landrum, p. 26.

264. Murray, p. 283, Dillon, *Burnt-Out Fires*, p. 310.

265. Landrum, p. 27.

266. House Documents, p. 173.

Chapter 14

267. Foster, pp. 10-11.

268. Landrum, pp. 38-42; Foster, p. 10.

269. Palmberg, p. 155; Foster, p. 12.

270. Dillon, *Burnt-Out Fires*, p. 329.

271. Landrum, p. 50.

272. House Documents, p. 326.

273. Ibid., p. 317.

274. Ibid., pp. 323-324.

275. Ibid., pp. 293-294; p. 314; Landrum, pp. 42-43.

276. Meacham, *Wigwam and War-path*, p. 643; Murray, p. 302; Dillon, *Burnt-Out Fires*, p. 327.

277. Riddle, p. 191; Palmberg, p. 155.

278. House Documents, p. 98.

279. Landrum, p. 70.

280. An original copy of one of these documents was purchased in 2005 for $4,000 by the Klamath County Museum in Klamath Falls. It was found on e-Bay by Bill Johnson.

281. Landrum, pp. 62-64.

282. Ibid., pp. 71-73.

283. Murray, p. 303.

284. Brady, p. 253; Landrum, p. 74; Dillon, *Burnt-Out Fires*, p. 331.

285. Dillon, *Burnt-Out Fires*, p. 333; Landrum, p. 74.

286. Trolinger, "List of Modoc Prisoners of War"; Murray, p. 312; *Dillon, Burnt-Out Fires,* p. 337.

287. Thompson, p. 171.

288. Dillon, *Burnt-Out Fires*, p. 335.

289. Author's note: The letter was passed on to Luella James, my mother, and is in my possession. The letter's poor grammar, construction, and misspellings indicate that Riddle had someone more adept at writing and editing working with him when he wrote his book, *Indian History of the Modoc War*.

End Notes
Part 2

Chapter 1

1. Martin, p. 435.
2. House documents, pp. 102-103.
3. Dillon, *Boyle's Personal Observations on the Conduct of the Modoc War*, p. 72.
4. *Yreka Journal*, Nov. 12, 1873.
5. *San Francisco Chronicle*, Nov. 9, 1873.
6. Martin, p. 421.
7. Ibid., p. 423.
8. Files: Indian Affairs, 1873, p. 82; Martin, p. 424.
9. Young, p.173. Bogus Charley was known for his flawless, "clear-cut English" (Brown, p.65; Dillon, *Burnt-Out Fires,* p. 194). He even confused soldiers during the war by perfectly mimicking military officers. It seems most unlikely he fell back to pidgin English. This may have been a reporter's embellishment, although the substance of Bogus Charley's comments is accurate.

Chapter 2

10. Johnston, p. 1.
11. Johnston; p. 4; *Klamath Falls Herald,* Part I, Oct. 9 1977. Two-part series, "A Page From The Past," by Harry Drew, Klamath County Museum Curator.
12. Ibid., Part II, Oct. 16, 1977.
13. Johnson, p. 35.
14. Putnam, p. 2.
15. *Klamath Falls Herald*, Oct. 9, 1977.
16. Ibid., Oct. 16, 1977.
17. Ibid.
18. Ibid.
19. Ibid.

20. www.sfgenealogy.com/sf/vitals/sfobica.htm.
21. Applegate, p.319.
22. Ibid.
23. Ibid.

Chapter 3
24. Martin, p. 426.
25. Files: Indian Affairs, 1873, p. 82; Martin, p. 424.
26. Young, p. 174; Martin, p. 426.
27. Young, p. 173.
28. Ibid.
29. Riddle, pp. 293-294; Martin, p. 430; http://soda.sou. edu: Indian Affairs Report from Indian Commissioner F. H. Smith to Hon. C. B. Fisk, Chairman Indian Committee, Nov. 21, 1874.
30. Riddle, pp. 294-295; http://soda.sou.edu.
31. Riddle, p. 295; Martin, p. 430; http://soda.sou.edu.
32. Martin, p. 431, Murray, p. 311.
33. Trolinger, "History of Modoc Tribe," p. 6.
34. Martin, p. 428.
35. Ibid., p. 430.
36. Murray, p. 312; Palmberg, p. 188; Riddle, p. 147; Trolinger, "History of Modoc Tribe," p. 8.
37. Riddle, p. 147.
38. Hubbard, p. 126.
39. Files: Indian Affairs, 1875, p. 282; Martin, p. 432.
40. Martin, p. 435.
41. Ibid.

Chapter 4
42. Smith, p. 100.
43. Ibid., p. 87.
44. Ibid.
45. Murray, p. 44; Smith, p. 87; Thompson, p. 6.
46. Smith, p. 89.
47. Martin, p. 422; Smith, p. 90.
48. Smith, p. 90.
49. Ibid. According to Hurtado, the education system set up and operated by the Tuttles did not conform to the fiscal legislation and intent of Congress. Money appropriated to the Modocs was earmarked for settlement, clothing,

food, agricultural implements, and seeds. Education
was not listed. William Nickolson, superintendent of the
Central Superintendency, justified these expenses to the
commissioner of Indian Affairs by claiming that because the
Modoc appropriation specified, "clothing and subsistence,
it would be applicable to feeding and clothing the Modoc
children at the Quapaw School."

50. Ibid.
51. Ibid., p. 99.
52. Ibid., p. 92.
53. Ibid., p. 97.
54. Ibid., p. 97. Author's note: Gregg is testimony to the fact
    that understanding and kindness is color/religion/gender
    blind. A major lesson of the Modoc saga is that good and
    bad are found among all people, in all situations.
55. Ibid., pp. 93-95.
56. Ibid., p. 100.
57. Ibid., pp. 99, 103.
58. Ibid., pp. 95-96. Author's note: The hypocrisy of criticizing
    Indian beliefs and then violating a major Christian belief,
    commandment number eight, "Thou shalt not steal," is a
    contradiction at the least. It is appalling when looked at
    in its full context of causing immense harm to a group of
    people.
59. Ibid., p. 105.

Chapter 5
60. Meacham, *Wi-ne-ma*, p. 16.
61. Murray, p. l91; Thompson p. 63.
62. Meacham, *Wi-ne-ma*, pp. 14-15.
63. Bland, p. 48.
64. Meacham, *Wi-ne-ma*, p. 93; www.libuiowa.ed/spec-coll/
    Bai/redpath.htm.
65. Dillon, *Burnt-Out Fires*, p. 342; Murray, p. 311.
66. Meacham, *Wi-ne-ma*, p. 91.
67. Martin, p. 437. Author's note: This story was told to Martin
    by my aunt, Viola Fryatt, Shacknasty Jim's granddaughter,
    who lived in Seneca, Missouri.
68. Murray, p. 313.
69. Young, p. 179.
70. Hubbard, p. 45.
71. Ibid., p. 46.

Chapter 6

72. Hubbard, p. 93.
73. Meacham, *Wi-ne-ma*, p. 86.
74. Hubbard, p. 92.
75. Ibid., p. 95.
76. Ibid.
77. *American Missionary Magazine*, p. 288.
78. www.rootsweb.com/~okottawa/modocemlist.html.
79. Trolinger, "Modoc Church," p. 1.
80. Martin, p. 433.
81. Trolinger, "Modoc Church," p. 1.
82. www.rootsweb.com/~okottawa/modocemlist.html; Trolinger, "Hist. of Modoc Tribe of OK".
83. Trolinger, "List of Modoc Prisoners of War".
84. Smith, pp. 28-30; Letters received: Haworth to Hayt, May 30, 1879.
85. Smith, pp. 29-31.
86. *Joplin Globe*, Oct. 2, 1949.
87. Smith, pp. 40-41.
88. Ibid., p. 44.
89. Ibid., p. 43; *Miami News Record*, October 21, 1932.

Chapter 7

90. Martin, p. 439.
91. Ibid., p. 437.
92. www.famousamericans.com/jeremiah-curtin; Curtin, *Memoirs*, p. 6. www.answers.com/topic/jeremiah-curtin.
93. Curtin referred to his older storyteller as Ko-a-lak'-ak-a. Riddle (p. 235) identifies this person as Princess Mary. I believe Riddle's identification in inaccurate. On p. 200, he also misidentifies Martha Lawver's "youngest child" as Jimmy rather than Jennie. The storyteller was certainly Martha Lawver, known among the Modocs themselves as a great storyteller. The storyteller had a daughter named Jennie, which Martha had, as reflected in Modoc genealogical records. Also, according to the introduction to Curtin's Myths (by M. A. Curtin), the storyteller "as late as Aug. 1, 1912, was still living, the oldest woman of the Klamath-Modoc tribe of Indians." Martha Lawver died March 31, 1913, according to the April 11, 1913 *Miami* (OK) *News Record*. Princess Mary died in 1906.
94. Curtin, *Memoirs*, p. 331.

95. Ibid., pp. 331-332.
96. Curtin, Alma. Letters to family, July 10, 1884.
97. National Anthropological Archives, NAA 3538.
98. Martin, p. 438.
99. Ibid., p. 440; September 30, 1945, Levi Gilbert letter; Watson.
100. Gilbert letter; Watson.
101. Martin, p. 440.
102. Ray, p, 70; Dillon, *Burnt-Out Fires*, p. 338.
103. Trolinger, "History of Modoc Tribe," p. 8.
104. Murray, p. 312.
105. Hubbard, p. 127; Tuning, p. 79.
106. www.rootsweb.com/~okottawa/modocemlist.html.

Chapter 8
107. Riddle, p. 147.
108. Ibid., p. 154.
109. Lawver, letters and papers; interviews with Bert Lawvor, Alvin Lawver, and Yvonne Lawver Kays.
110. Ibid.
111. Interview with Arnold Richardson, born near Quapaw Agency, Oklahoma Indian Territory, June 1906.
112. www.dallashistory.org/cgi-bin/webbbs_config. pl?noframes;read=4215.
113. Wright, under "Modoc Indians".

Chapter 9
114. Martin, p. 441.
115. *Klamath Echoes*, p. 7.
116. http://soda.sou.edu; No. 13, p. 347: Annual Report, Commissioner of Indian Affairs, 1876.
117. *Klamath Echoes*, pp. 9-10; *Klamath Falls Herald and News*, October 27, 1986.
118. *Klamath Echoes*, p. 9.
119. Ibid., p. 13.
120. Ibid., p. 15.
121. Ibid., pp. 13-15.
122. Ibid., p. 14.
123. Lawver, letters and papers.
124. Ibid..

125. Ibid.
126. Tuning, p. 87; Trolinger, "List of Modoc Prisoners of War".
127. Tuning, pp. 79, 87; Watson, p. 6.
128. Author's note: November 15, 2002, *Portland Oregonian* - "Gov. John Kitzhaber plans to acknowledge that the state forcibly sterilized hundreds of vulnerable Oregonians over more than 60 years...but evidence of what occurred was scanty...the records of the Board of Eugenics...were lost or destroyed. Between January 1987 and June 1988, a nonprofit contractor in Portland shredded hundreds of detailed documents of the board's work at the request of the state." But during the summer of 2002, state archives workers discovered seven boxes of records. Among the records were copies of 1921 meetings that show that six board members met quarterly and ordered sterilization for people whom "procreation would produce children with an inherited tendency to feeble-mindedness, insanity, epilepy, criminality, or degenercy." Letters to Alice Lawver indicate that all four of her children were sterilized by order of the Board of Eugenics.
129. Tuning, p. 88; interviews with Bert Lawvor and Coke Crume.

Chapter 10
130. Interview with Herrera.
131. Interviews with Bert Lawvor and Coke Crume.
132. Interview with Magee.
133. Interview with Kays and Bert Lawvor.
134. Interview with Bodner and Duffy.
135. Wright, under "Modoc Indians".
136. Interviews with Richardson and Potts.
137. Interview with author's father on "Public Eye" Author's note: I have in my possession one of the brass buttons from my father's uniform.
138. "Public Eye".
139. Interview with Shadwick.
140. Martin, p. 444.
141. Daniel Clinton letter.
142. "Public Eye".
143. Interview with Hayworth.
144. Interview with Crume-Smith and Magee.
145. Interview with Coke Crume.
146. Ibid.

147. Interview with Wright.
148. June 25, 1873, *San Francisco Call*; House Documents, p. 188.
149. *The Oregonian*, July 1, 2007.
150. Thompson, p. 173.
151. Brown, p. 102; Murray, p. 277.

Chapter 11
152. www.nps.gov/labe.
153. www.klamathtribes.org.
154. www.answers.com/topic/klamath-tribes; www.klamathtribes.org.
155. Written information from Follis.
156. www.eighttribes.org.
157. Written information from Follis.
158. *Miami News-Record*. Insight, On Site - Vision 2001.
159. Written information from Follis.
160. Interview with Foreman; www.klamathtribes.org/; Klamath Tribes brochure.
161. Ibid.
162. Ibid.
163. Trolinger, "Modoc Church".
164. Interview with Adams; Tuning, p. 88.
165. Interview with Bert Lawvor.
166. *Klamath Falls Herald and News*, November 18,1979.
167. Ibid., March 3,1974.
168. Letters in possession of Klamath Tribes.
169. Ibid.
170. *Klamath News*, Feb/March, 1994, p. 2; letters in possession of Klamath Tribes; interview with Garcia.
171. Ibid.

Bibliography

Books

Applegate, Shannon. *Skokum*. Corvallis, OR: Oregon State University Press, 2005.

Bancroft, Hubert Howe. *The History of Oregon, Vol. II*. San Francisco: The History Company, 1888.

Bland, T. A. *Life of Alfred Meacham*. "The Tragedy of the Lava Beds." Washington D.C.: T.A. and M.C. Bland, 1883.

Brady, Cyrus Townsend, LL.D. *Northwestern Fights and Fighters*. New York: McClure, 1907.

Brown, William S. *California Northeast, The Bloody Ground*. Oakland, CA: Biobooks, 1951.

Curtin, Jeremiah. *Memoirs of Jeremiah Curtin*. Madison: The State Historical Society of Wisconsin, 1940.

_____. *Myths of the Modocs*. Boston: Little, Brown, 1912.

Dillon, Richard. *Burnt-Out Fires: California's Modoc Indian Wars*. Englewood Cliffs, NJ: Prentice-Hall, Inc., 1973.

_____, editor. *William Henry Boyle's Personal Observations on the Conduct of the Modoc War*. Los Angeles, Dawson, 1959

Faulk, Odie B. *The Modoc People*. Phoenix, AZ: Indian Tribal Series, 1976.

Highberger, Mark, editor. *The Soldiers' Side of the Modoc War*. Wallowa, OR: Bear Creek Press, 2003.

Howe, Carrol B. *Ancient Modocs of California and Oregon*. Portland, OR: Binford & Mort, 1979.

Hubbard, Jeremiah. *Forty Years Among the Indians*. Knightstown, IN: The Bookmark, Reprinted, 1975.

Jones, J. Roy. *Saddle Bags in Siskiyou*. Yreka, CA: News-Journal Print Shop, 1953.

Knight, Oliver. *Following the Indian Wars: The Story of the Newspaper Correspondent Among the Indian Campaigners*. Norman: University of Oklahoma Press, 1960.

Kroeber, A. L. *Handbook of the Indians of California.* Washington, D. C.: Government Printing Office, 1925.

Landrum, Francis. *Guardhouse, Gallows, and Graves.* Klamath Falls, OR: Klamath County Museum, 1988.

Meacham, Alfred B. *Wigwam and War-path.* Boston: John P. Dale, 1875.

_____, *Wi-ne-ma.* Hartford, CT: American Publishing Co., 1876.

Murray, Keith. *The Modocs and Their War.* Norman, OK: University of Oklahoma, 1959.

Odeneal, T. B. *Modoc War: Statement of its Origin and Causes Containing an Account of the Treaty, Copies of Petitions, and Official Correspondence.* Portland, OR: Bulletin Steam Book and Job Printing Office, 1873.

Palmberg, Walter H. *Copper Paladin.* Bryn Mawr, PA: Dorrance and Company, Inc., 1982.

Quinn, Arthur. *Hell with the Fire Out.* Boston: Faber and Faber, Inc., 1997.

Ray, Verne F. *Primitive Pragmatists, the Modoc Indians.* Seattle: University of Washington, 1963.

Riddle, Jeff C. *The Indian History of the Modoc War and the Causes That Led to It.* San Francisco: Marnell Co., 1914.

Smith, Robert E., editor. *Oklahoma's Forgotten Indians.* Oklahoma City: Oklahoma Historical Society, 1981.

Stone, Buena Cobb. *Old Fort Klamath: An Oregon Frontier Post 1863-1890.* Medford, OR: Pacific Northwest Books Company, 1990.

Thompson, Erwin. *Modoc War: Its Military History and Topography.* Sacramento, CA: Argus, 1971.

Wright, Muriel. *A Guide to the Indian Tribes of Oklahoma.* Norman, OK: University of Oklahoma Press, 1951, 1986.

Journals and Magazines

Cornwall, Robert. "Oliver Cromwell Applegate: Paternalistic Friend of the Indians." *The Journal of the Shaw Historical Library* (Vol. 6, 1992): pp. 17-32.

Foster, Doug. "Heroes or Villains: The 1873 Modoc War Crimes Trial." *Southern Oregon Heritage Today* (Vol. 3, No. 8), pp. 8-14.

Gates, Paul W. "Carpetbaggers join the rush for California land." *California Historical Society* (Vol. 56, Summer 1977), pp. 98-127.

James, Cheewa. "Modoc Exile." *The Journal of the Modoc County Historical Society* (No. 5, 1953), pp. 11-23.

Johnson, Robert B. "Two Jesses and the Modoc War." *The Journal of the Shaw Historical Library* (Vol. 5, Nos. 1 and 2, 1991), pp. 1-44.

Martin, Lucille J. "A History of the Modoc Indians: An Acculturation Study." *The Chronicles of Oklahoma* (Vol. XLVII, No. 4), pp. 398-446.

Palmquist, Peter. "Imagemakers of the Modoc War: Louis Heller and Eadweard Muybridge." *The Journal of the Shaw Historical Library* (Vol. 8, 1994): pp. 29-48.

Putnam, Charles. "Incidents of the Modoc War." *The Journal of the Shaw Historical Library* (Vol. 1, No. 2, 1987), pp. 1-12.

Smith, Robert E. "A Life For a Pair of Boots: The Murder of Shepalina." *The Chronicles of Oklahoma* (Vol. LXIX, No. 1), pp. 26-46.

Tuning, Virena. "Friends' Work on the Klamath Indian Reservation." *Women's Missionary Society of Oregon Yearly Meeting of Friends Churches (Quaker)*, Friends Circle the Globe, pp. 86-89, date unknown, approx. early 1950s.

"Yainax." *Klamath Echoes* 12: 1974, pp. 6-17. Klamath County Historical Society, Klamath Falls, Oregon.

Young, Claiborne Addison. "A Walking Tour in the Indian Territory, 1874." *The Chronicles of Oklahoma* (Vol. XXXVI, No. 2), pp. 167-180.

Government Publications

Annual Report of the Commissioner of Indian Affairs to the Secretary of the Interior for the Year 1876. Washington: U. S. Government Printing Office.

House Documents, 43rd Congress, 1st Session, No. 122, Correspondence and papers relative to the Modoc War.

National Archives. *Special Files of the Office of Indian Affairs.* 1807-1904. Record Group 75, Washington D. C.

National Anthropological Archives, Smithsonian Institution. NAA 3538, folder 2, NAA.

Unpublished Manuscripts and Material

Clinton, Alice Lawver. Unpublished letters, 1920-25, and papers. In Alvin Lawver and author's possession.

Clinton, Daniel. Unpublished letter, December 8, 1916. In author's possession.

Curtin, Alma. Letters and journals as transcribed by Jose M. de Prada-Samper. Milwaukee County Historical Society.

Gilbert, Levi. September 30, 1945 letter, including list of 1890 Yainax Modoc Quaker Church members. In author's possession.

Howard, Jason. "Jason Howard Field Notes, 1920-1926, H2017." Compiled by Chief Interpreter Gary Hathaway, Lava Beds National Monument, CA. July 21, 1988.

Howard, Sam. "Tangled Web: Behind the Ben Wright Legend."

Klamath Tribes. Brochure: "We Are the Klamath Tribes," Klamath Falls, Oregon, 2000.

Klamath Tribes. Letters on four Modoc skulls. Klamath Tribes office.

Lawver family. Letters and papers. Copies in author's possession.

Moore, Harry De Witt. Unpublished letters, 1872-73. Email copies in author's possession.

Pentz, Charles. Unpublished letters, 1873-75, Klamath Falls, OR: Shaw Historical Library and copies in author's possession.

Trolinger, Patricia S. "History of the Modoc Tribe of Oklahoma." Miami, OK: Modoc Tribe of Oklahoma Tribal Office, 2001.

_____, "Modoc Church, Quapaw Agency, Indian Territory." Miami, OK: personal notes, 2001.

_____, "List of Modoc Prisoners of War." Miami, OK: Modoc Tribe of Oklahoma Tribal Office.

Watson, Floyd. "My Sprague River Story." 2004.

Web Sites

Answers.com, "Hubert Howe Bancroft" http://www.answers.com/topic/hubert-howe-bancroft

Answers.com, "Jeremiah Curtin" http://www.answers.com/topic/jeremiah-curtin [external links: his memoirs]

Arlington Cemetery http://www.arlingtoncemetery.net/johnosca.htm

Austin Genealogical Society http://www.austintxgensoc.org/calculatecpi.php

Dallas Historical Society, "Re: bois d'arc in Texas." http://www.dallashistory.org/cgi-bin/webbbs_config. pl?noframes;read=4215

Famous Americans, "Jeremiah Curtin" http://www.famousamericans.net/jeremiahcurtin/

Home of Heroes, Medal of Honor

http://www.homeofheroes.com

Intertribal Council, Inc. of Northeastern Oklahoma
http://www.eighttribes.com

Klamath Tribes
http://www.klamathtribes.org/

Lava Beds National Monument
http://www.nps.gov/labe/

Maxpages.com, "Modoc War"
http://maxpages.com/modocwar

Modoc Tribe of Oklahoma
http://www.modoctribe.net/

Rootsweb.com, "Modoc Cemetery"
http://www.rootsweb.com/~okottawa/modocemlist.html

San Francisco Genealogy, "Jesse Carr"
http://www.sfgenealogy.com/sf/vitals/sfobica.htm

Southern Oregon Digital Archives, "First Nations Collection:
Modoc Indians"
http://soda.sou.edu/

Tule Lake Butte Valley Museum of Local History, "Time Line."
http://www.cot.net/~tulefair/tbvmuseum/history.htm

University of Houston, "The Applegate Trail"
http://www.uh.edu/~jbutler/gean/applegatetrail.html

University of Iowa Books, "Redpath Lyceum Bureau"
http://www.lib.uiowa.edu/spec-coll/Bai/redpath.htm

Television

"Public Eye." KOBI-TV, Medford, Oregon. Host and Producer,
Cheewa James. 1979-80

Newspapers and Magazines

American Missionary Magazine, Vol. XI, No. 10. 1886. Cornell
University Library, 2005.

Army and Navy Journal

Boston Beacon

Daily Eastern Argus (Portland, Maine)

Hallaquah

Joplin Globe (Missouri)

Klamath Falls Evening Herald (Oregon)

Klamath Falls Herald and News

Klamath News (Official Publication of the Klamath Tribes)

Miami Daily News-Record (Oklahoma)
New York Herald
New York Star
The Portland Oregonian
Sacramento Record
San Francisco Call
San Francisco Chronicle
Yreka Union

Interviews by Author - 2006

Adams, Robert (oral)
Bodner, Vincent "Buttons" (oral)
Crume, Coleen "Coke" (oral)
Duffy, Bill AKA Tupper, Phil (oral)
Follis, Bill (written)
Foreman, Allen (oral)
Garcia, Marvin (oral)
Hayworth, Viola (email through daughter Gerry Milhorn)
Herrera, Deborah Riddle (oral)
Kays, Yvonne Lawver (oral)
Lawver, Alvin (oral)
Lawvor, Bert (oral)
Magee, Jo Anne Tuning (oral)
Miles, Ann (oral and email)
Porterfield, Harold (oral)
Shadwick, Jack (oral)
Smith, Helen Crume (oral)
Watson, Floyd (email)
Wright, Harold (oral)

Interviews - 2007

Potts, Oma (oral)
Prada-Samper, Jose M. de (email)
Richardson, Arnold (oral)

Index

Page numbers in bold type indicate photographs.